G.I. JOE

FUTURE NOIR

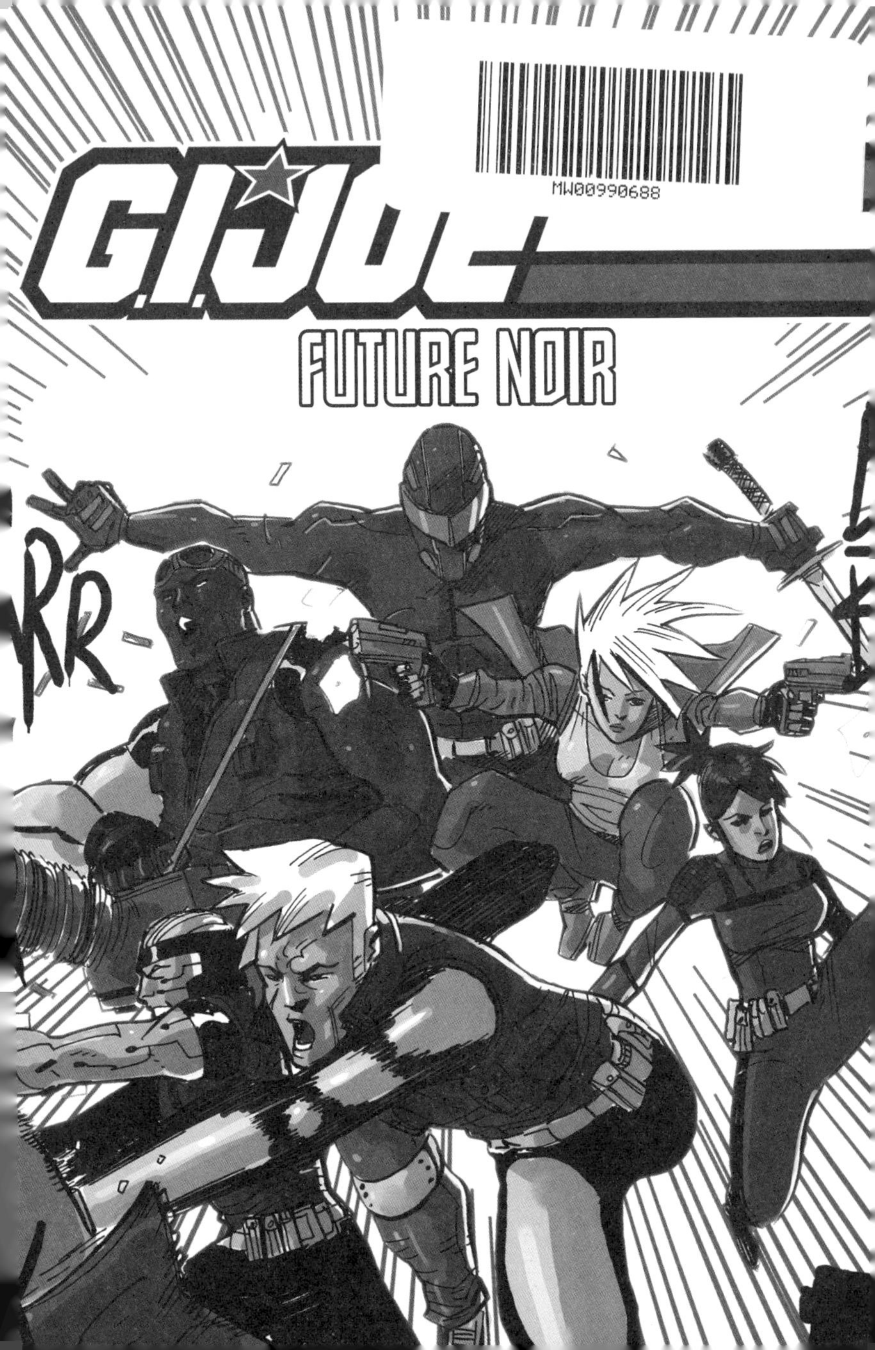

Licensed By: Special thanks to Hasbro's Aaron Archer, Michael Kelly, Amie Lozanski, Ed Lane, Joe Furfaro, Jos Huxley, Samantha Lomow, and Michael Verrecchia for their invaluable assistance.

www.IDWPUBLISHING.com   ISBN: 978-1-60010-865-5   14 13 12 11   1 2 3

IDW Publishing is: Operations: Ted Adams, CEO & Publisher • Greg Goldstein, Chief Operating Officer • Matthew Ruzicka, CPA, Chief Financial Officer • Alan Payne, VP of Sales • Lorelei Bunjes, Director of Digital Services • Jeff Webber, Director of ePublishing • AnnaMaria White, Dir., Marketing and Public Relations • Dirk Wood, Dir., Retail Marketing • Marci Hubbard, Executive Assistant • Alonzo Simon, Shipping Manager • Angela Loggins, Staff Accountant • Cherrie Go, Assistant Web Designer • Editorial: Chris Ryall, Chief Creative Officer, Editor-In-Chief • Scott Dunbier, Senior Editor, Special Projects • Andy Schmidt, Senior Editor • Justin Eisinger, Senior Editor, Books • Kris Oprisko, Editor/Foreign Lic. • Denton J. Tipton, Editor • Tom Waltz, Editor • Mariah Huehner, Editor • Carlos Guzman, Assistant Editor • Bobby Curnow, Assistant Editor • Design: Robbie Robbins, EVP/Sr. Graphic Artist • Neil Uyetake, Senior Art Director • Chris Mowry, Senior Graphic Artist • Amauri Osorio, Graphic Artist • Gilberto Lazcano, Production Assistant • Shawn Lee, Graphic Artist

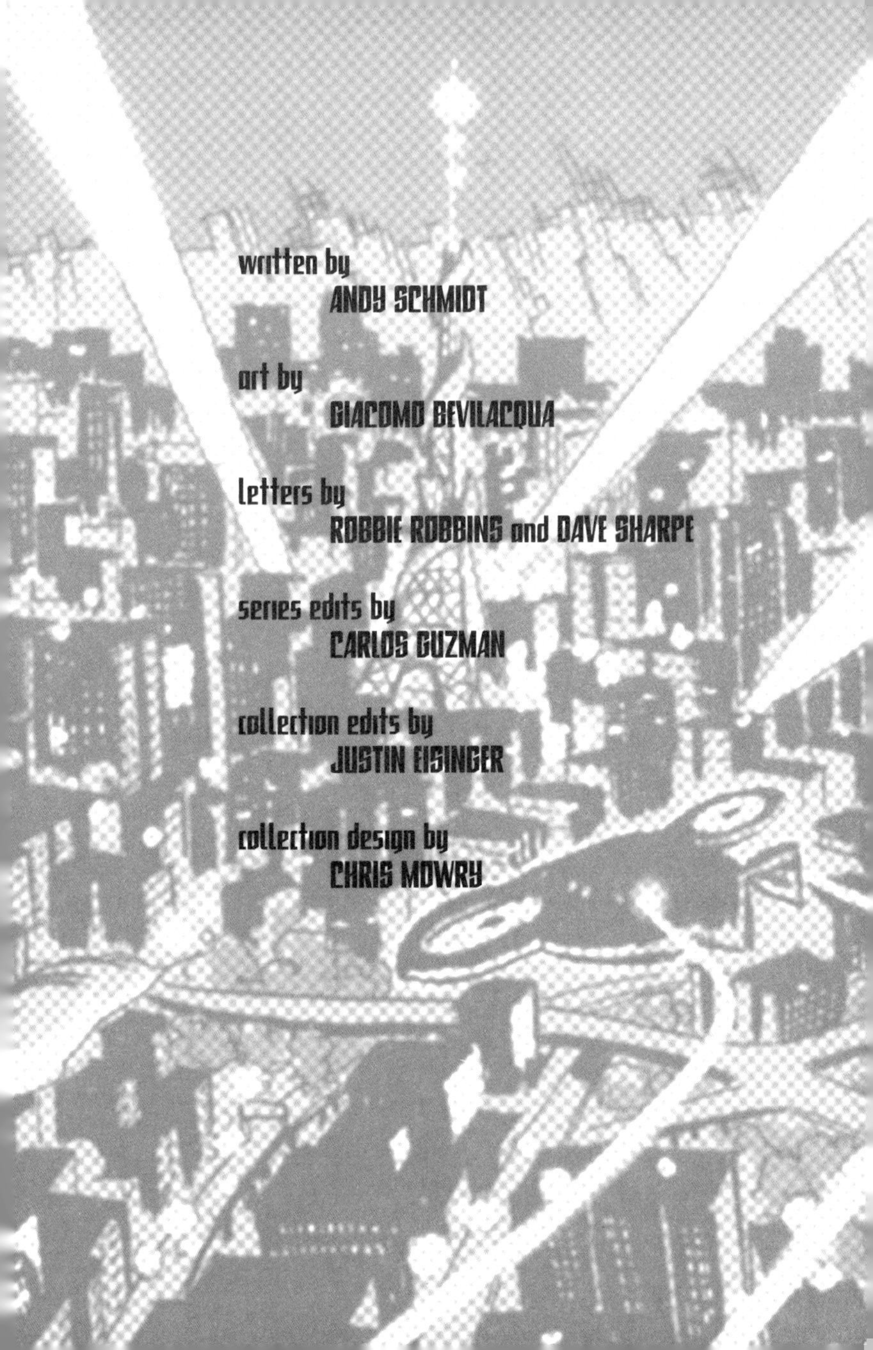

written by
ANDY SCHMIDT

art by
GIACOMO BEVILACQUA

letters by
ROBBIE ROBBINS and DAVE SHARPE

series edits by
CARLOS GUZMAN

collection edits by
JUSTIN EISINGER

collection design by
CHRIS MOWRY

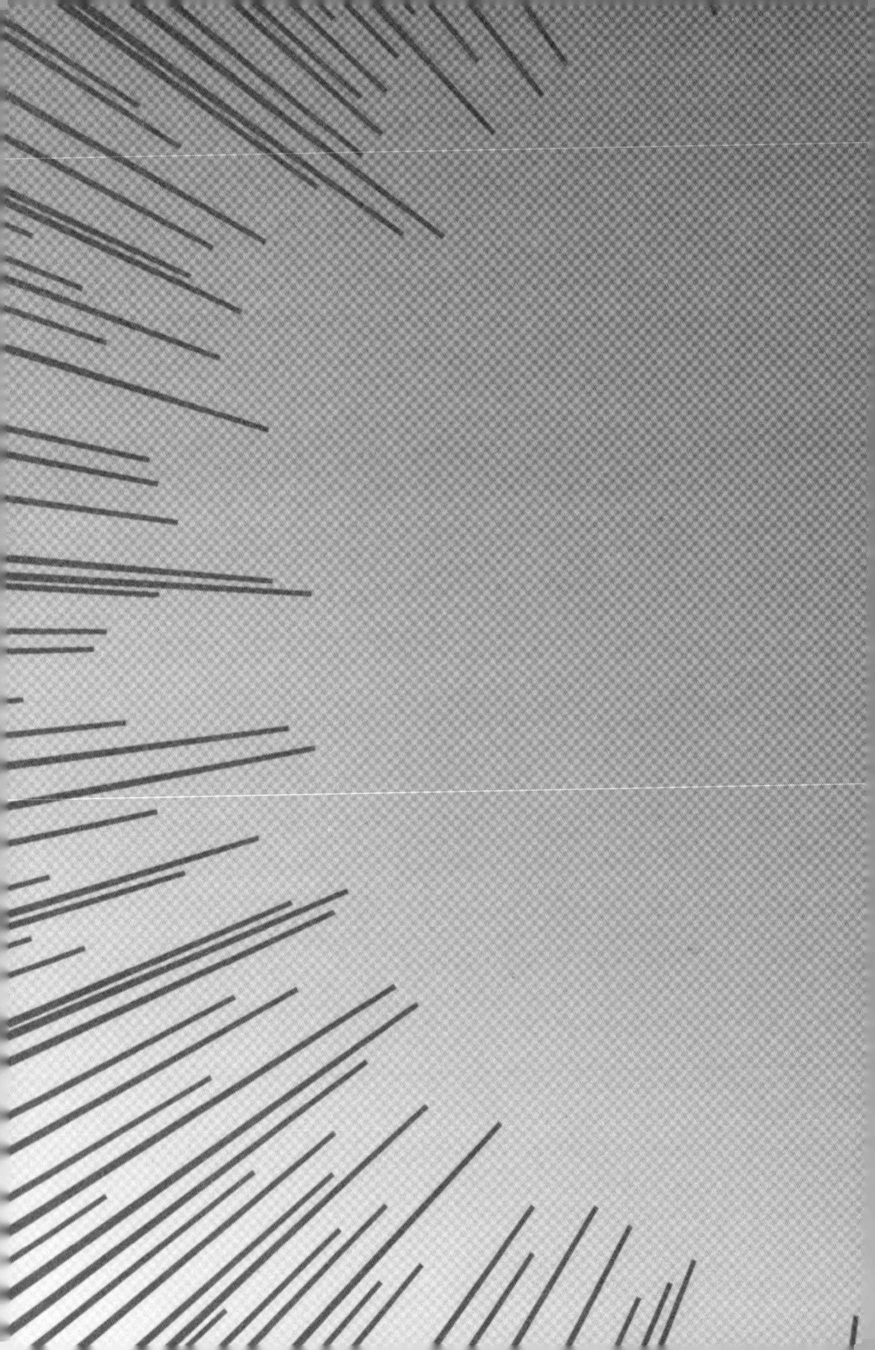

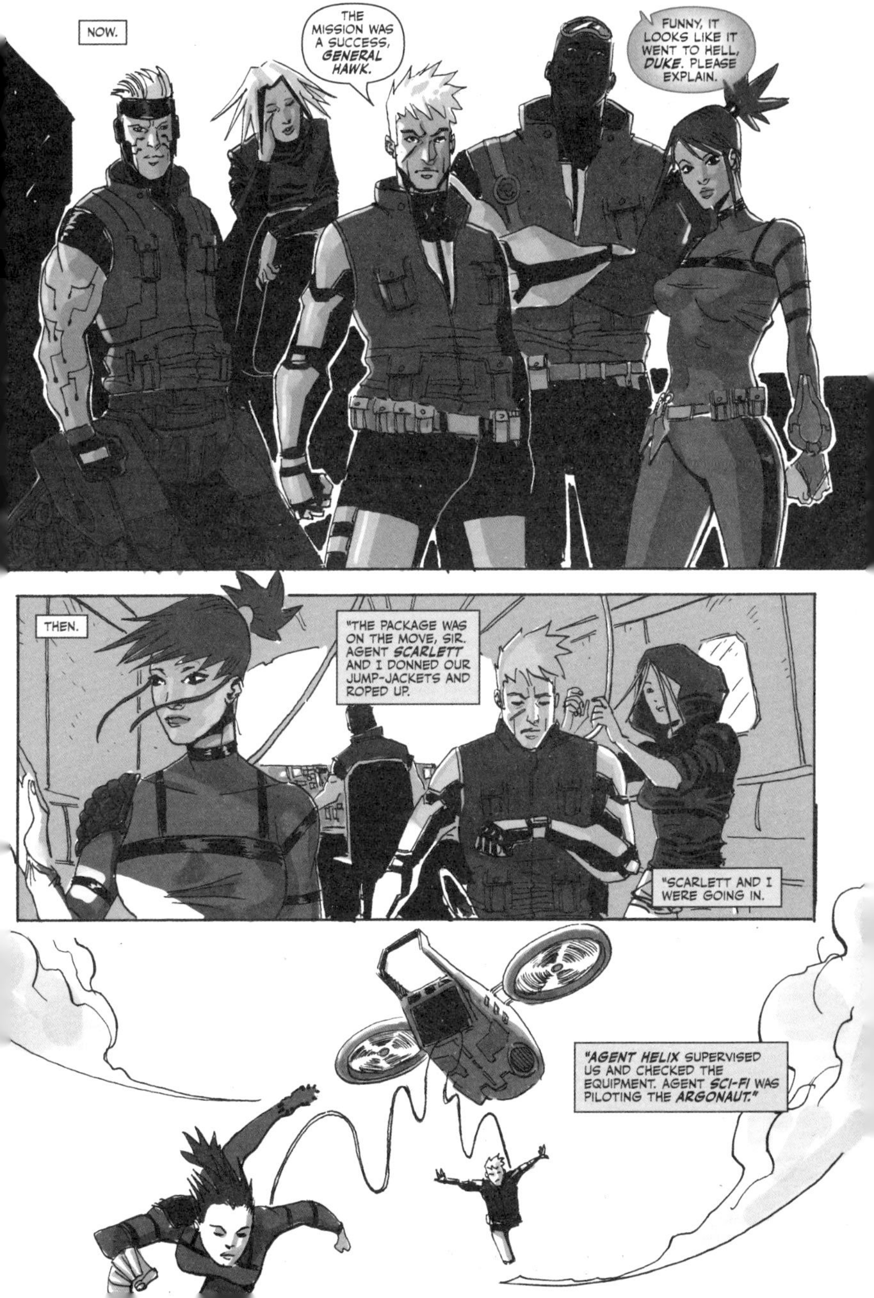
NOW.
THE MISSION WAS A SUCCESS, GENERAL HAWK.
FUNNY, IT LOOKS LIKE IT WENT TO HELL, DUKE. PLEASE EXPLAIN.
THEN.
"THE PACKAGE WAS ON THE MOVE, SIR. AGENT SCARLETT AND I DONNED OUR JUMP-JACKETS AND ROPED UP.
"SCARLETT AND I WERE GOING IN.
"AGENT HELIX SUPERVISED US AND CHECKED THE EQUIPMENT. AGENT SCI-FI WAS PILOTING THE ARGONAUT."

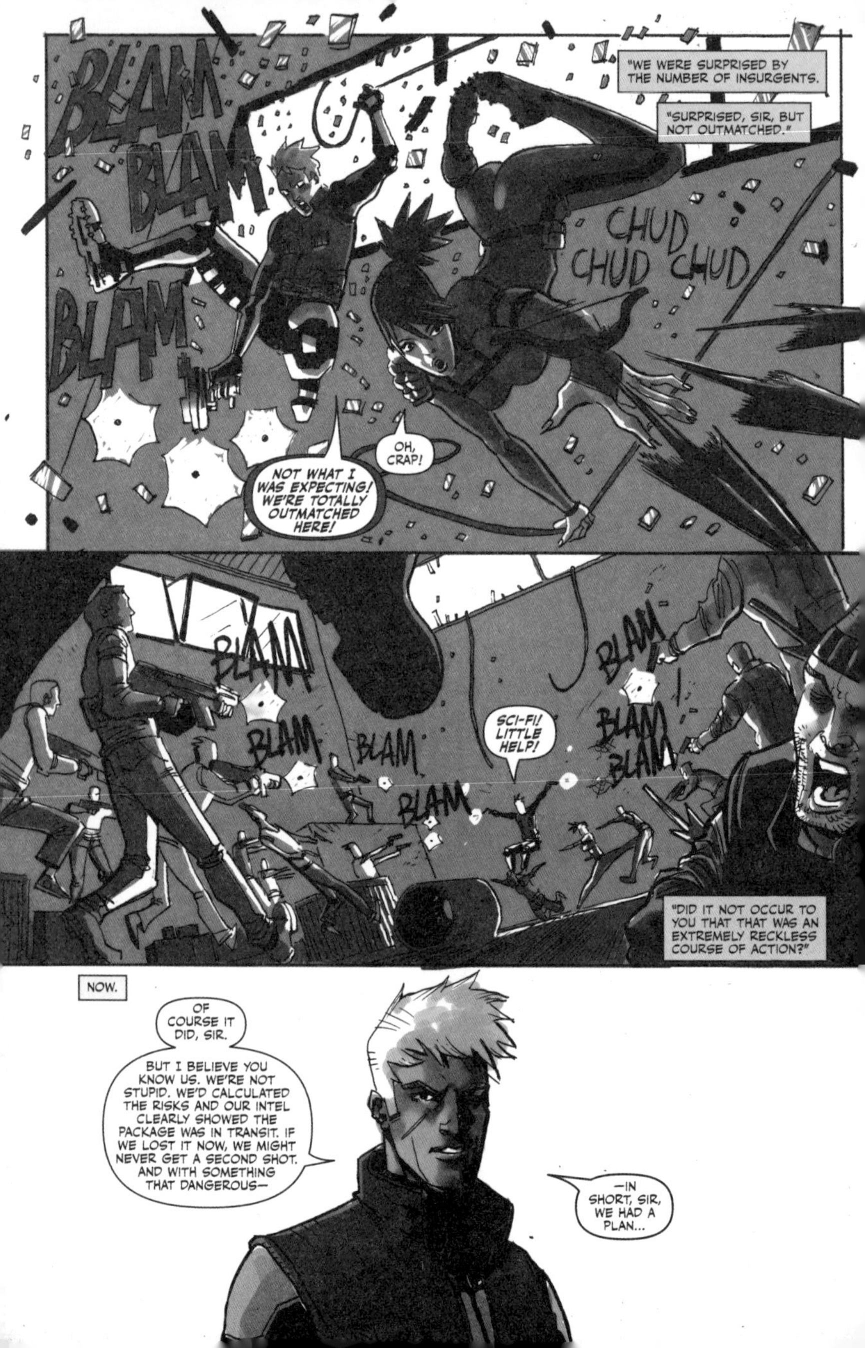
BLAM
BLAM
BLAM
"WE WERE SURPRISED BY THE NUMBER OF INSURGENTS.
"SURPRISED, SIR, BUT NOT OUTMATCHED."
CHUD CHUD CHUD
NOT WHAT I WAS EXPECTING! WE'RE TOTALLY OUTMATCHED HERE!
OH, CRAP!
BLAM
BLAM
BLAM
BLAM
SCI-FI! LITTLE HELP!
BLAM
BLAM
BLAM
"DID IT NOT OCCUR TO YOU THAT THAT WAS AN EXTREMELY RECKLESS COURSE OF ACTION?"
NOW.
OF COURSE IT DID, SIR.
BUT I BELIEVE YOU KNOW US. WE'RE NOT STUPID. WE'D CALCULATED THE RISKS AND OUR INTEL CLEARLY SHOWED THE PACKAGE WAS IN TRANSIT. IF WE LOST IT NOW, WE MIGHT NEVER GET A SECOND SHOT. AND WITH SOMETHING THAT DANGEROUS—
—IN SHORT, SIR, WE HAD A PLAN...

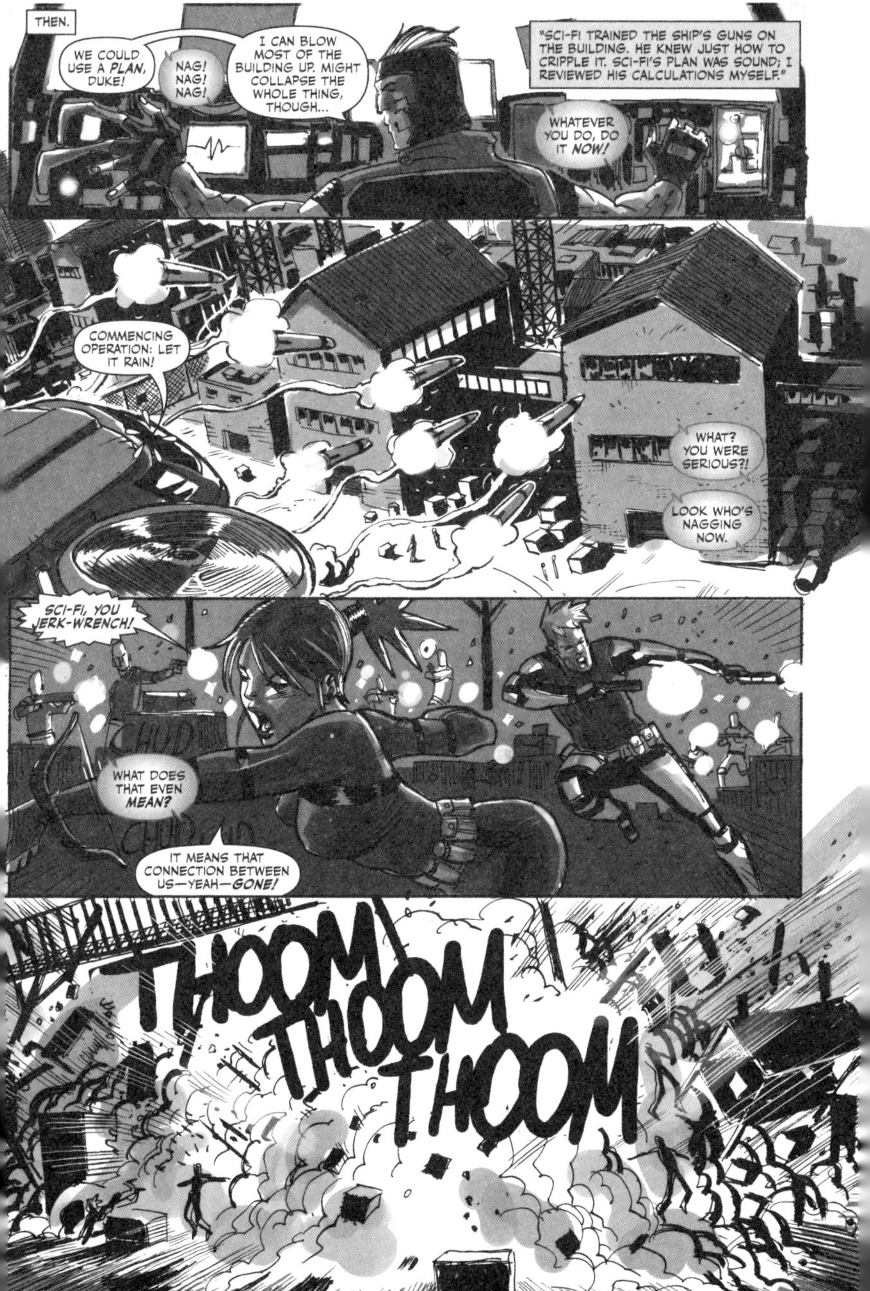
THEN.
WE COULD USE A *PLAN*, DUKE!
NAG! NAG! NAG!
I CAN BLOW MOST OF THE BUILDING UP. MIGHT COLLAPSE THE WHOLE THING, THOUGH...
"SCI-FI TRAINED THE SHIP'S GUNS ON THE BUILDING. HE KNEW JUST HOW TO CRIPPLE IT. SCI-FI'S PLAN WAS SOUND; I REVIEWED HIS CALCULATIONS MYSELF."
WHATEVER YOU DO, DO IT *NOW!*
COMMENCING OPERATION: LET IT RAIN!
WHAT? YOU WERE SERIOUS?!
LOOK WHO'S NAGGING NOW.
SCI-FI, YOU JERK-WRENCH!
CHUD
WHAT DOES THAT EVEN *MEAN?*
CHUD
IT MEANS THAT CONNECTION BETWEEN US—YEAH—*GONE!*
THOOM
THOOM
THOOM

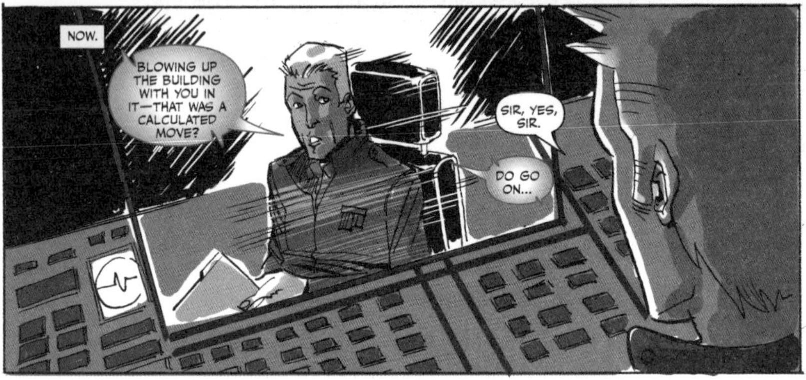
NOW.
BLOWING UP THE BUILDING WITH YOU IN IT—THAT WAS A CALCULATED MOVE?
SIR, YES, SIR.
DO GO ON...

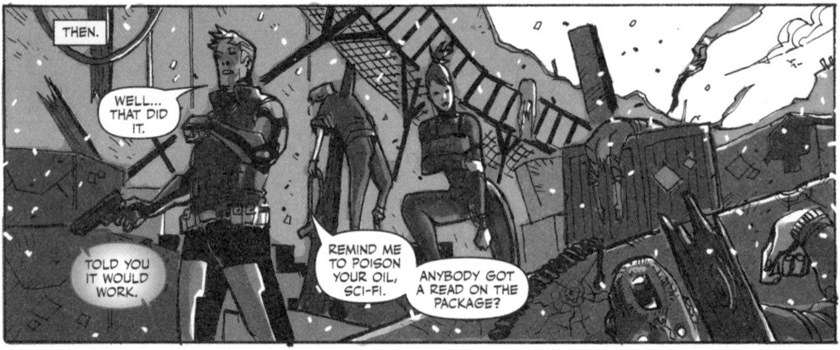
THEN.
WELL... THAT DID IT.
TOLD YOU IT WOULD WORK.
REMIND ME TO POISON YOUR OIL, SCI-FI.
ANYBODY GOT A READ ON THE PACKAGE?

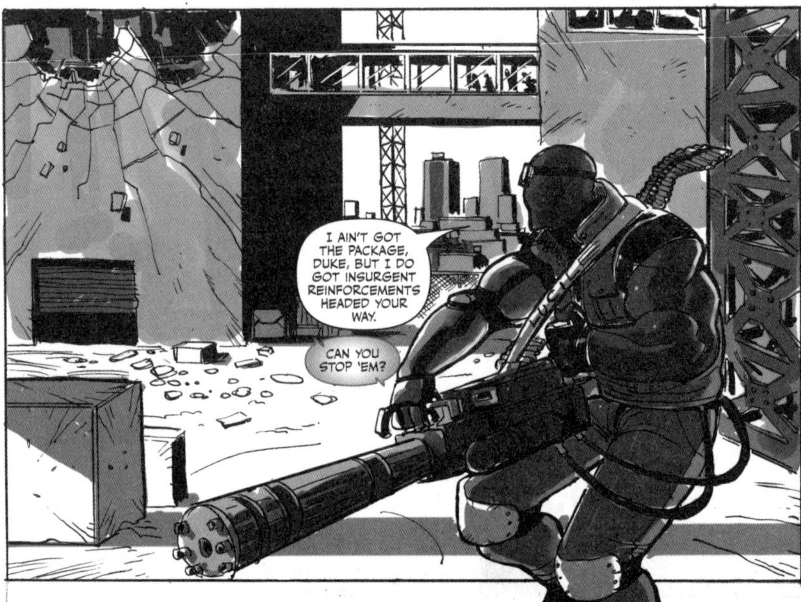
I AIN'T GOT THE PACKAGE, DUKE, BUT I DO GOT INSURGENT REINFORCEMENTS HEADED YOUR WAY.
CAN YOU STOP 'EM?

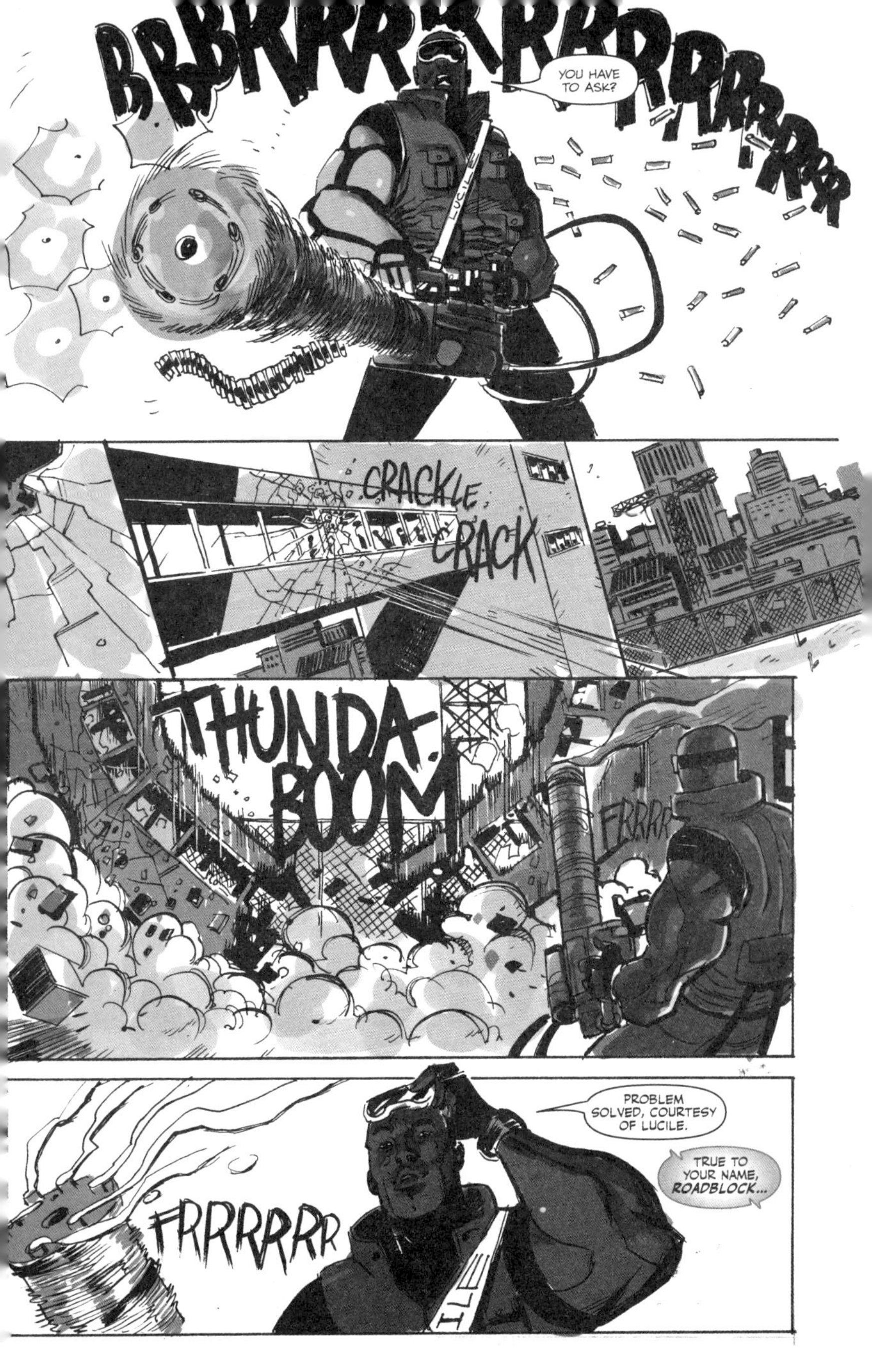

YOU HAVE TO ASK?
CRACKLE
CRACK
THUNDA BOOM
FRRRR
PROBLEM SOLVED, COURTESY OF LUCILE.
TRUE TO YOUR NAME, *ROADBLOCK*...
FRRRRRRR

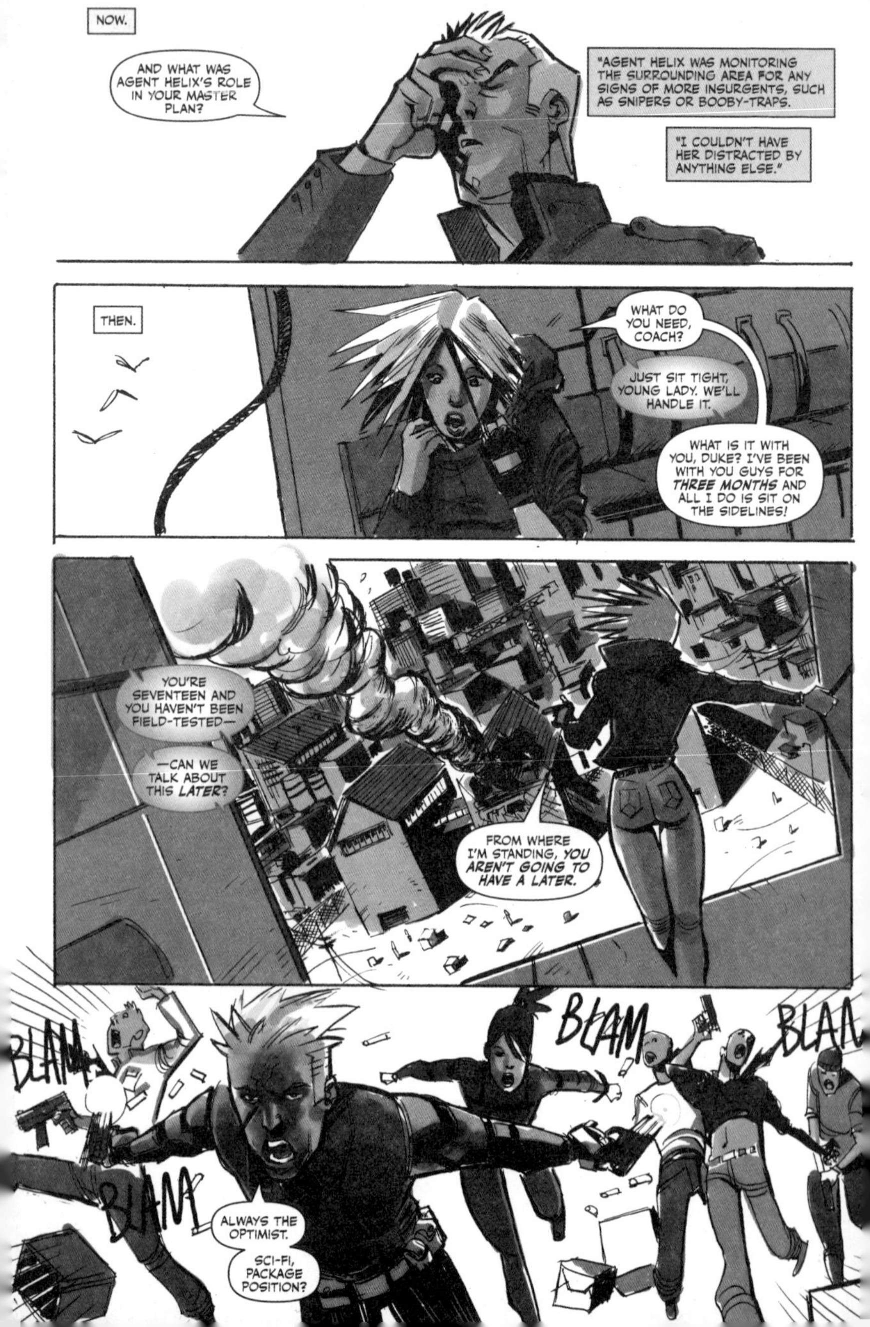
NOW.
AND WHAT WAS AGENT HELIX'S ROLE IN YOUR MASTER PLAN?
"AGENT HELIX WAS MONITORING THE SURROUNDING AREA FOR ANY SIGNS OF MORE INSURGENTS, SUCH AS SNIPERS OR BOOBY-TRAPS.
"I COULDN'T HAVE HER DISTRACTED BY ANYTHING ELSE."
THEN.
WHAT DO YOU NEED, COACH?
JUST SIT TIGHT, YOUNG LADY. WE'LL HANDLE IT.
WHAT IS IT WITH YOU, DUKE? I'VE BEEN WITH YOU GUYS FOR THREE MONTHS AND ALL I DO IS SIT ON THE SIDELINES!
YOU'RE SEVENTEEN AND YOU HAVEN'T BEEN FIELD-TESTED—
—CAN WE TALK ABOUT THIS LATER?
FROM WHERE I'M STANDING, YOU AREN'T GOING TO HAVE A LATER.
BLAM
BLAM
BLAM
BLAM
ALWAYS THE OPTIMIST.
SCI-FI, PACKAGE POSITION?

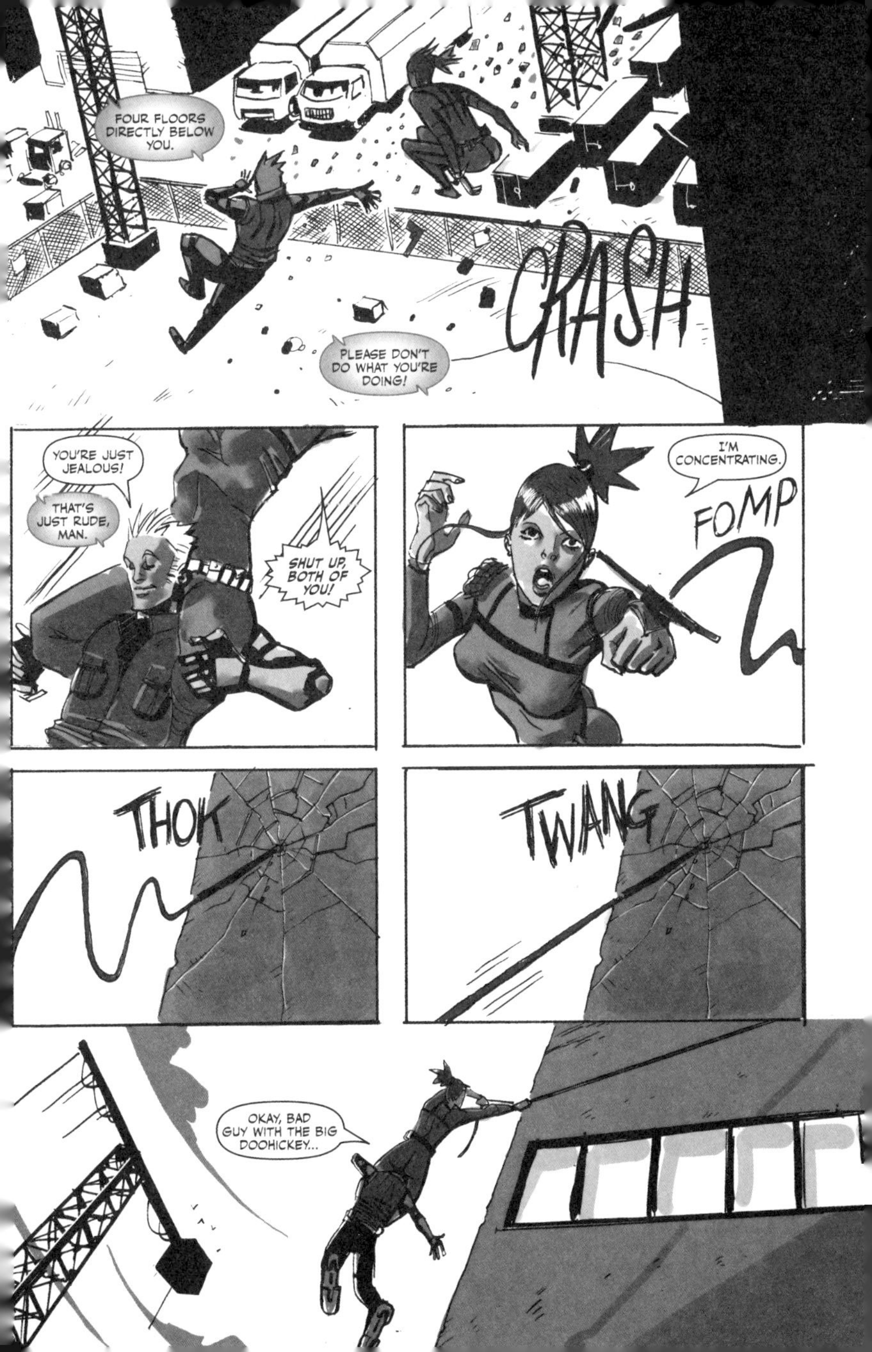
FOUR FLOORS DIRECTLY BELOW YOU.
CRASH
PLEASE DON'T DO WHAT YOU'RE DOING!
YOU'RE JUST JEALOUS!
THAT'S JUST RUDE, MAN.
SHUT UP, BOTH OF YOU!
I'M CONCENTRATING.
FOMP
THOK
TWANG
OKAY, BAD GUY WITH THE BIG DOOHICKEY...

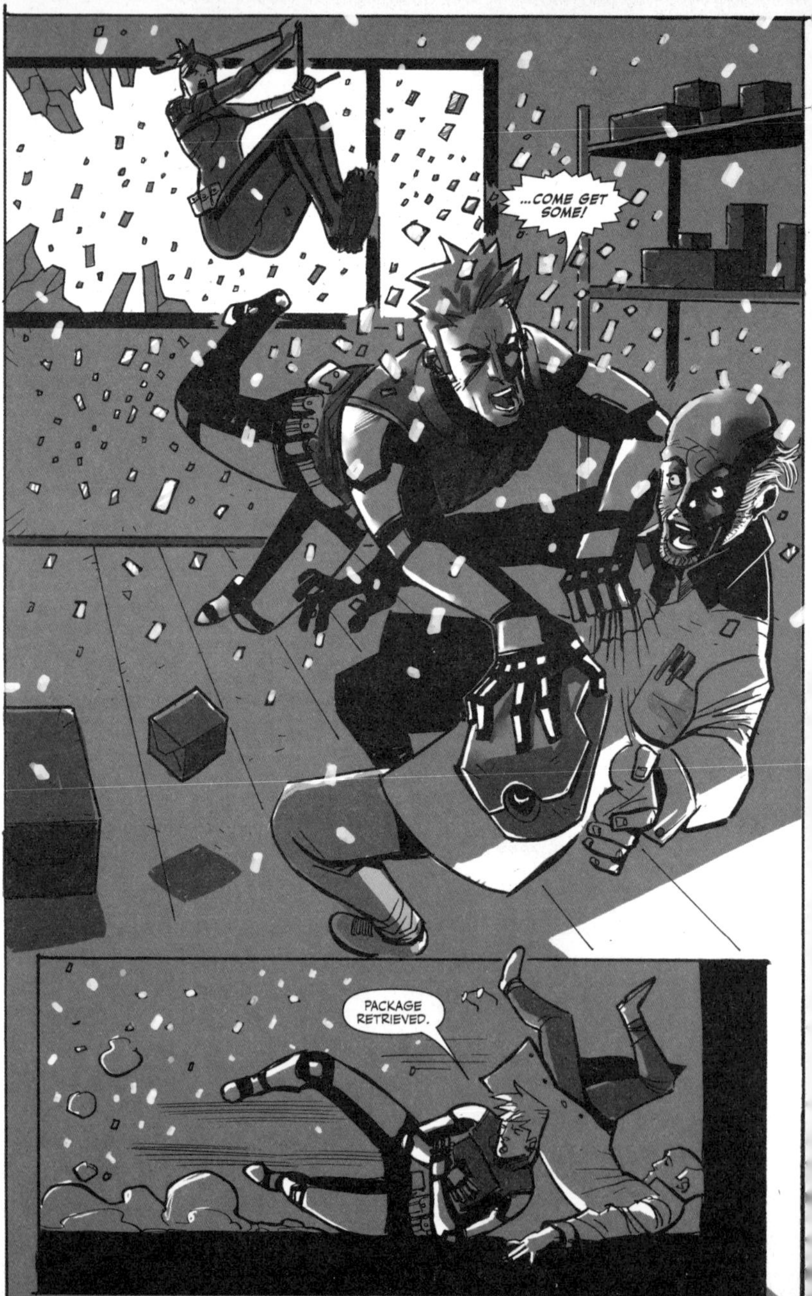
...COME GET SOME!
PACKAGE RETRIEVED.

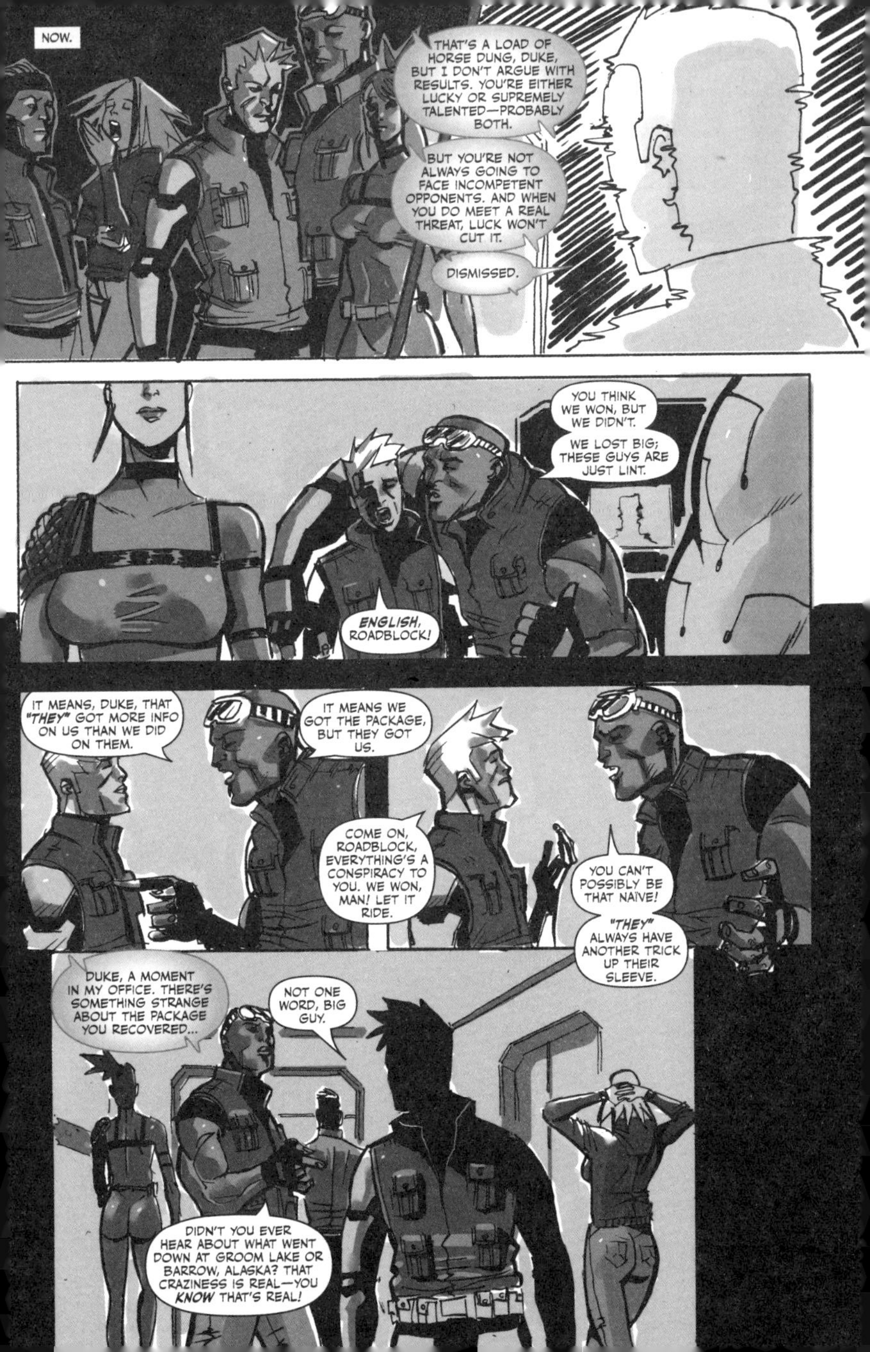
NOW.
THAT'S A LOAD OF HORSE DUNG, DUKE, BUT I DON'T ARGUE WITH RESULTS. YOU'RE EITHER LUCKY OR SUPREMELY TALENTED—PROBABLY BOTH.
BUT YOU'RE NOT ALWAYS GOING TO FACE INCOMPETENT OPPONENTS. AND WHEN YOU DO MEET A REAL THREAT, LUCK WON'T CUT IT.
DISMISSED.
YOU THINK WE WON, BUT WE DIDN'T.
WE LOST BIG; THESE GUYS ARE JUST LINT.
ENGLISH, ROADBLOCK!
IT MEANS, DUKE, THAT *"THEY"* GOT MORE INFO ON US THAN WE DID ON THEM.
IT MEANS WE GOT THE PACKAGE, BUT THEY GOT US.
COME ON, ROADBLOCK, EVERYTHING'S A CONSPIRACY TO YOU. WE WON, MAN! LET IT RIDE.
YOU CAN'T POSSIBLY BE THAT NAÏVE!
"THEY" ALWAYS HAVE ANOTHER TRICK UP THEIR SLEEVE.
DUKE, A MOMENT IN MY OFFICE. THERE'S SOMETHING STRANGE ABOUT THE PACKAGE YOU RECOVERED...
NOT ONE WORD, BIG GUY.
DIDN'T YOU EVER HEAR ABOUT WHAT WENT DOWN AT GROOM LAKE OR BARROW, ALASKA? THAT CRAZINESS IS REAL—YOU *KNOW* THAT'S REAL!

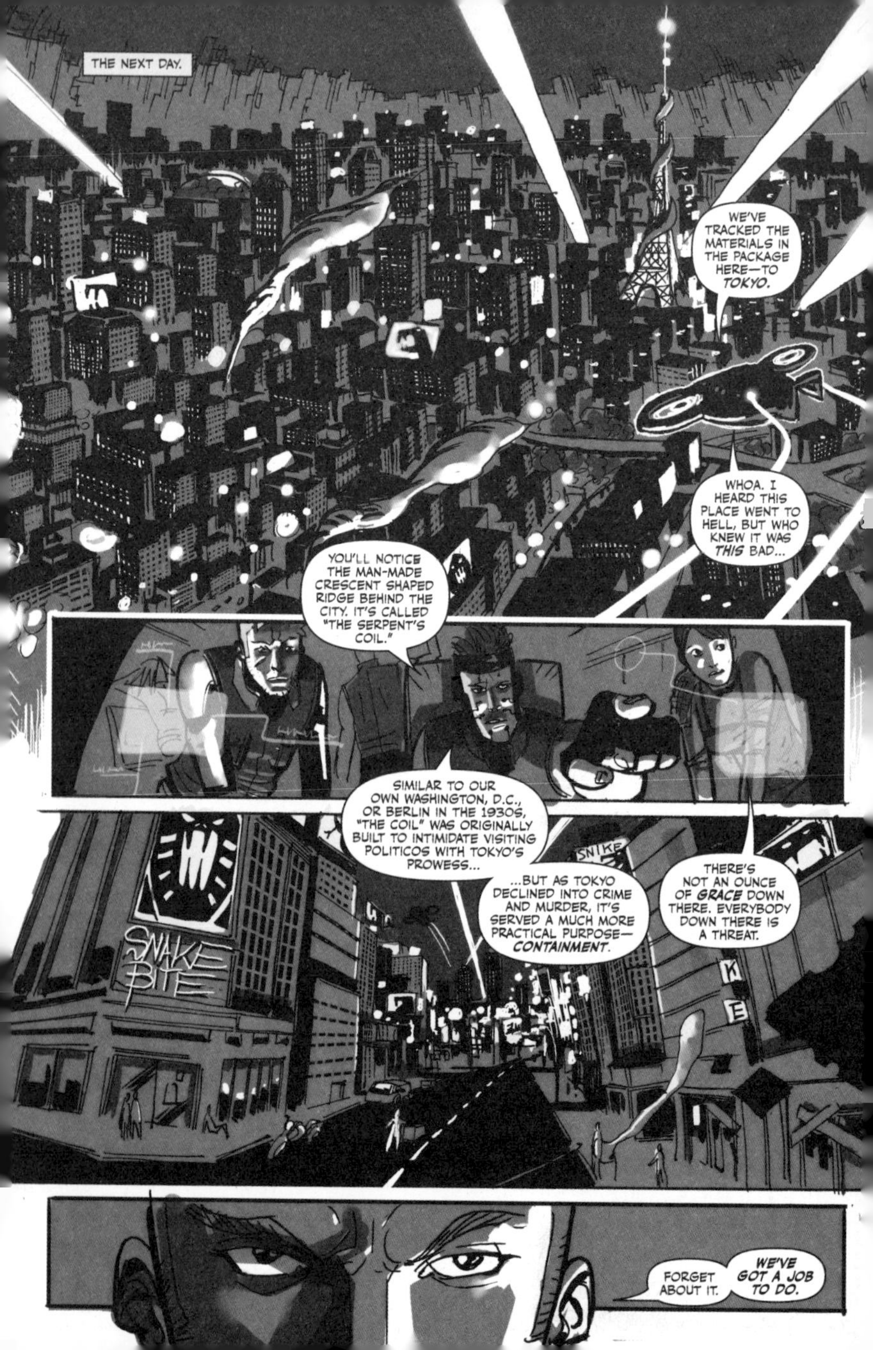
THE NEXT DAY.
WE'VE TRACKED THE MATERIALS IN THE PACKAGE HERE—TO TOKYO.
WHOA. I HEARD THIS PLACE WENT TO HELL, BUT WHO KNEW IT WAS THIS BAD...
YOU'LL NOTICE THE MAN-MADE CRESCENT SHAPED RIDGE BEHIND THE CITY. IT'S CALLED "THE SERPENT'S COIL."
SIMILAR TO OUR OWN WASHINGTON, D.C., OR BERLIN IN THE 1930S, "THE COIL" WAS ORIGINALLY BUILT TO INTIMIDATE VISITING POLITICOS WITH TOKYO'S PROWESS...
...BUT AS TOKYO DECLINED INTO CRIME AND MURDER, IT'S SERVED A MUCH MORE PRACTICAL PURPOSE—CONTAINMENT.
THERE'S NOT AN OUNCE OF GRACE DOWN THERE. EVERYBODY DOWN THERE IS A THREAT.
SNAKE BITE
FORGET ABOUT IT.
WE'VE GOT A JOB TO DO.

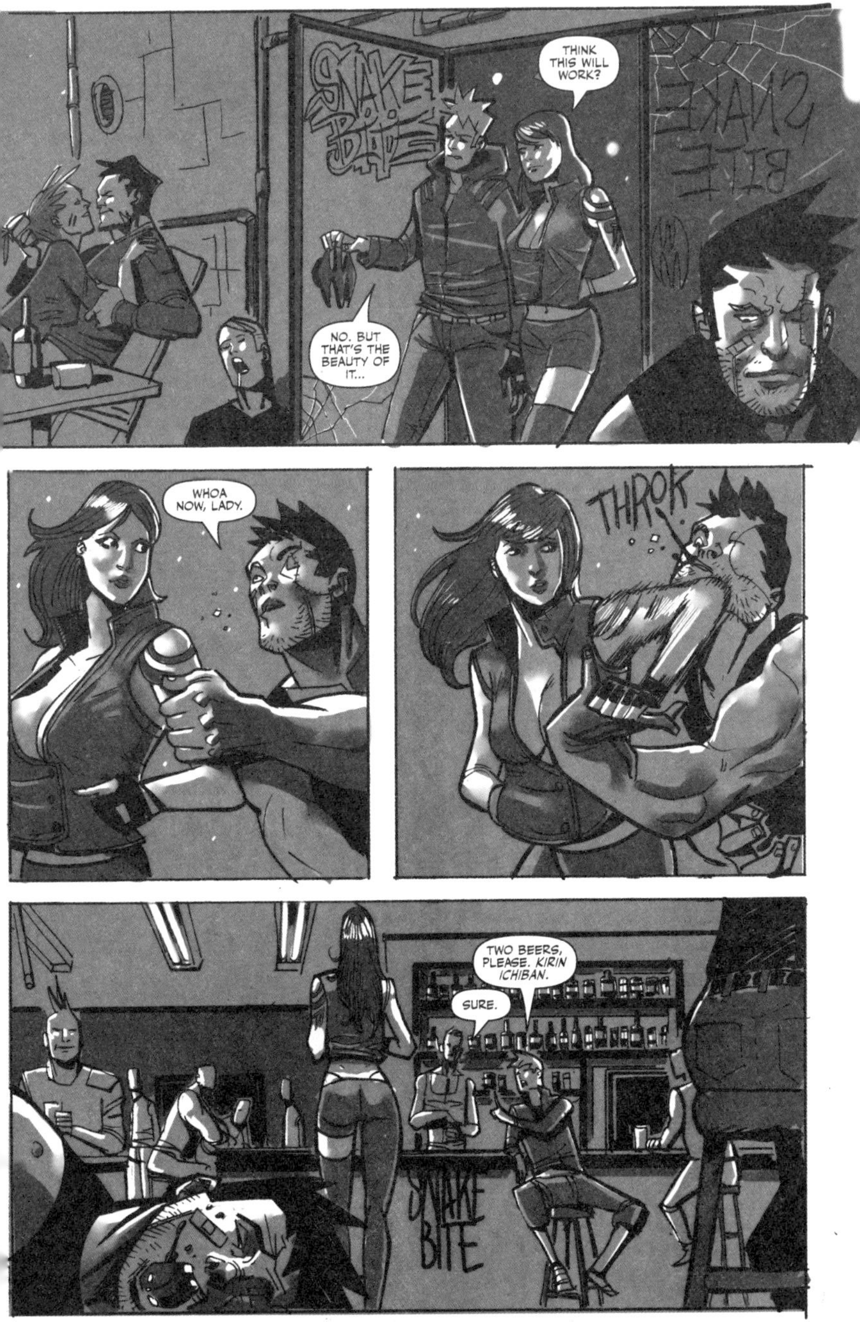
SNAKE BITE
THINK THIS WILL WORK?
NO. BUT THAT'S THE BEAUTY OF IT...
SNAKE BITE
WHOA NOW, LADY.
THROK!
TWO BEERS, PLEASE. KIRIN ICHIBAN.
SURE.
SNAKE BITE

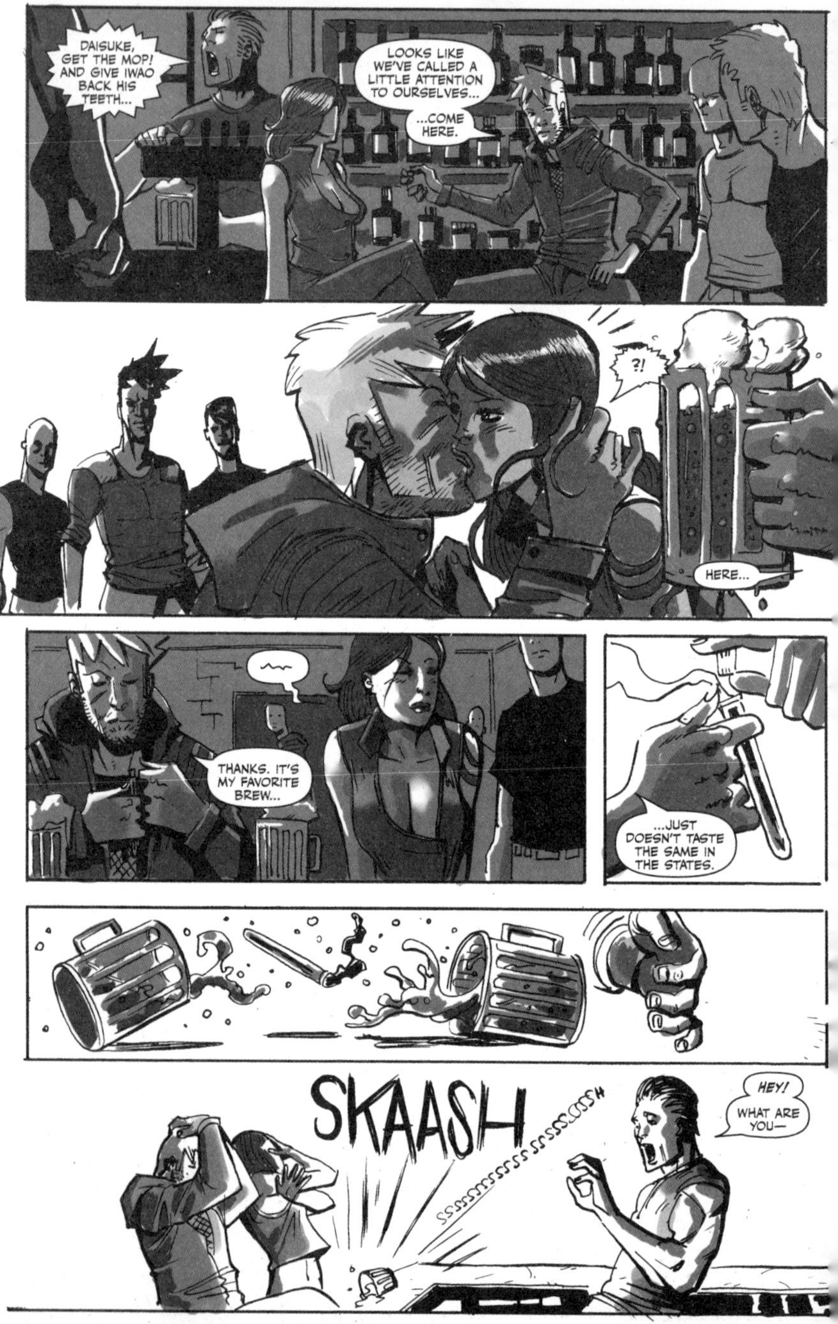
DAISUKE, GET THE MOP! AND GIVE IWAO BACK HIS TEETH...
LOOKS LIKE WE'VE CALLED A LITTLE ATTENTION TO OURSELVES...
...COME HERE.
?!
HERE...
~
THANKS. IT'S MY FAVORITE BREW...
...JUST DOESN'T TASTE THE SAME IN THE STATES.
SKAASH
SSSSSSSSSSSSSSSSSSSSSSSSSH
HEY!
WHAT ARE YOU—

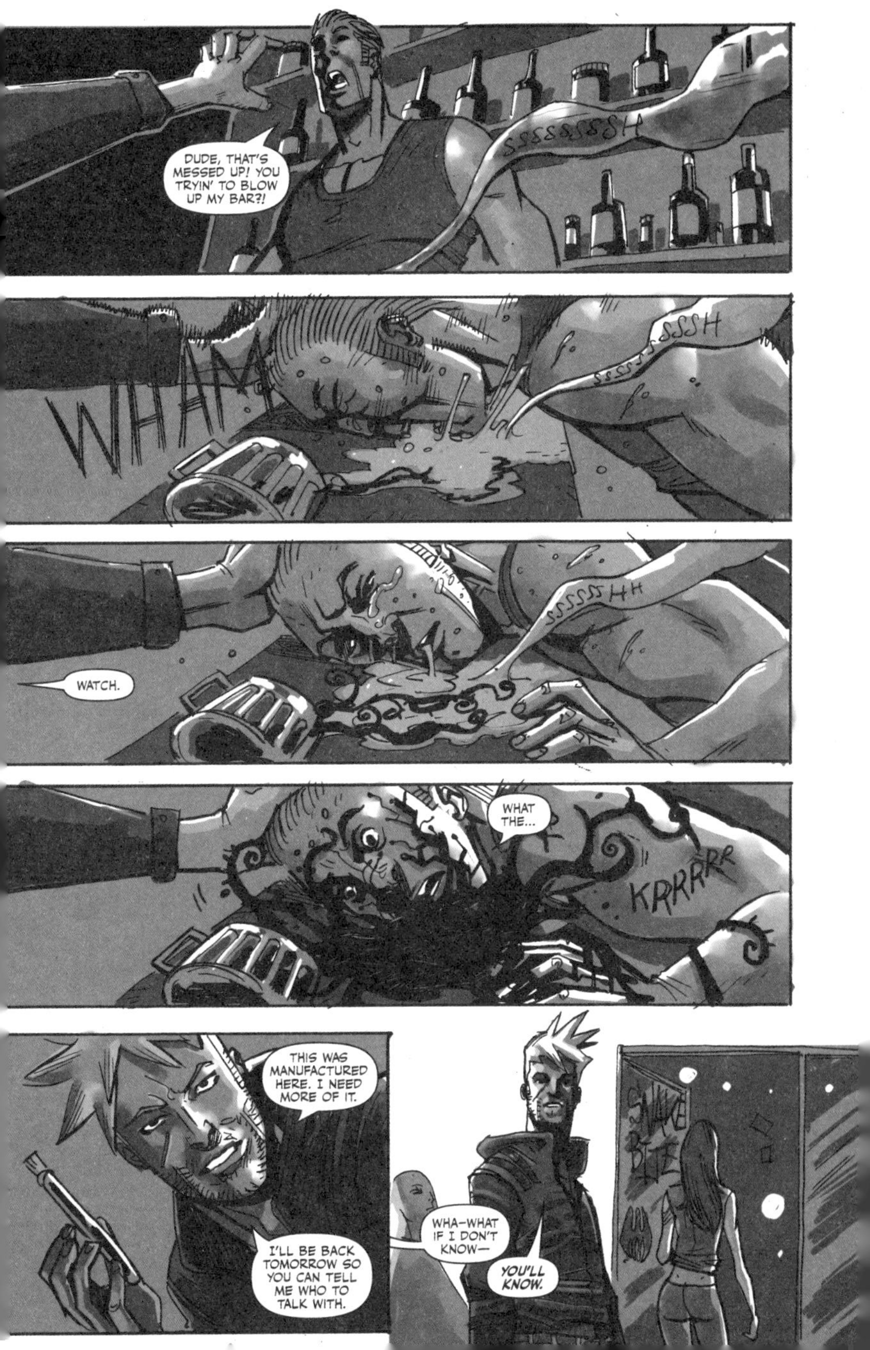

DUDE, THAT'S MESSED UP! YOU TRYIN' TO BLOW UP MY BAR?!
SSSSSSSSSH
WHAM
SSSSSSSSSH
WATCH.
SSSSSSHH
WHAT THE...
KRRRRRR
THIS WAS MANUFACTURED HERE. I NEED MORE OF IT.
I'LL BE BACK TOMORROW SO YOU CAN TELL ME WHO TO TALK WITH.
WHA–WHAT IF I DON'T KNOW—
YOU'LL KNOW.

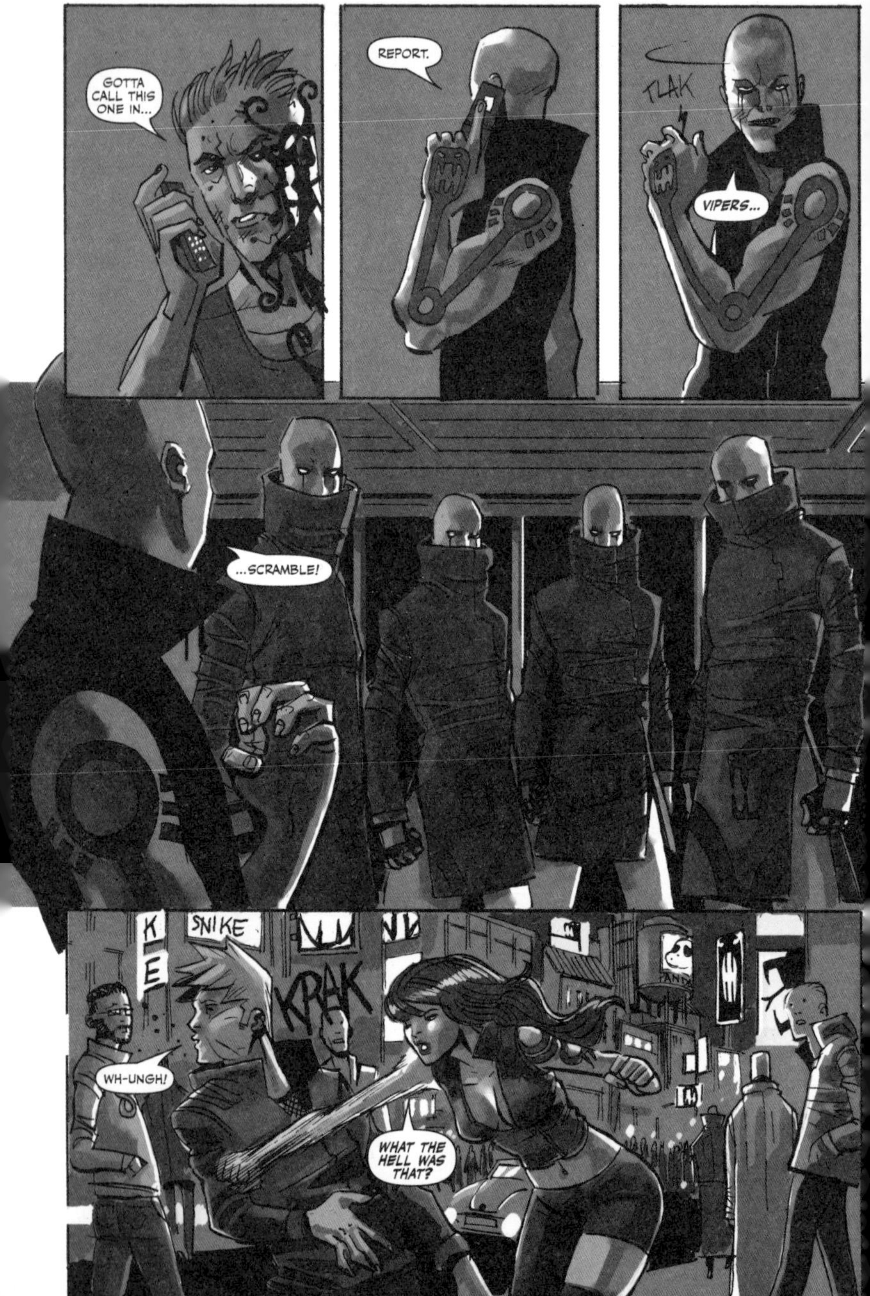
GOTTA CALL THIS ONE IN...
REPORT.
TLAK
VIPERS...
...SCRAMBLE!
SNIKE
KRAK
WH-UNGH!
WHAT THE HELL WAS THAT?

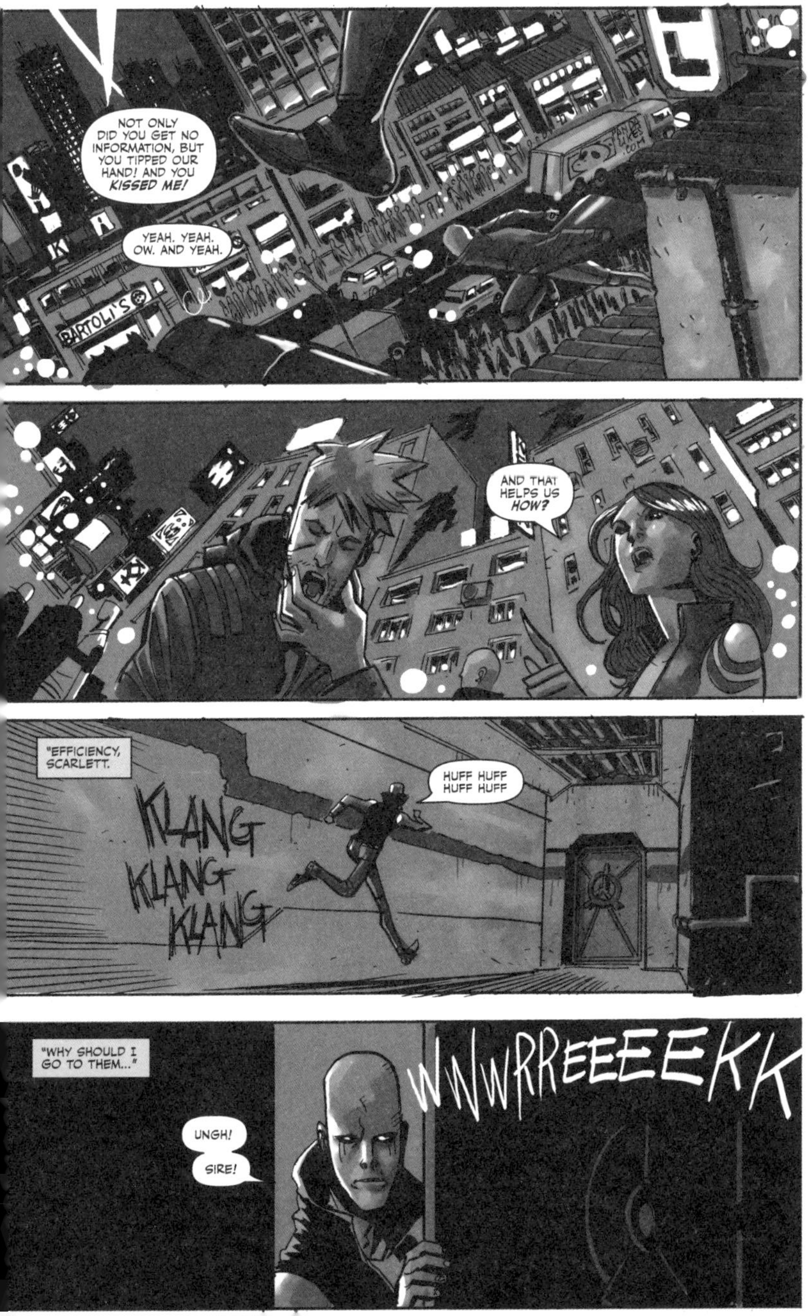
NOT ONLY DID YOU GET NO INFORMATION, BUT YOU TIPPED OUR HAND! AND YOU *KISSED ME!*
YEAH. YEAH. OW. AND YEAH.
BARTOLI'S
AND THAT HELPS US *HOW?*
"EFFICIENCY, SCARLETT.
HUFF HUFF HUFF HUFF
KLANG KLANG KLANG
"WHY SHOULD I GO TO THEM..."
UNGH!
SIRE!
WWWRREEEEEKK

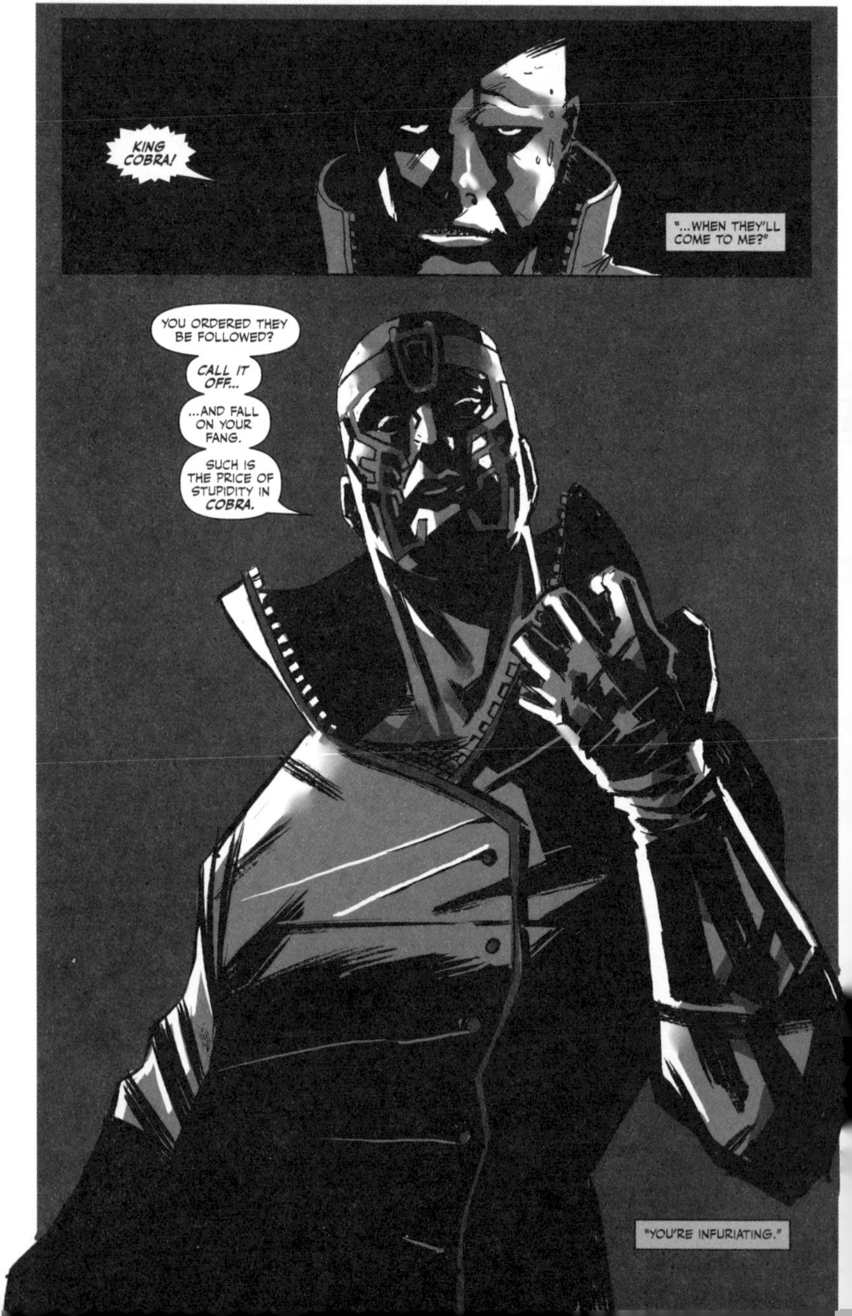
KING COBRA!
"...WHEN THEY'LL COME TO ME?"
YOU ORDERED THEY BE FOLLOWED?
CALL IT OFF...
...AND FALL ON YOUR FANG.
SUCH IS THE PRICE OF STUPIDITY IN COBRA.
"YOU'RE INFURIATING."

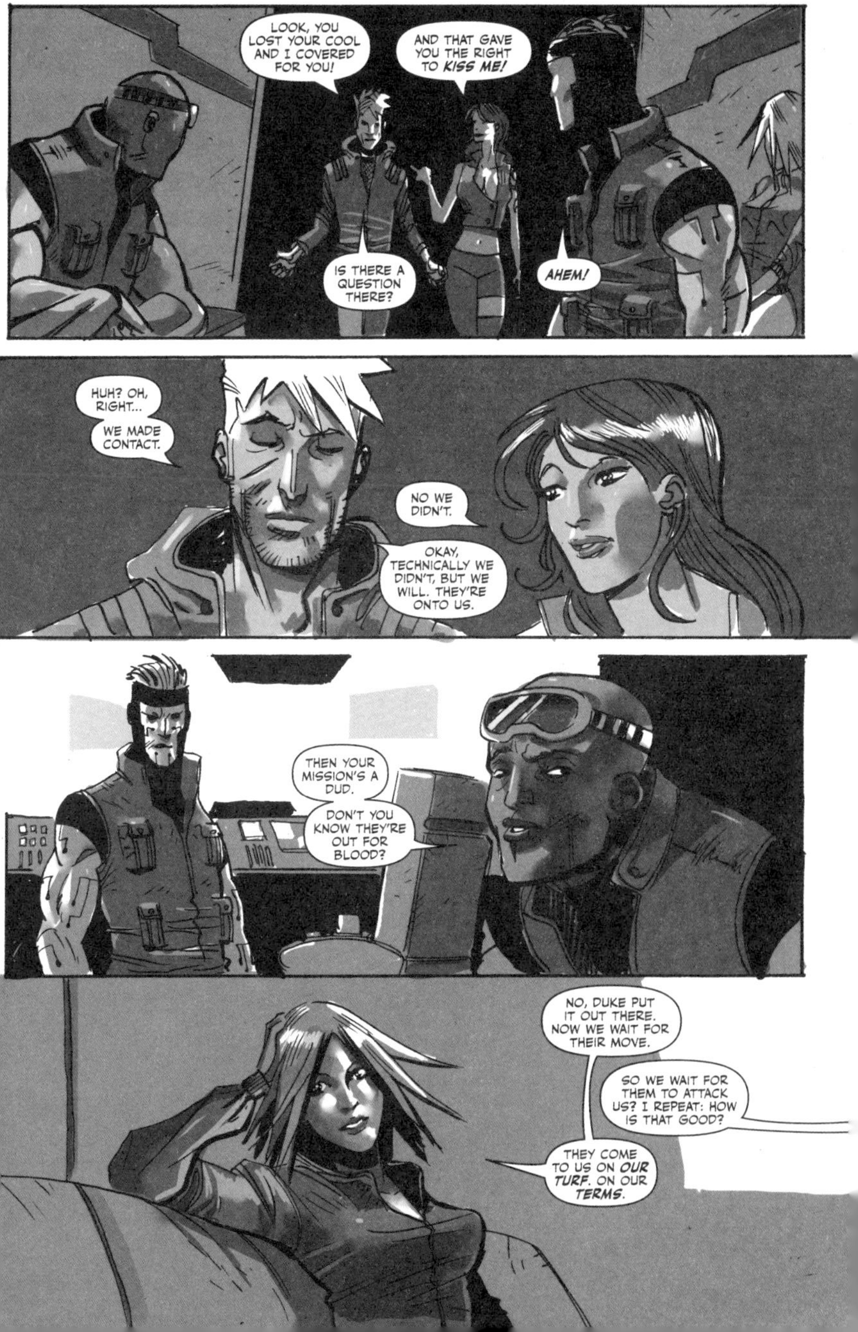
LOOK, YOU LOST YOUR COOL AND I COVERED FOR YOU!
AND THAT GAVE YOU THE RIGHT TO KISS ME!
IS THERE A QUESTION THERE?
AHEM!
HUH? OH, RIGHT...
WE MADE CONTACT.
NO WE DIDN'T.
OKAY, TECHNICALLY WE DIDN'T, BUT WE WILL. THEY'RE ONTO US.
THEN YOUR MISSION'S A DUD.
DON'T YOU KNOW THEY'RE OUT FOR BLOOD?
NO, DUKE PUT IT OUT THERE. NOW WE WAIT FOR THEIR MOVE.
SO WE WAIT FOR THEM TO ATTACK US? I REPEAT: HOW IS THAT GOOD?
THEY COME TO US ON OUR TURF. ON OUR TERMS.

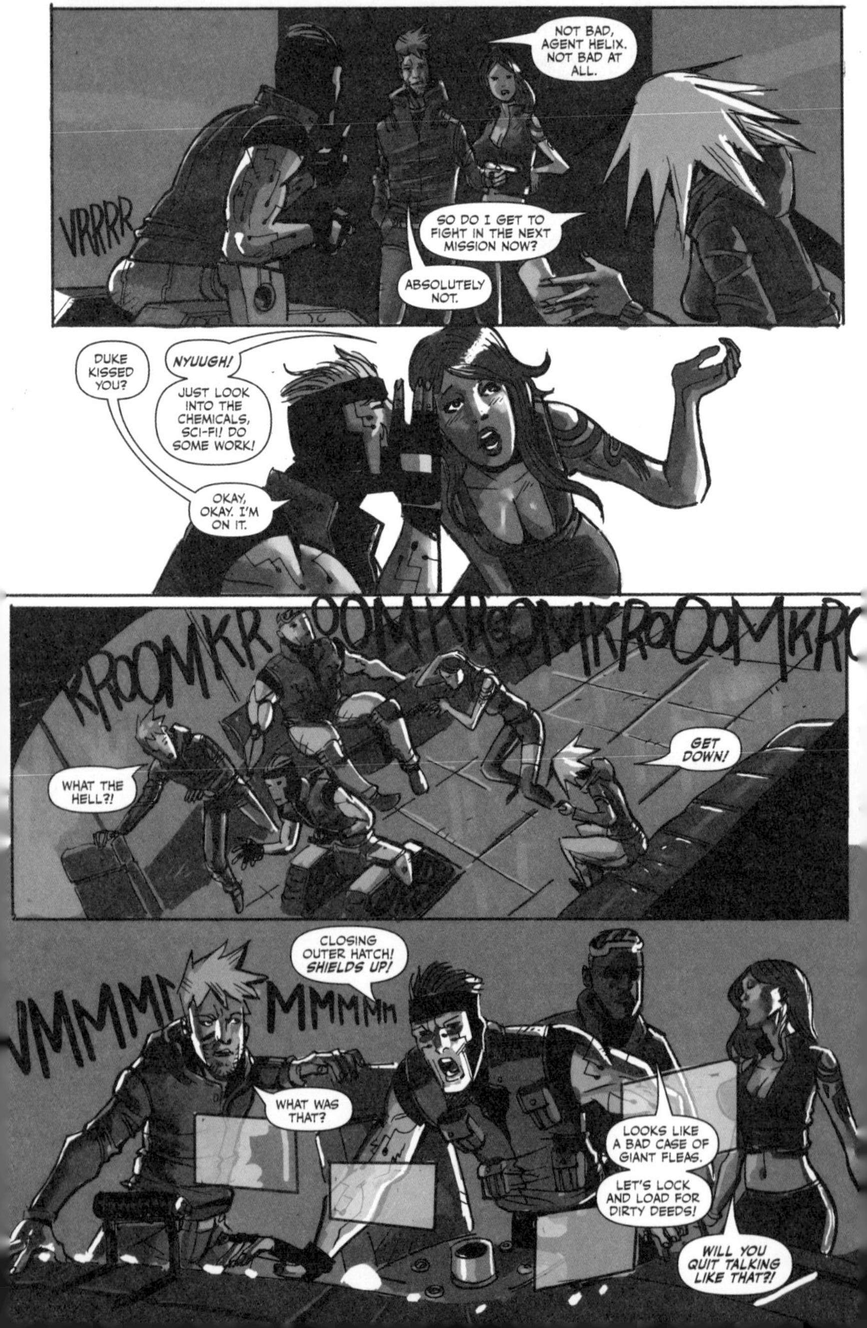
NOT BAD, AGENT HELIX. NOT BAD AT ALL.
VRRRR
SO DO I GET TO FIGHT IN THE NEXT MISSION NOW?
ABSOLUTELY NOT.
DUKE KISSED YOU?
NYUUGH!
JUST LOOK INTO THE CHEMICALS, SCI-FI! DO SOME WORK!
OKAY, OKAY. I'M ON IT.
KROOMKROOMKROOMKROOMKRO
WHAT THE HELL?!
GET DOWN!
CLOSING OUTER HATCH! SHIELDS UP!
VMMMMMMMMm
WHAT WAS THAT?
LOOKS LIKE A BAD CASE OF GIANT FLEAS.
LET'S LOCK AND LOAD FOR DIRTY DEEDS!
WILL YOU QUIT TALKING LIKE THAT?!

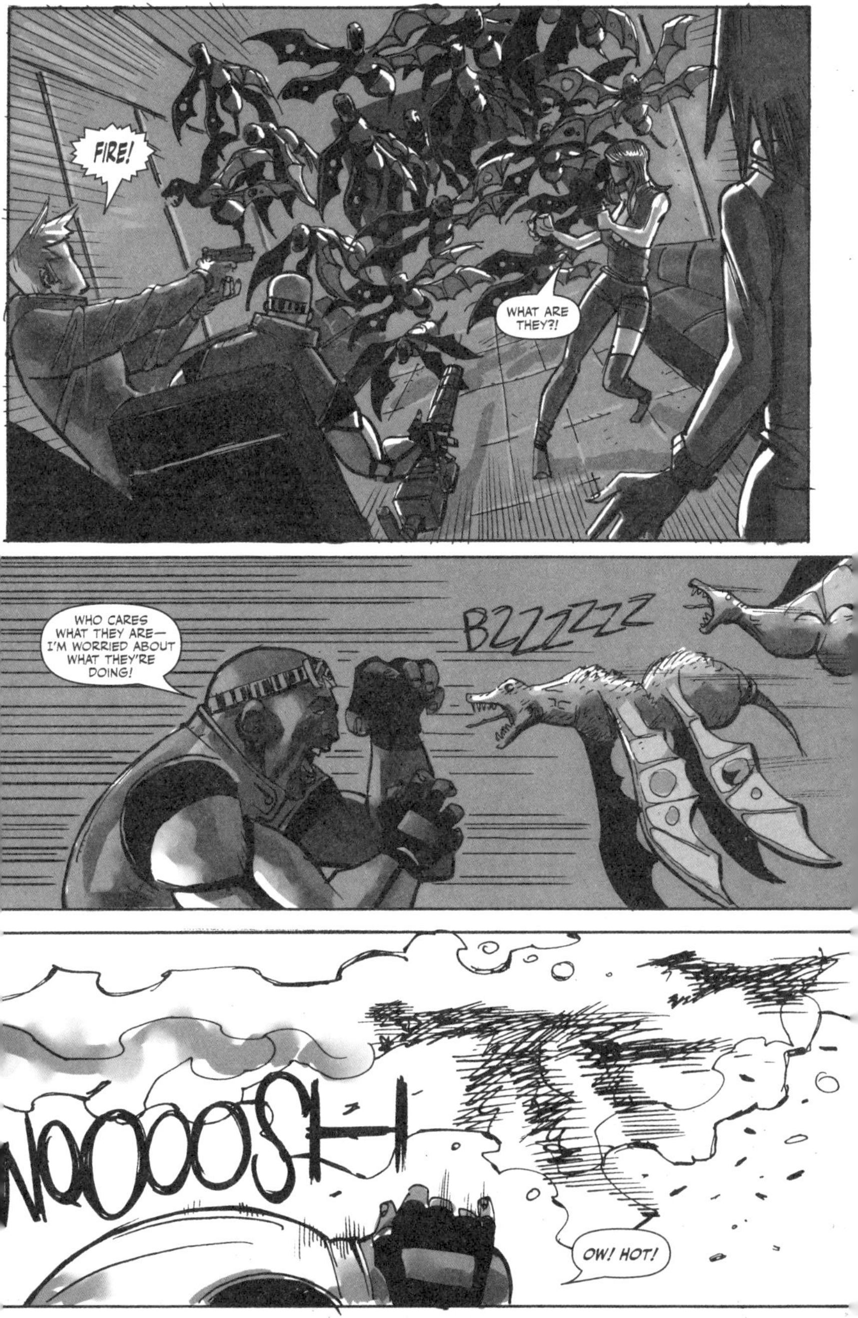
FIRE!
WHAT ARE THEY?!
WHO CARES WHAT THEY ARE— I'M WORRIED ABOUT WHAT THEY'RE DOING!
BZZZZZZ
WOOOOSH
OW! HOT!

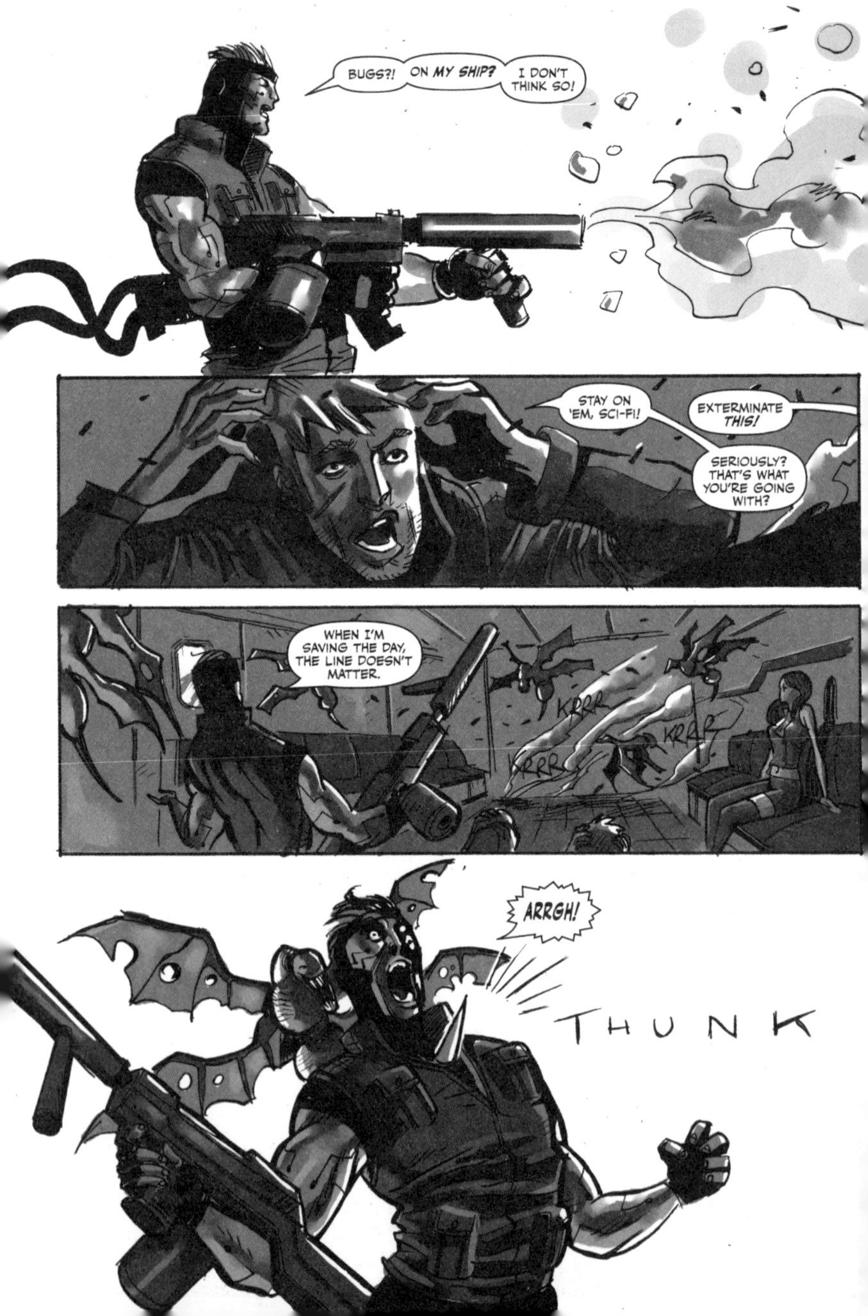
BUGS?!
ON MY SHIP?
I DON'T THINK SO!
STAY ON 'EM, SCI-FI!
EXTERMINATE THIS!
SERIOUSLY? THAT'S WHAT YOU'RE GOING WITH?
WHEN I'M SAVING THE DAY, THE LINE DOESN'T MATTER.
KRRR
KRRR
KRRR
ARRGH!
THUNK

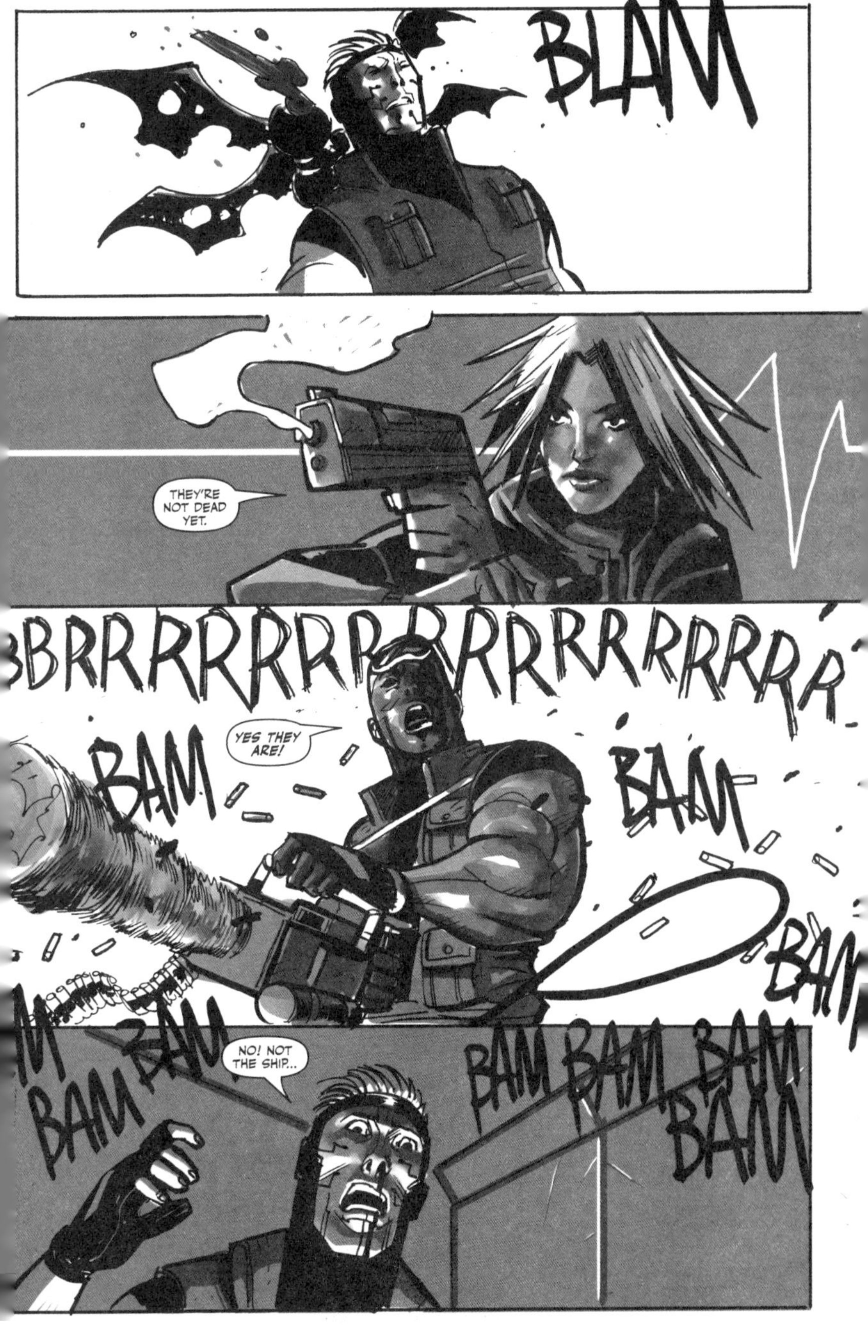
BLAM
THEY'RE NOT DEAD YET.
BRRRRRRRRRRRRRRRR
YES THEY ARE!
BAM
BAM
BAM
BAM BAM BAM
NO! NOT THE SHIP...
BAM BAM BAM BAM

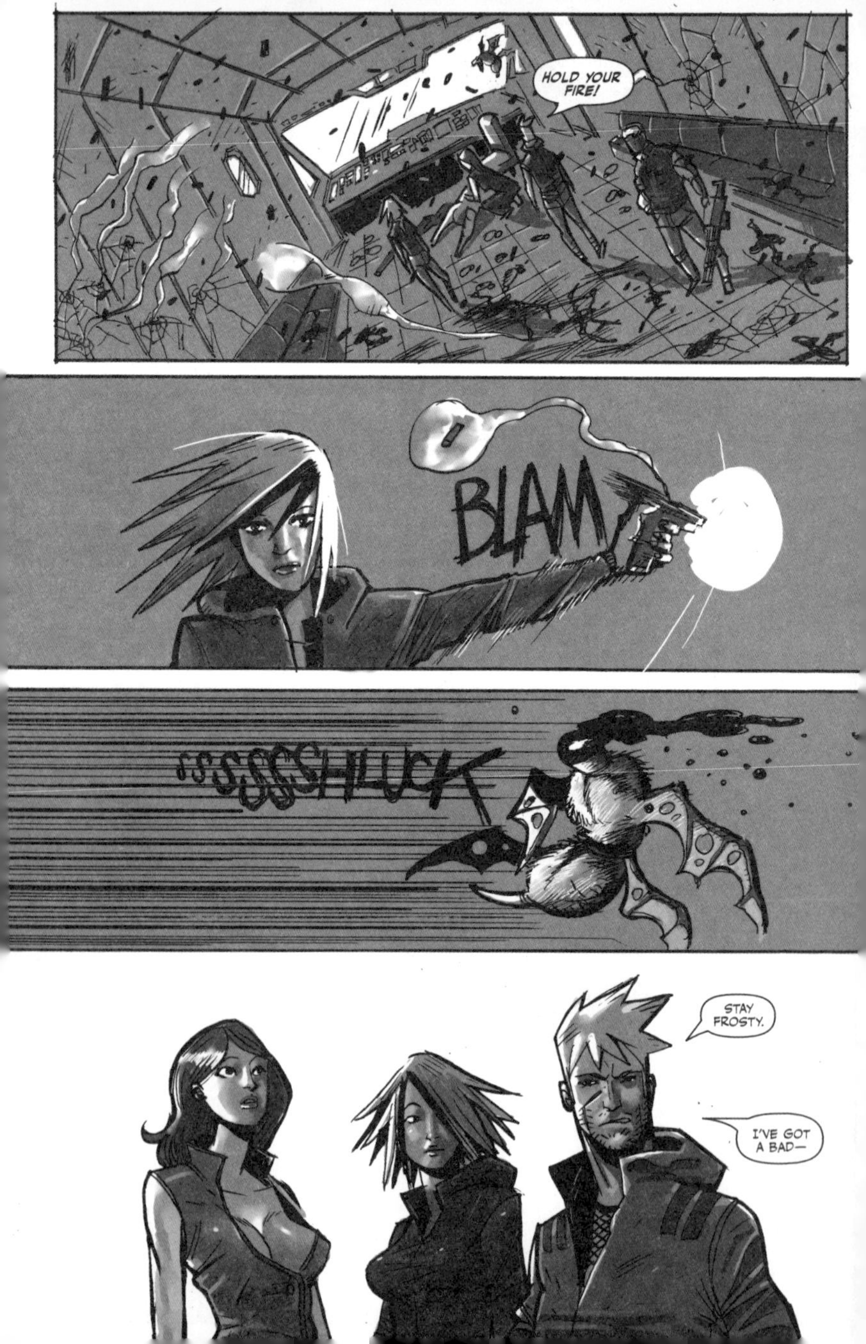
HOLD YOUR FIRE!
BLAM
SSSSSSHLUCK
STAY FROSTY.
I'VE GOT A BAD—

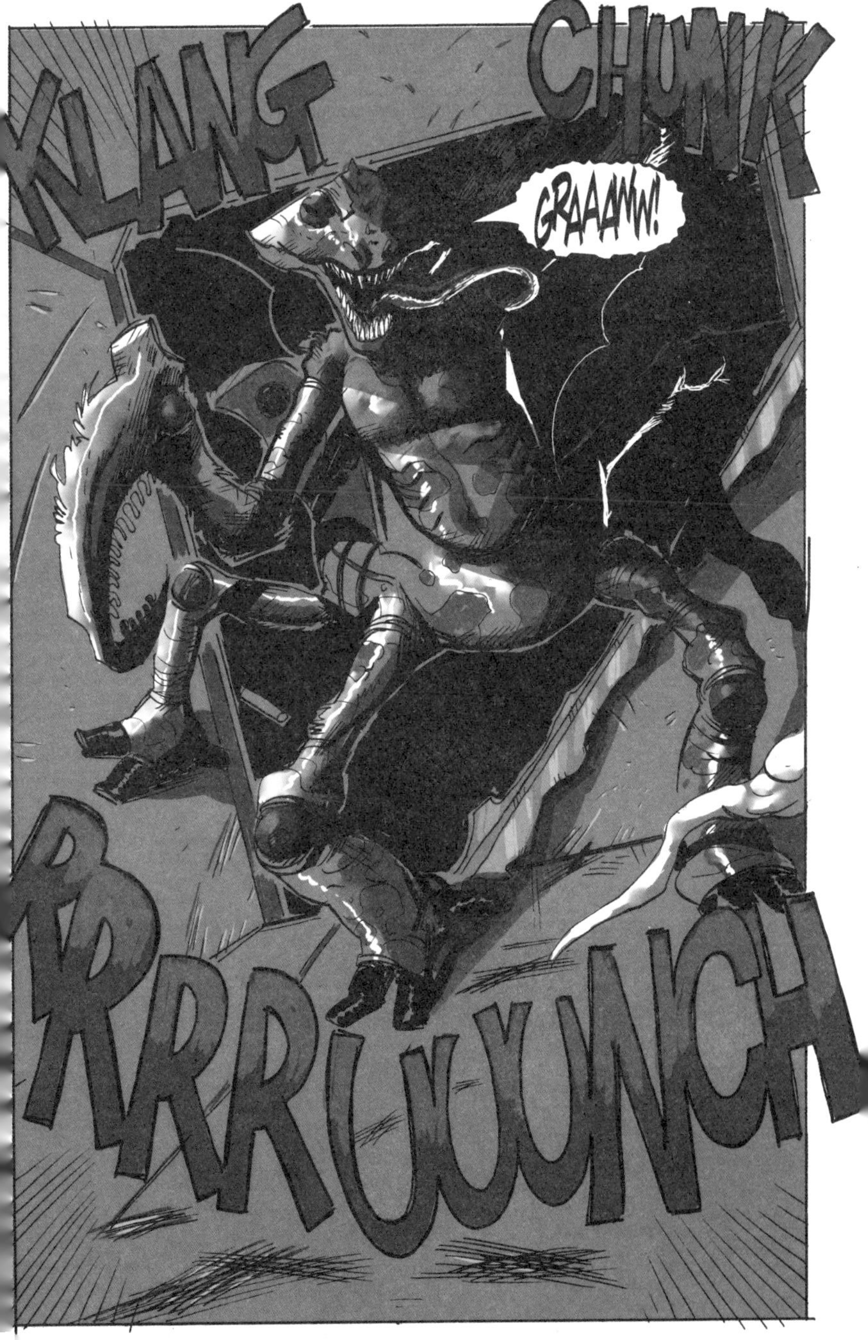
KLANG
CHUNK
GRAAAWW!
RRRRUUUNCH

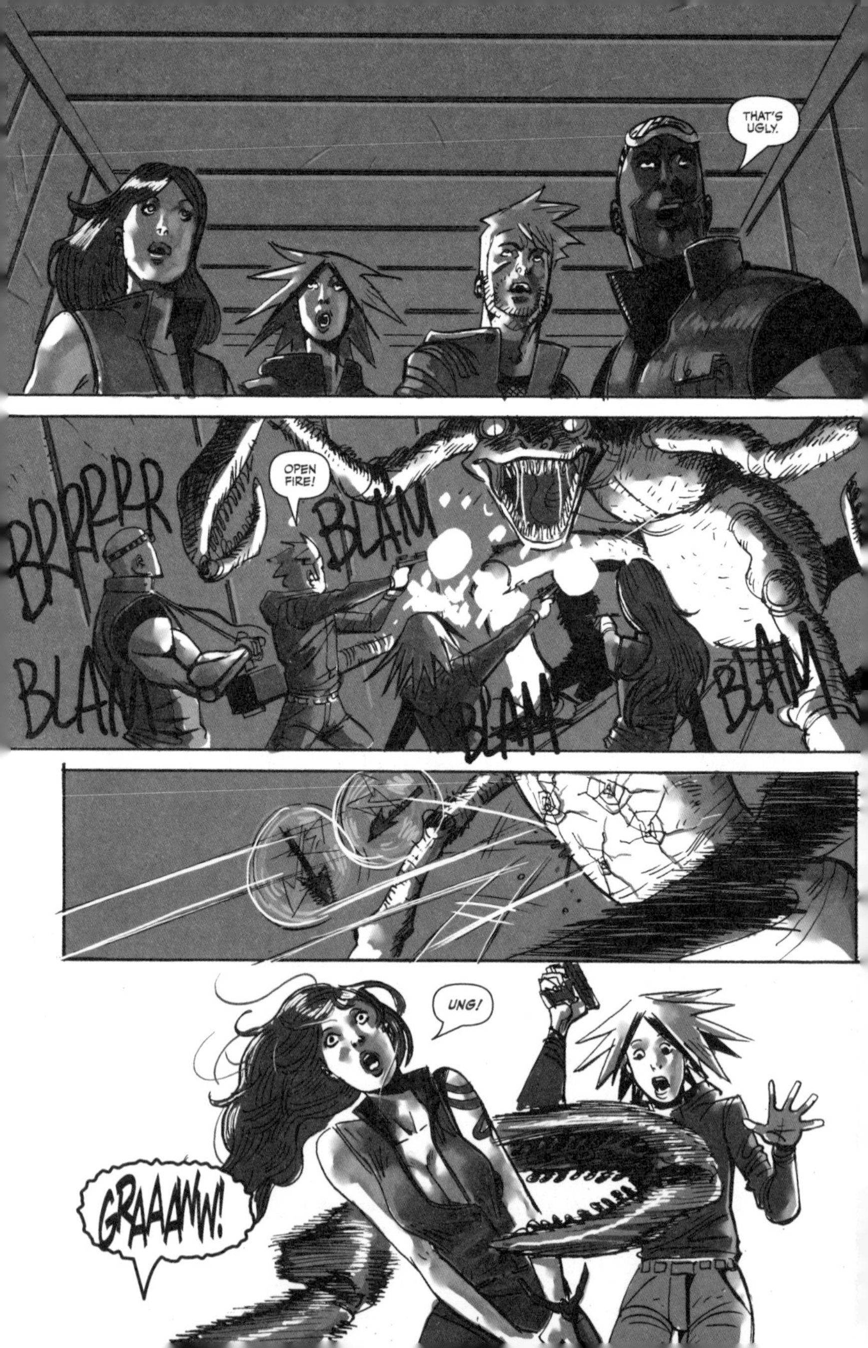
THAT'S UGLY.
OPEN FIRE!
BRRRRR
BLAM
BLAM
BLAM
BLAM
BLAM
UNG!
GRAAAWW!

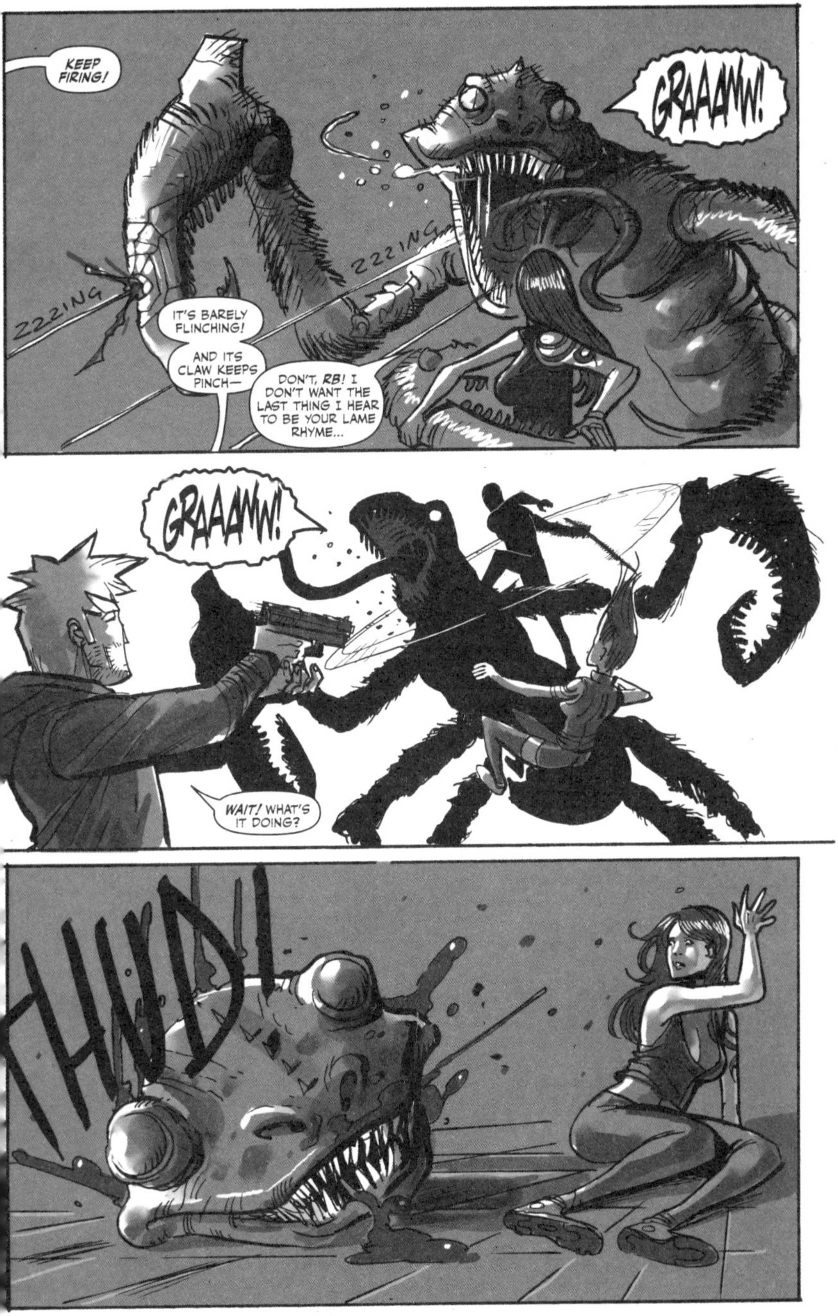
KEEP FIRING!
GRAAAWW!
ZZZING
ZZZING
IT'S BARELY FLINCHING!
AND ITS CLAW KEEPS PINCH—
DON'T, *RB!* I DON'T WANT THE LAST THING I HEAR TO BE YOUR LAME RHYME...
GRAAAWW!
WAIT! WHAT'S IT DOING?
THUD!

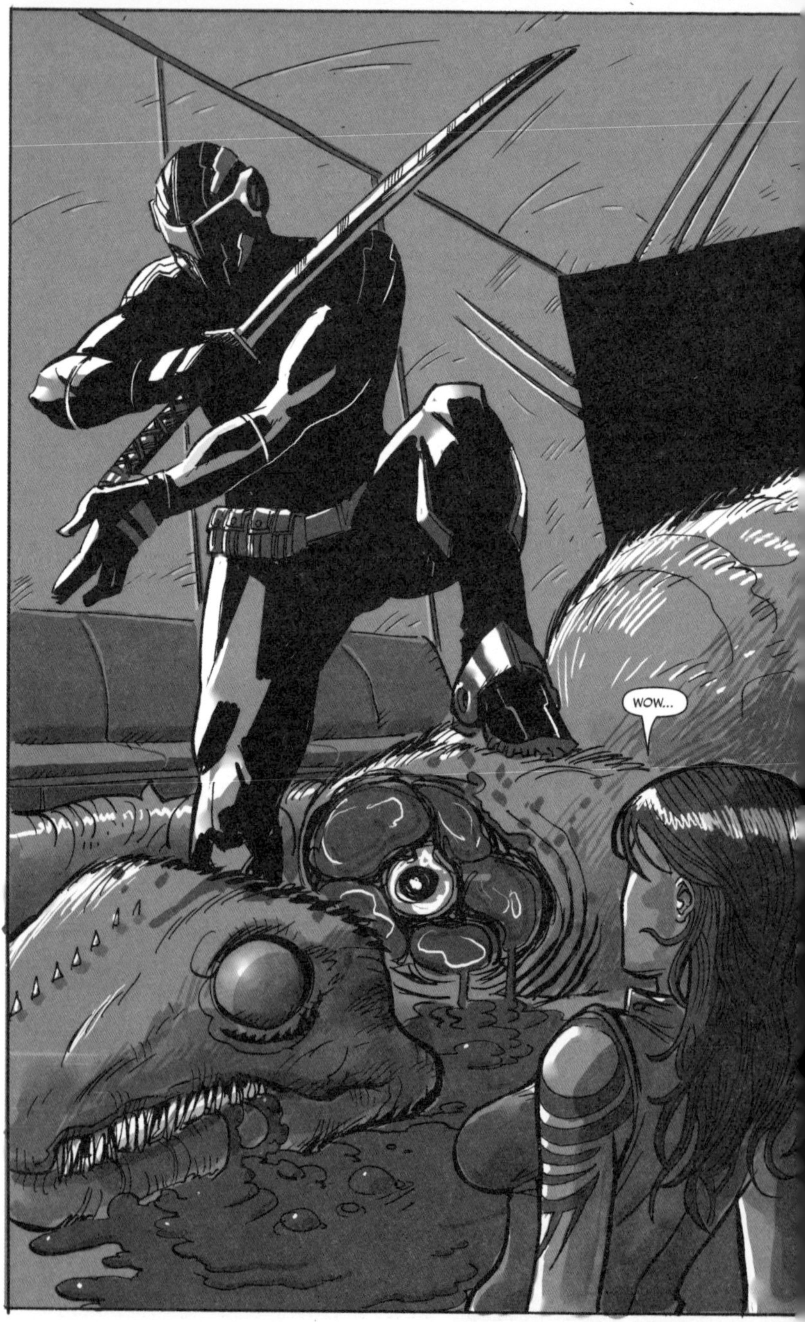
WOW...

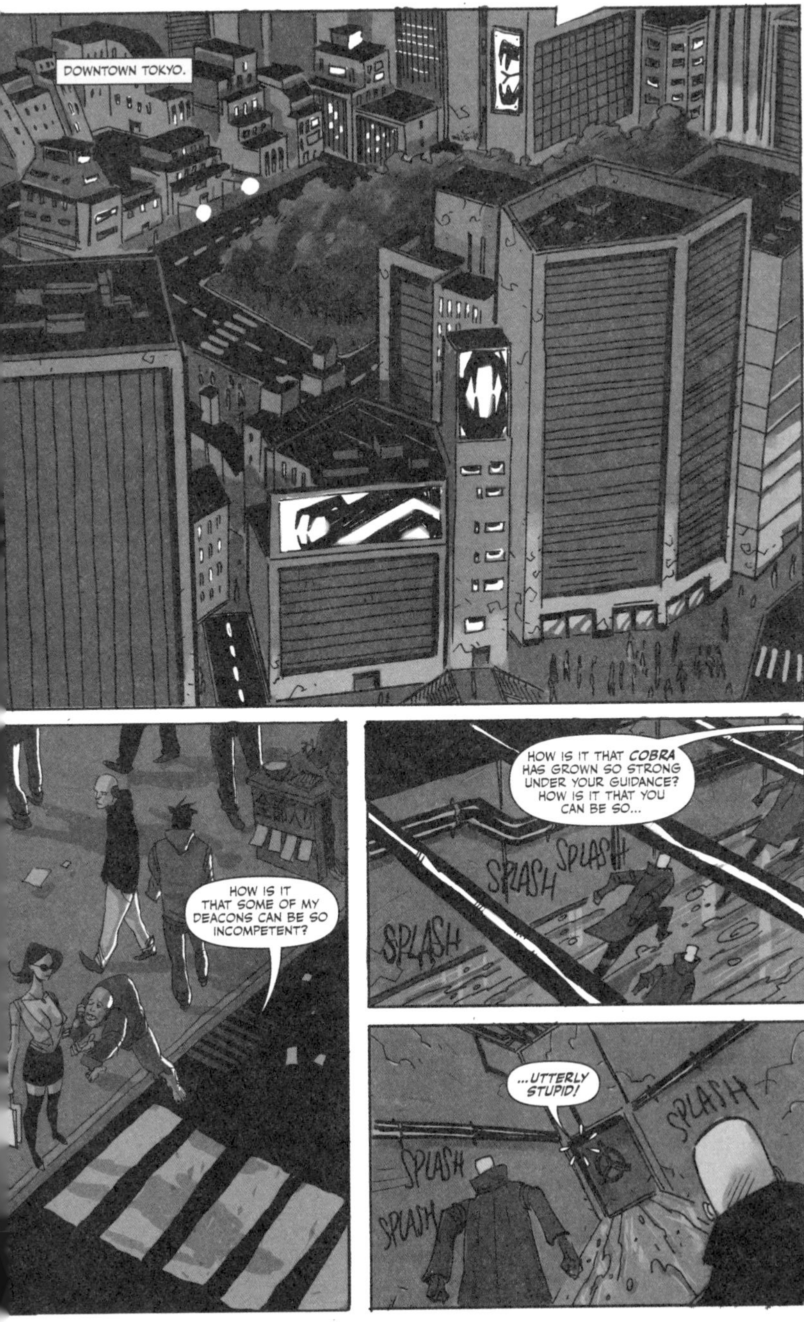
DOWNTOWN TOKYO.
HOW IS IT THAT SOME OF MY DEACONS CAN BE SO INCOMPETENT?
HOW IS IT THAT COBRA HAS GROWN SO STRONG UNDER YOUR GUIDANCE? HOW IS IT THAT YOU CAN BE SO...
SPLASH
SPLASH
SPLASH
...UTTERLY STUPID!
SPLASH
SPLASH
SPLASH

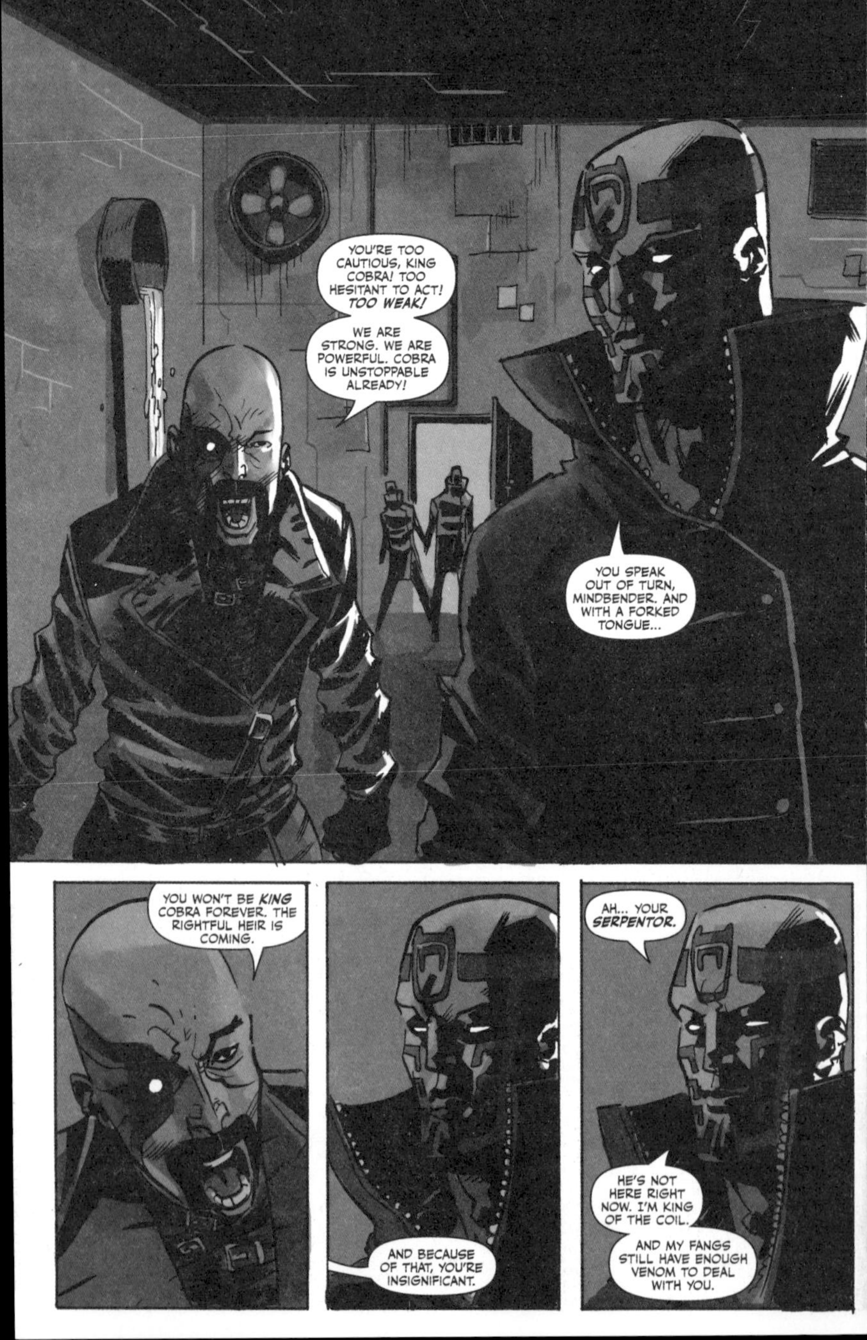
YOU'RE TOO CAUTIOUS, KING COBRA! TOO HESITANT TO ACT! TOO WEAK!
WE ARE STRONG. WE ARE POWERFUL. COBRA IS UNSTOPPABLE ALREADY!
YOU SPEAK OUT OF TURN, MINDBENDER. AND WITH A FORKED TONGUE...
YOU WON'T BE KING COBRA FOREVER. THE RIGHTFUL HEIR IS COMING.
AND BECAUSE OF THAT, YOU'RE INSIGNIFICANT.
AH... YOUR SERPENTOR.
HE'S NOT HERE RIGHT NOW. I'M KING OF THE COIL.
AND MY FANGS STILL HAVE ENOUGH VENOM TO DEAL WITH YOU.

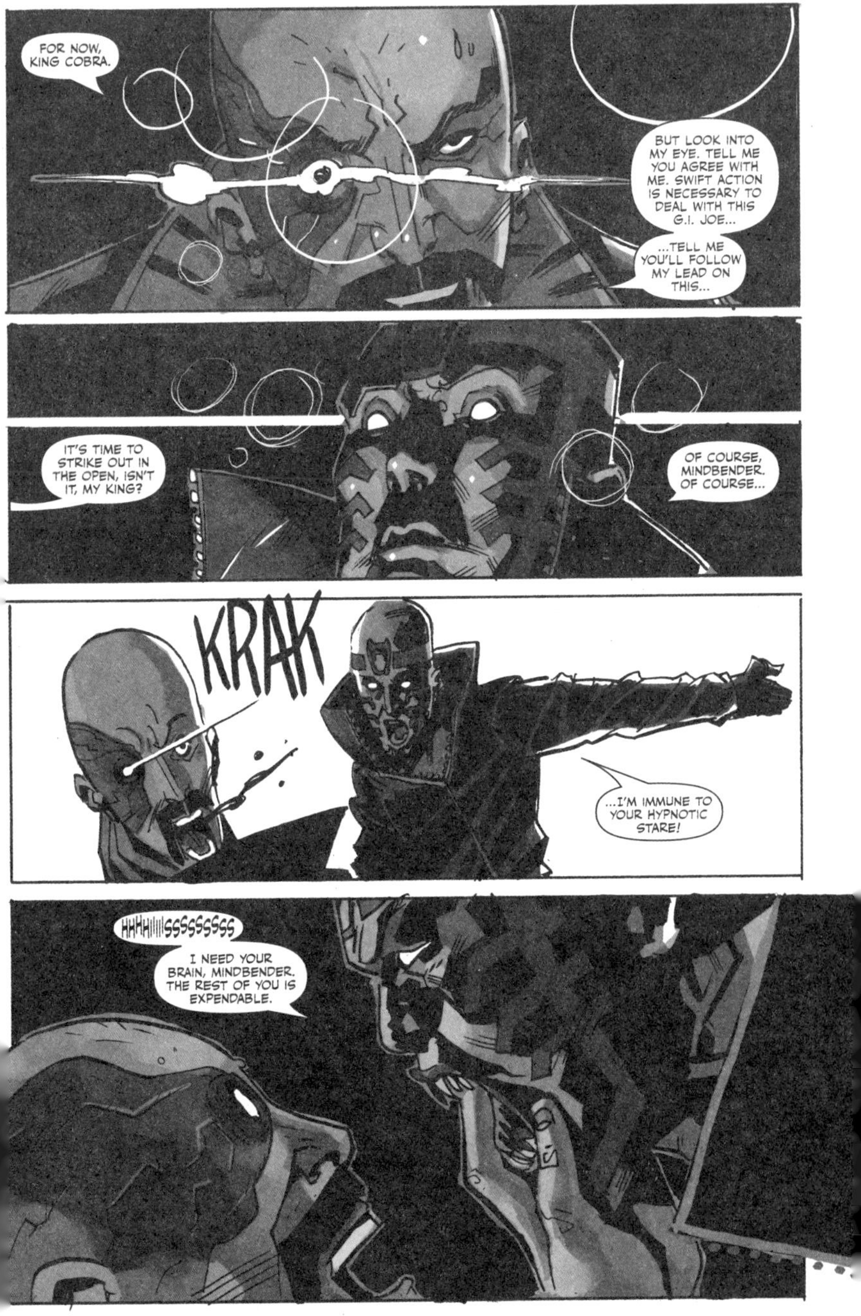
FOR NOW, KING COBRA.
BUT LOOK INTO MY EYE. TELL ME YOU AGREE WITH ME. SWIFT ACTION IS NECESSARY TO DEAL WITH THIS G.I. JOE...
...TELL ME YOU'LL FOLLOW MY LEAD ON THIS...
IT'S TIME TO STRIKE OUT IN THE OPEN, ISN'T IT, MY KING?
OF COURSE, MINDBENDER. OF COURSE...
KRAK
...I'M IMMUNE TO YOUR HYPNOTIC STARE!
HHHHIIIIISSSSSSSSS
I NEED YOUR BRAIN, MINDBENDER. THE REST OF YOU IS EXPENDABLE.

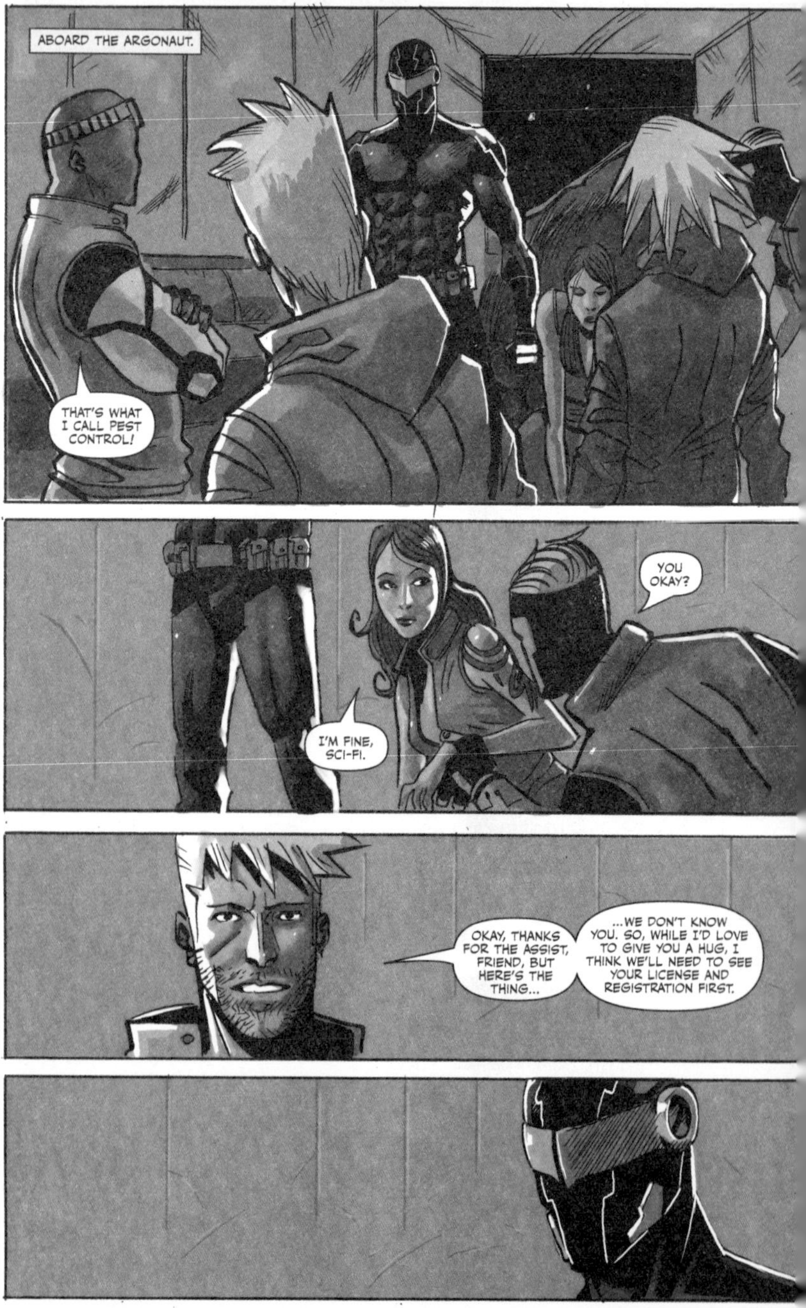
ABOARD THE ARGONAUT.
THAT'S WHAT I CALL PEST CONTROL!
YOU OKAY?
I'M FINE, SCI-FI.
OKAY, THANKS FOR THE ASSIST, FRIEND, BUT HERE'S THE THING...
...WE DON'T KNOW YOU. SO, WHILE I'D LOVE TO GIVE YOU A HUG, I THINK WE'LL NEED TO SEE YOUR LICENSE AND REGISTRATION FIRST.

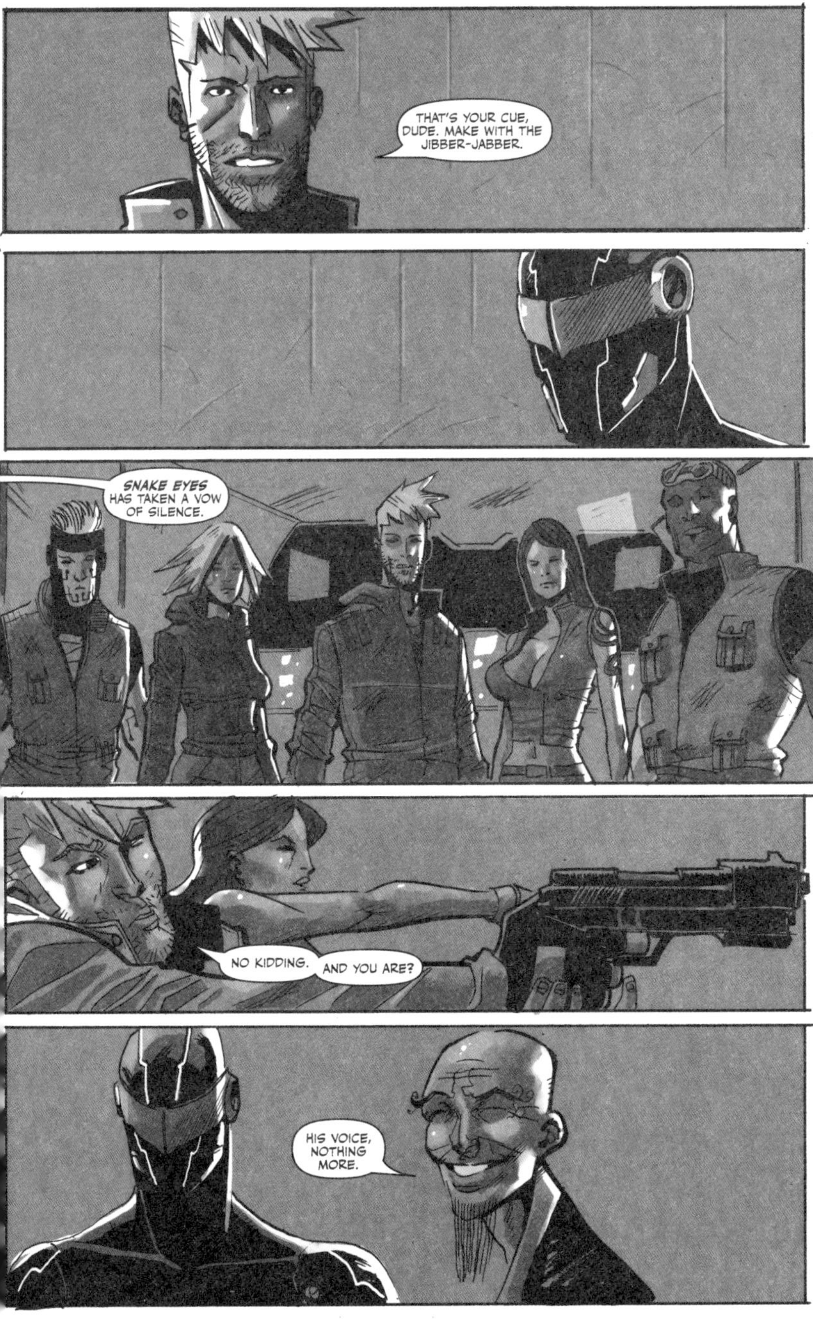
THAT'S YOUR CUE, DUDE. MAKE WITH THE JIBBER-JABBER.
SNAKE EYES HAS TAKEN A VOW OF SILENCE.
NO KIDDING.
AND YOU ARE?
HIS VOICE, NOTHING MORE.

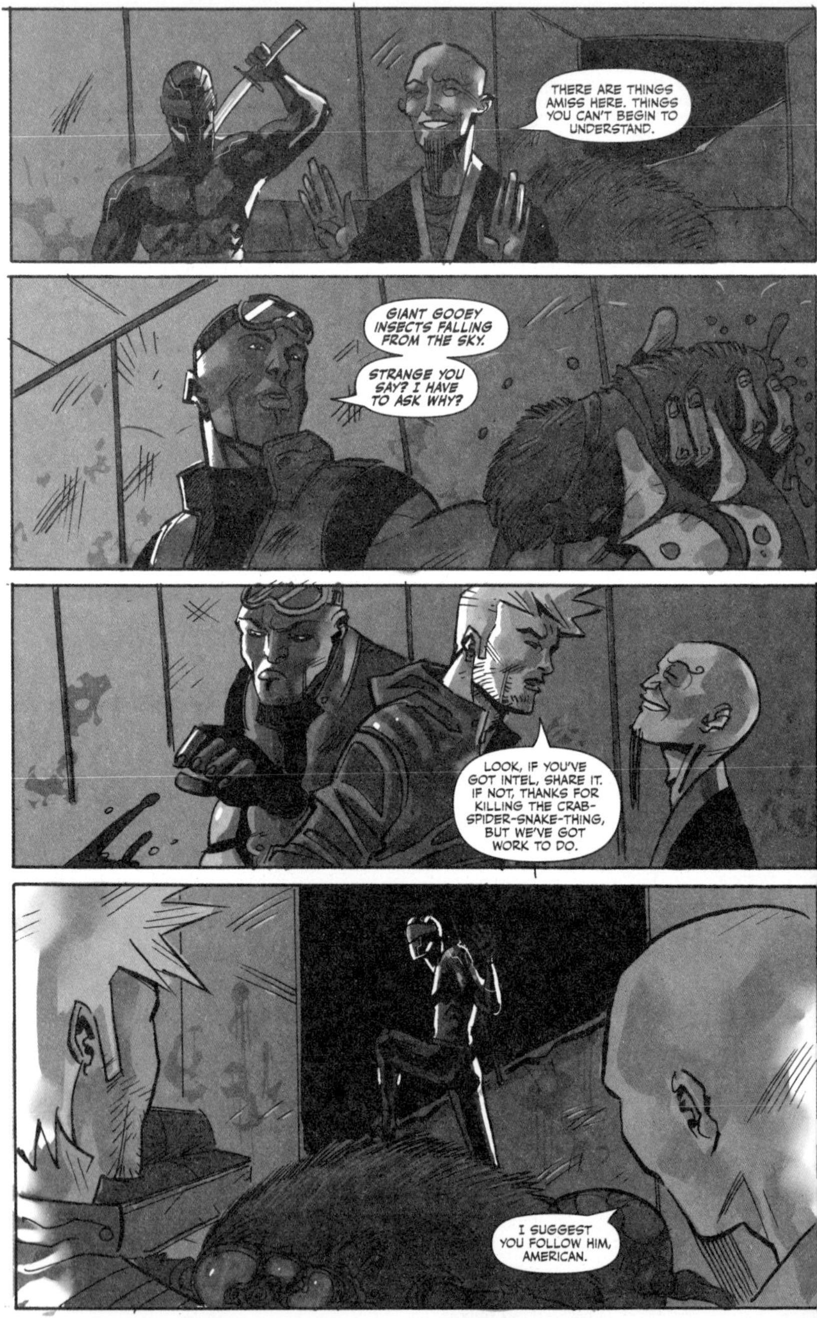
THERE ARE THINGS AMISS HERE. THINGS YOU CAN'T BEGIN TO UNDERSTAND.
GIANT GOOEY INSECTS FALLING FROM THE SKY.
STRANGE YOU SAY? I HAVE TO ASK WHY?
LOOK, IF YOU'VE GOT INTEL, SHARE IT. IF NOT, THANKS FOR KILLING THE CRAB-SPIDER-SNAKE-THING, BUT WE'VE GOT WORK TO DO.
I SUGGEST YOU FOLLOW HIM, AMERICAN.

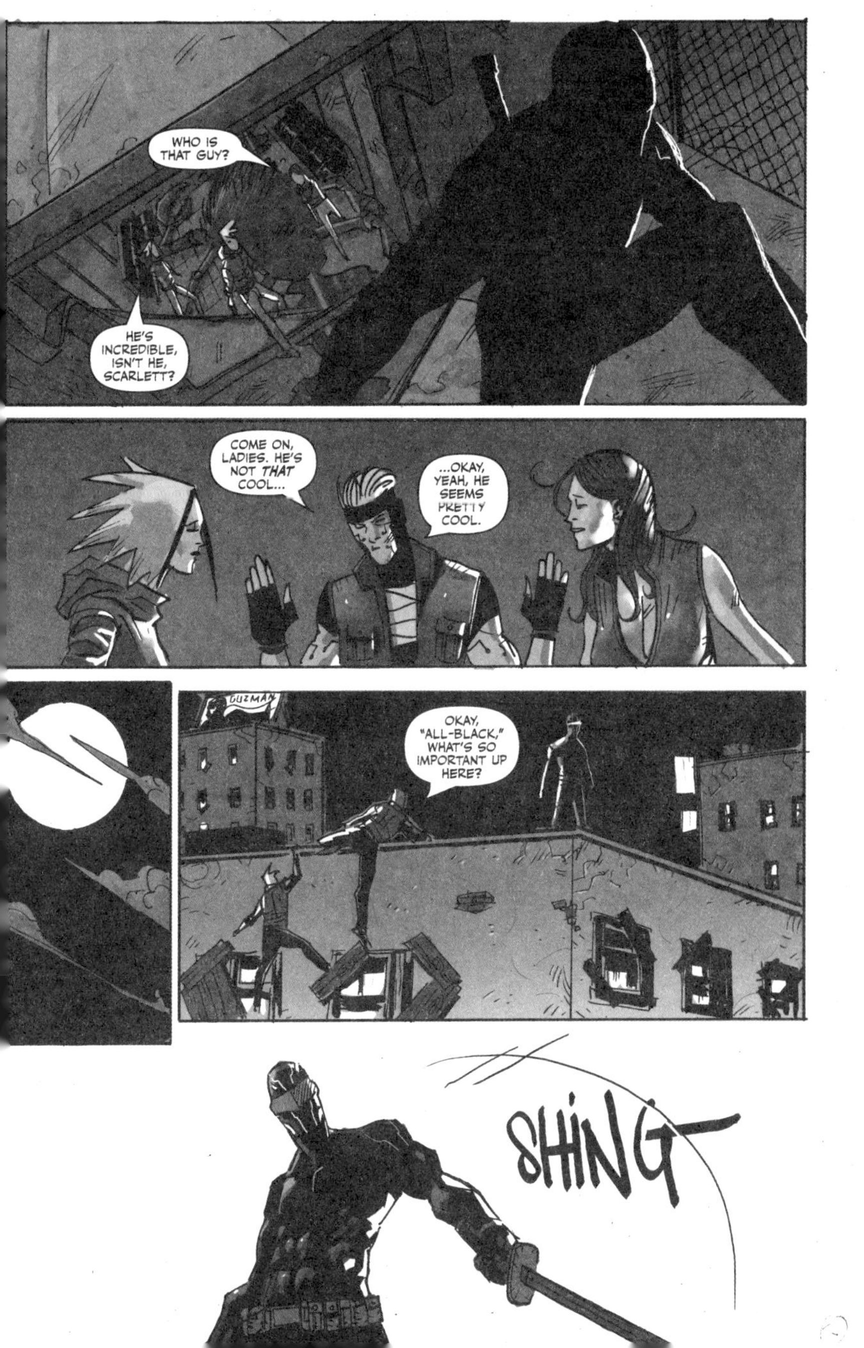
WHO IS THAT GUY?
HE'S INCREDIBLE, ISN'T HE, SCARLETT?
COME ON, LADIES. HE'S NOT *THAT* COOL...
...OKAY, YEAH, HE SEEMS PRETTY COOL.
GUZMAN
OKAY, "ALL-BLACK," WHAT'S SO IMPORTANT UP HERE?
SHING

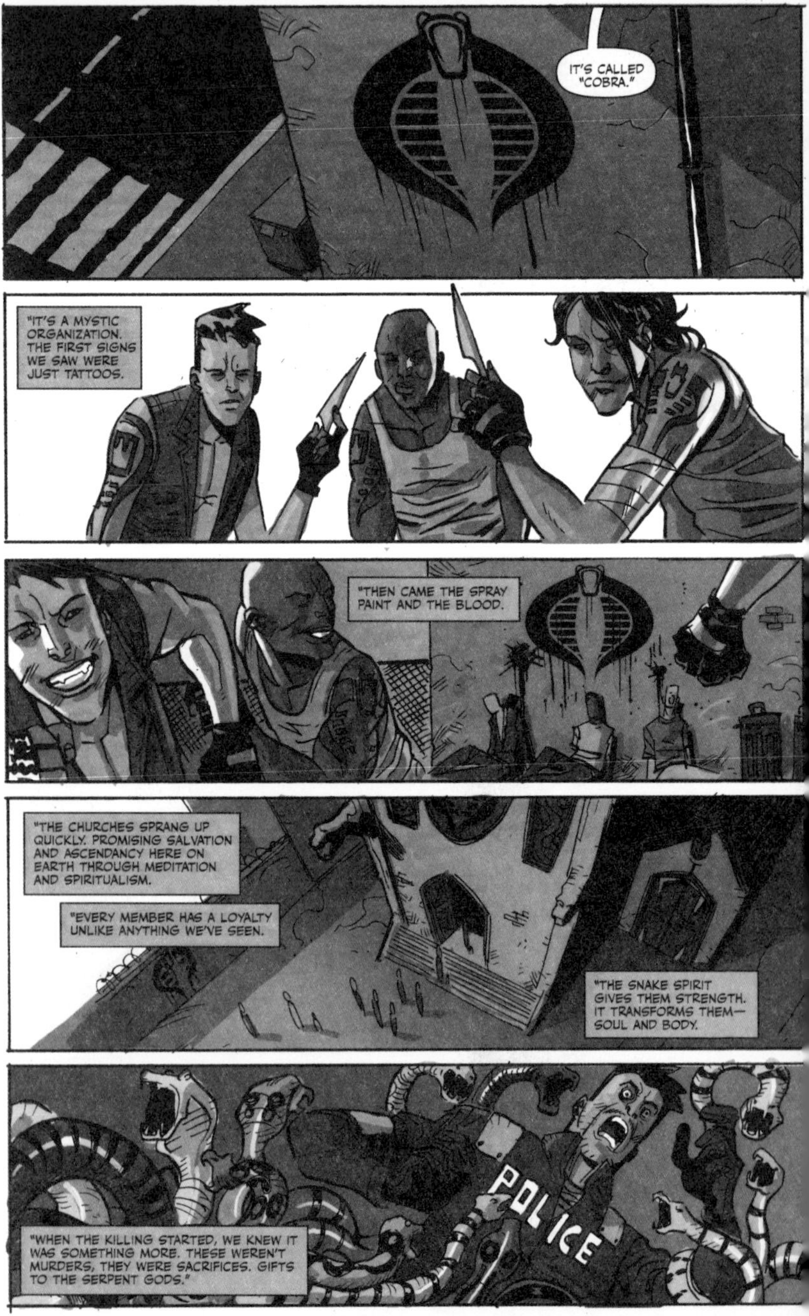
IT'S CALLED "COBRA."
"IT'S A MYSTIC ORGANIZATION. THE FIRST SIGNS WE SAW WERE JUST TATTOOS.
"THEN CAME THE SPRAY PAINT AND THE BLOOD.
"THE CHURCHES SPRANG UP QUICKLY. PROMISING SALVATION AND ASCENDANCY HERE ON EARTH THROUGH MEDITATION AND SPIRITUALISM.
"EVERY MEMBER HAS A LOYALTY UNLIKE ANYTHING WE'VE SEEN.
"THE SNAKE SPIRIT GIVES THEM STRENGTH. IT TRANSFORMS THEM—SOUL AND BODY.
POLICE
"WHEN THE KILLING STARTED, WE KNEW IT WAS SOMETHING MORE. THESE WEREN'T MURDERS, THEY WERE SACRIFICES. GIFTS TO THE SERPENT GODS."

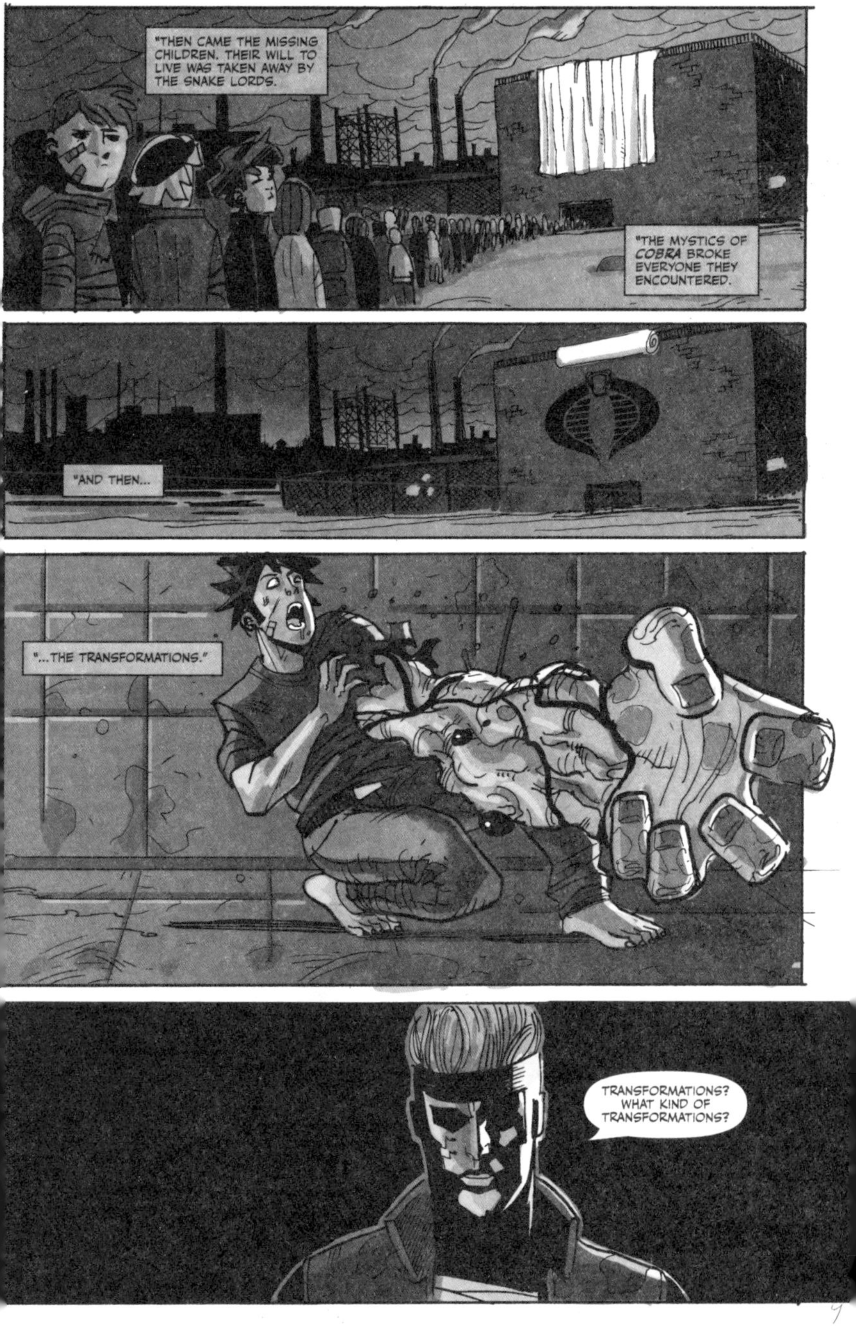
"THEN CAME THE MISSING CHILDREN. THEIR WILL TO LIVE WAS TAKEN AWAY BY THE SNAKE LORDS.
"THE MYSTICS OF COBRA BROKE EVERYONE THEY ENCOUNTERED.
"AND THEN...
"...THE TRANSFORMATIONS."
TRANSFORMATIONS? WHAT KIND OF TRANSFORMATIONS?

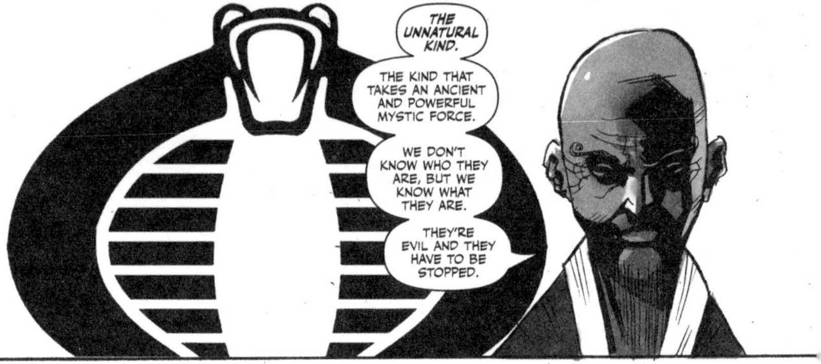
THE UNNATURAL KIND.
THE KIND THAT TAKES AN ANCIENT AND POWERFUL MYSTIC FORCE.
WE DON'T KNOW WHO THEY ARE, BUT WE KNOW WHAT THEY ARE.
THEY'RE EVIL AND THEY HAVE TO BE STOPPED.

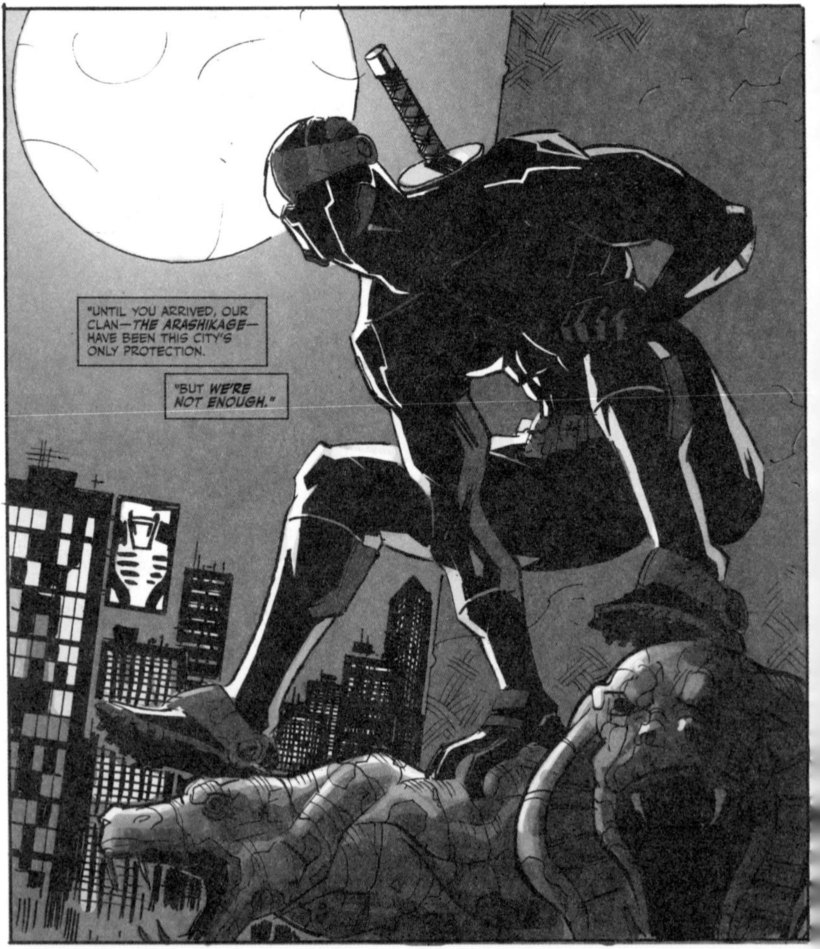
"UNTIL YOU ARRIVED, OUR CLAN—THE ARASHIKAGE—HAVE BEEN THIS CITY'S ONLY PROTECTION.
"BUT WE'RE NOT ENOUGH."

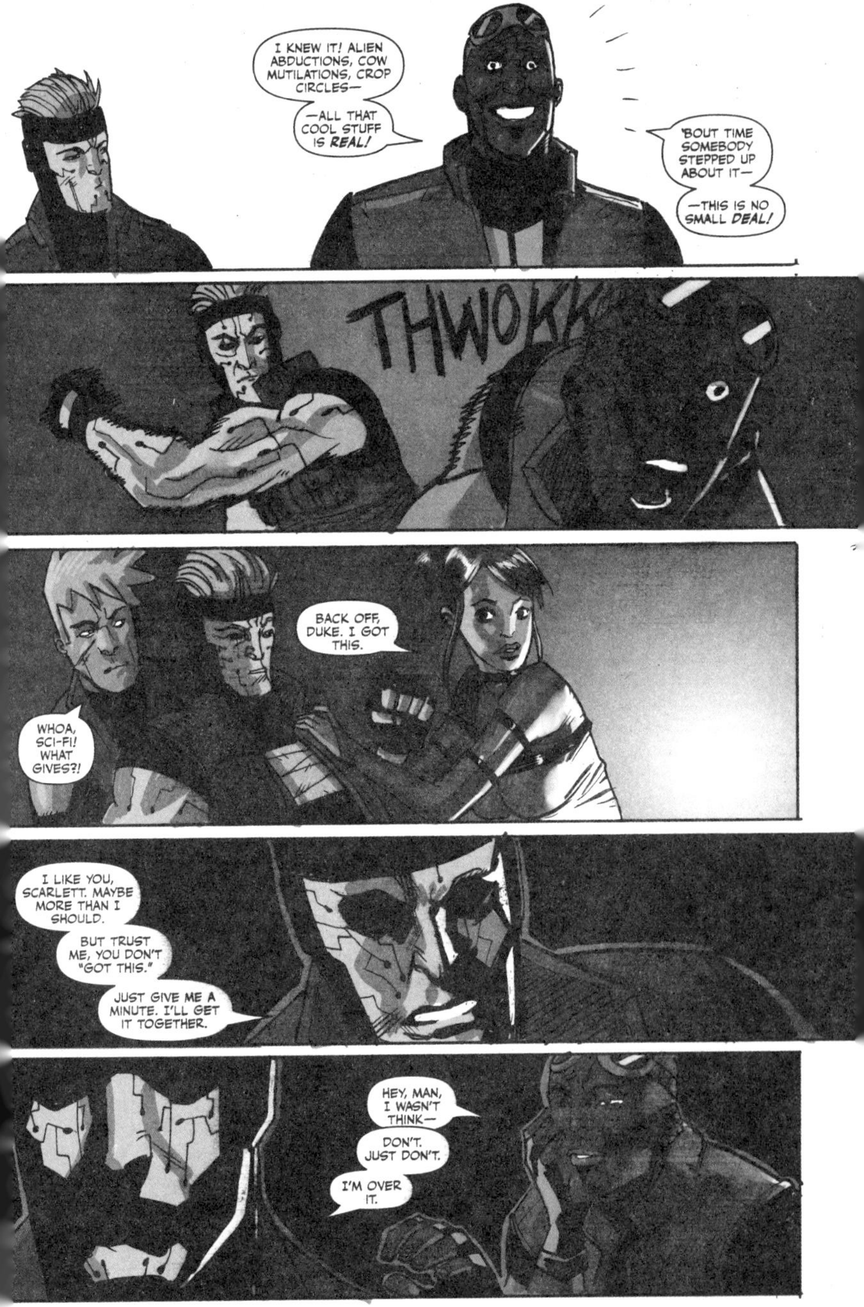
I KNEW IT! ALIEN ABDUCTIONS, COW MUTILATIONS, CROP CIRCLES—
—ALL THAT COOL STUFF IS *REAL!*
'BOUT TIME SOMEBODY STEPPED UP ABOUT IT—
—THIS IS NO SMALL *DEAL!*
THWOKK
BACK OFF, DUKE. I GOT THIS.
WHOA, SCI-FI! WHAT GIVES?!
I LIKE YOU, SCARLETT. MAYBE MORE THAN I SHOULD.
BUT TRUST ME, YOU DON'T "GOT THIS."
JUST GIVE ME A MINUTE. I'LL GET IT TOGETHER.
HEY, MAN, I WASN'T THINK—
DON'T. JUST DON'T.
I'M OVER IT.

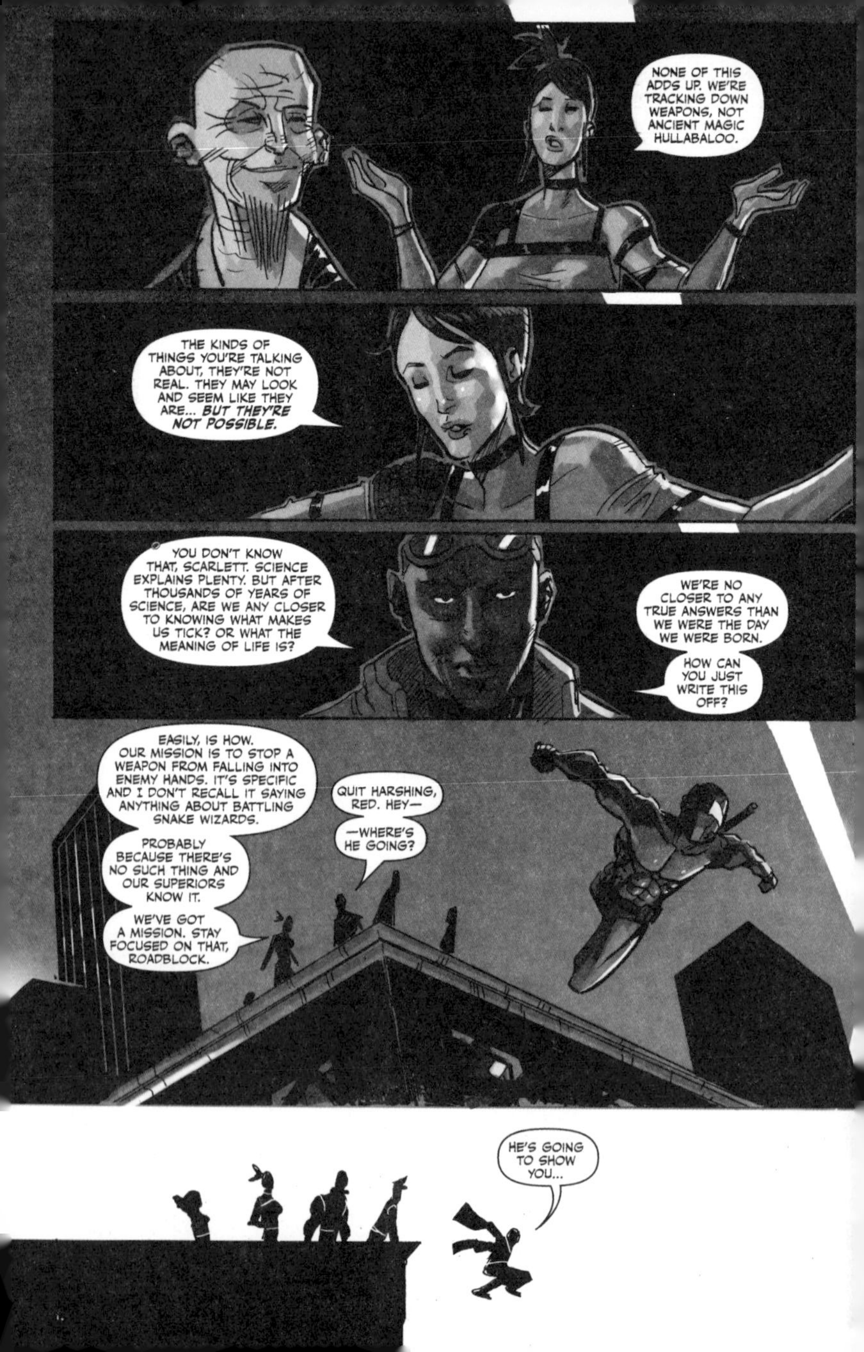
NONE OF THIS ADDS UP. WE'RE TRACKING DOWN WEAPONS, NOT ANCIENT MAGIC HULLABALOO.
THE KINDS OF THINGS YOU'RE TALKING ABOUT, THEY'RE NOT REAL. THEY MAY LOOK AND SEEM LIKE THEY ARE... ***BUT THEY'RE NOT POSSIBLE.***
YOU DON'T KNOW THAT, SCARLETT. SCIENCE EXPLAINS PLENTY. BUT AFTER THOUSANDS OF YEARS OF SCIENCE, ARE WE ANY CLOSER TO KNOWING WHAT MAKES US TICK? OR WHAT THE MEANING OF LIFE IS?
WE'RE NO CLOSER TO ANY TRUE ANSWERS THAN WE WERE THE DAY WE WERE BORN.
HOW CAN YOU JUST WRITE THIS OFF?
EASILY, IS HOW. OUR MISSION IS TO STOP A WEAPON FROM FALLING INTO ENEMY HANDS. IT'S SPECIFIC AND I DON'T RECALL IT SAYING ANYTHING ABOUT BATTLING SNAKE WIZARDS.
PROBABLY BECAUSE THERE'S NO SUCH THING AND OUR SUPERIORS KNOW IT.
WE'VE GOT A MISSION. STAY FOCUSED ON THAT, ROADBLOCK.
QUIT HARSHING, RED. HEY—
—WHERE'S HE GOING?
HE'S GOING TO SHOW YOU...

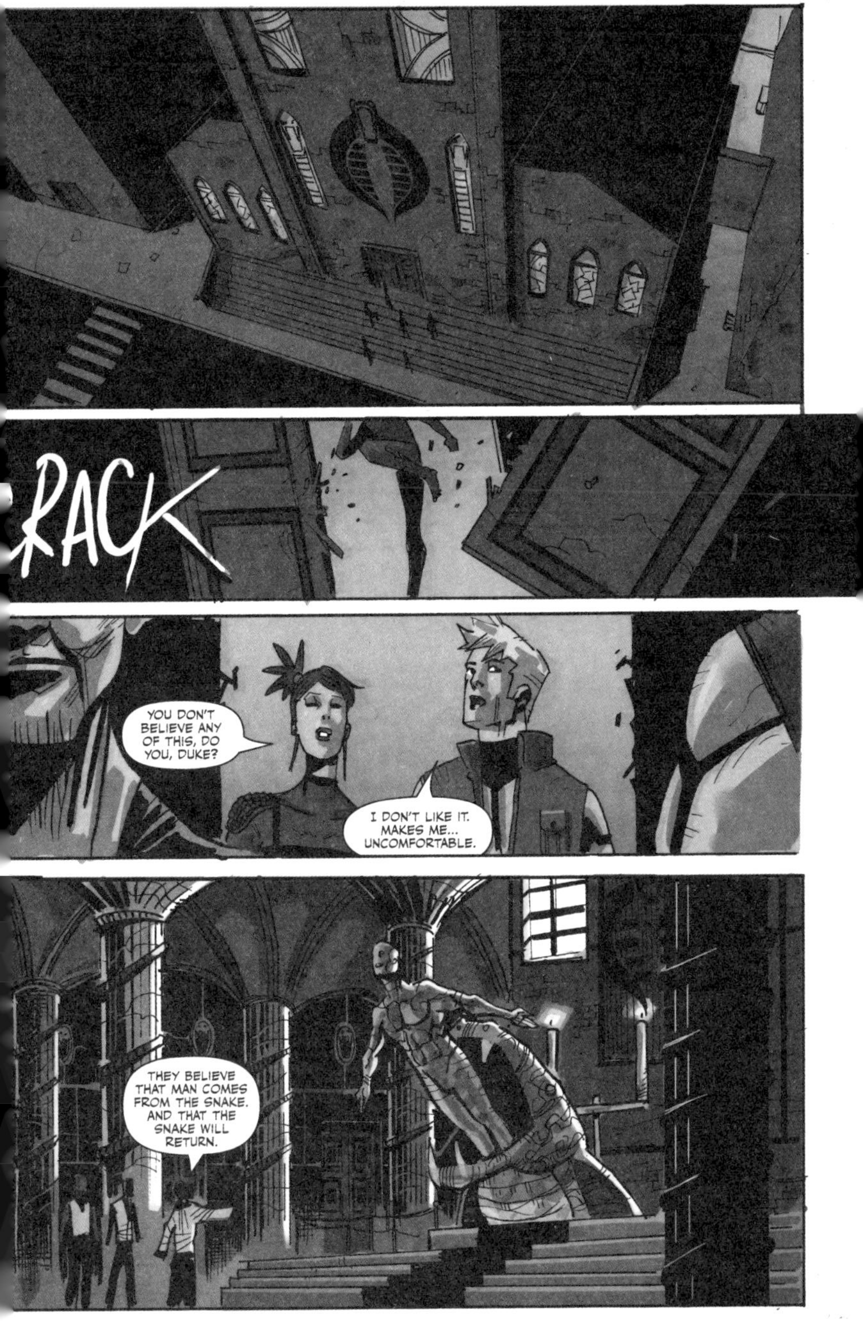
RACK
YOU DON'T BELIEVE ANY OF THIS, DO YOU, DUKE?
I DON'T LIKE IT. MAKES ME... UNCOMFORTABLE.
THEY BELIEVE THAT MAN COMES FROM THE SNAKE. AND THAT THE SNAKE WILL RETURN.

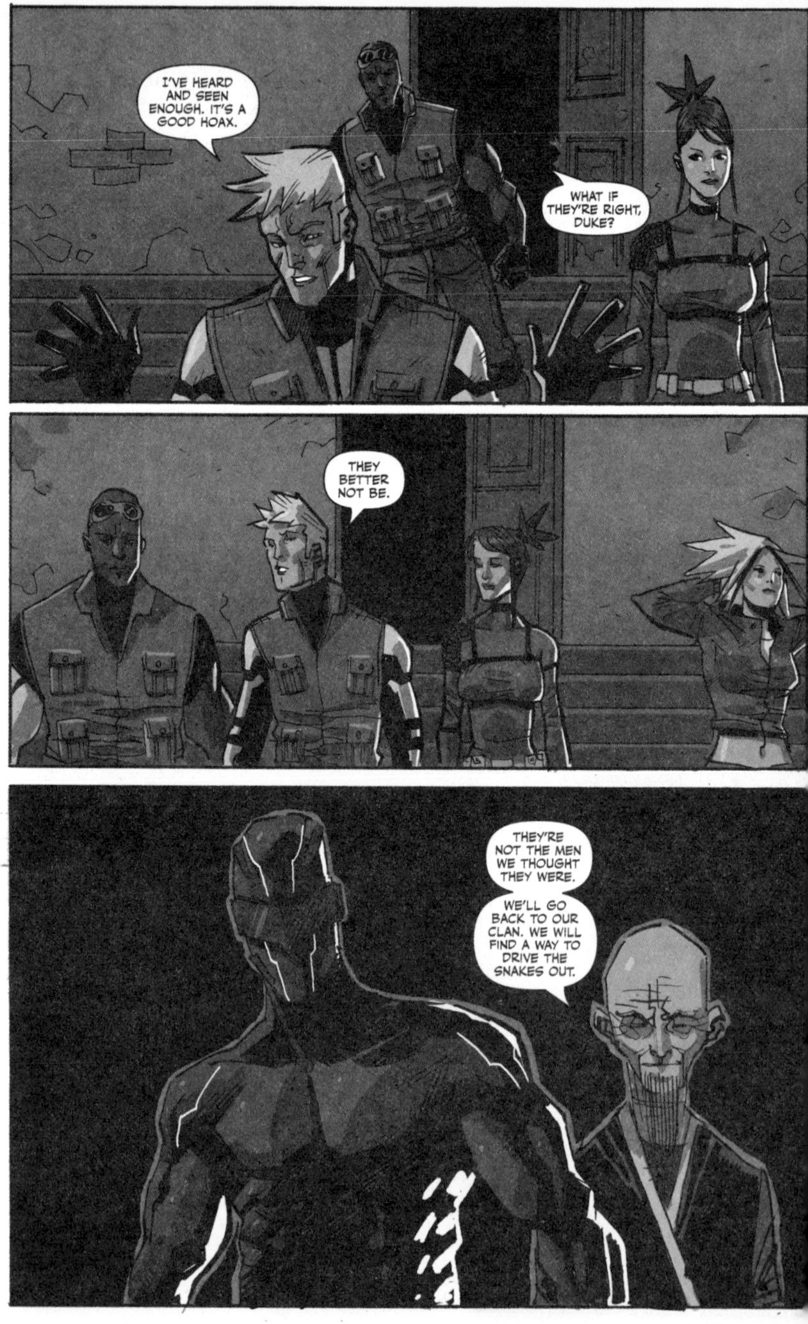
I'VE HEARD AND SEEN ENOUGH. IT'S A GOOD HOAX.
WHAT IF THEY'RE RIGHT, DUKE?
THEY BETTER NOT BE.
THEY'RE NOT THE MEN WE THOUGHT THEY WERE.
WE'LL GO BACK TO OUR CLAN. WE WILL FIND A WAY TO DRIVE THE SNAKES OUT.

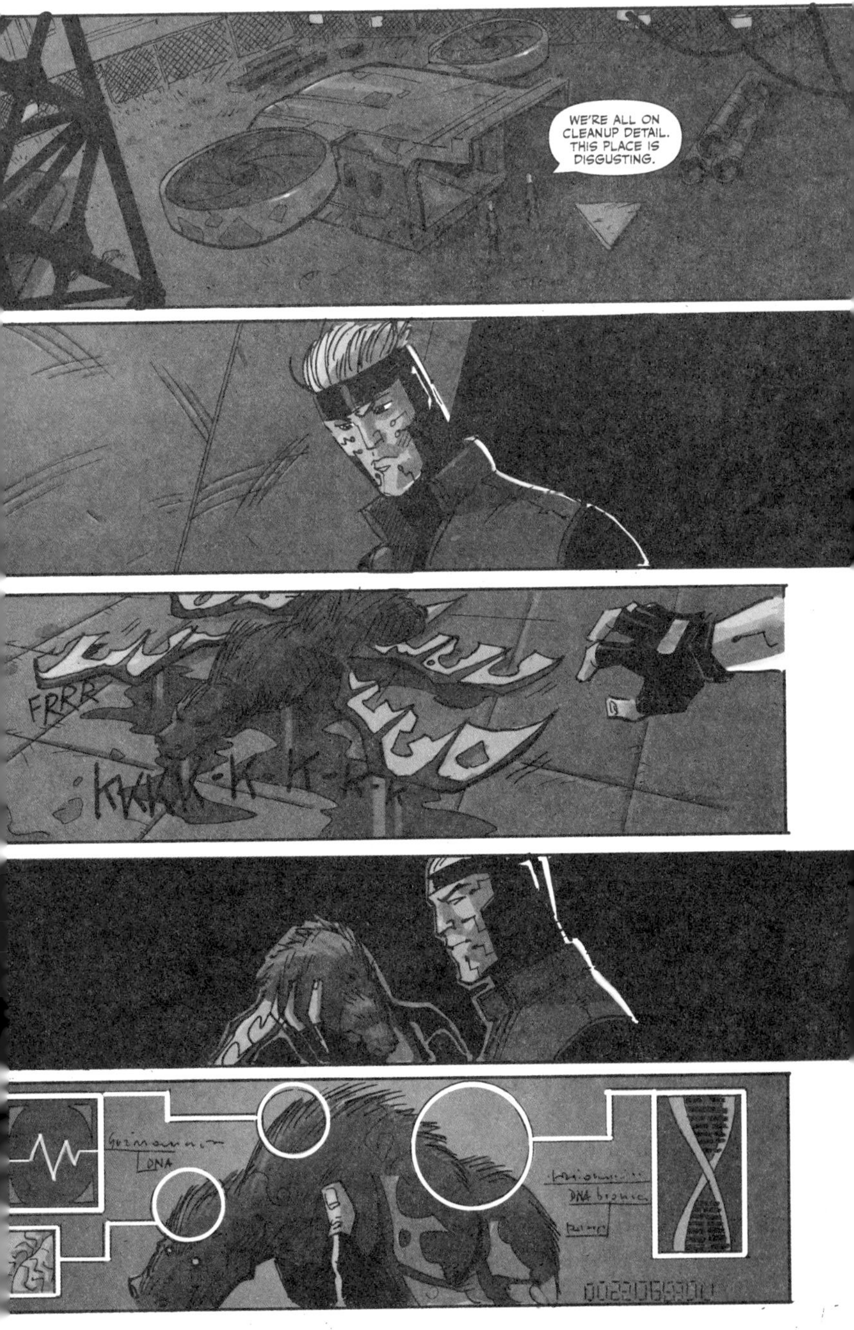
WE'RE ALL ON CLEANUP DETAIL. THIS PLACE IS DISGUSTING.
FRRR

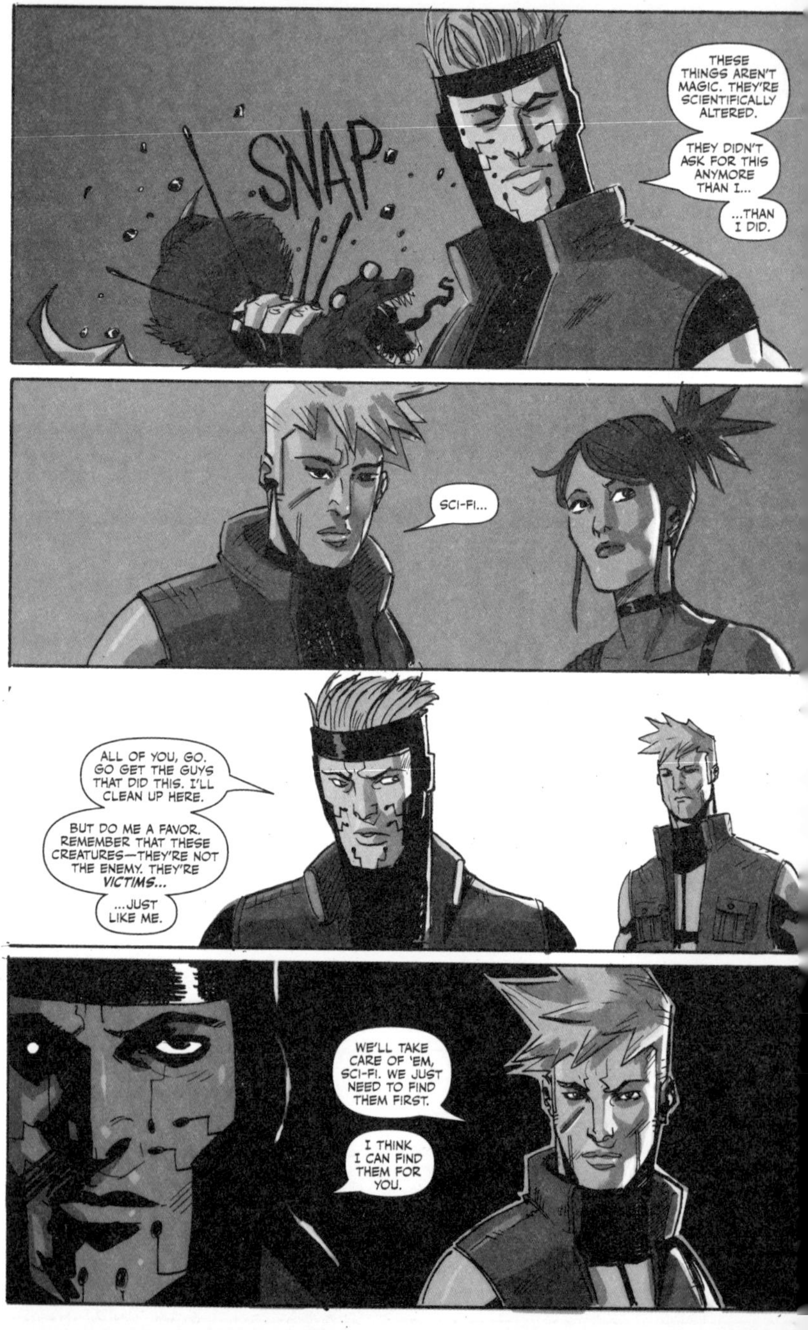
THESE THINGS AREN'T MAGIC. THEY'RE SCIENTIFICALLY ALTERED.
THEY DIDN'T ASK FOR THIS ANYMORE THAN I...
...THAN I DID.
SNAP
SCI-FI...
ALL OF YOU, GO. GO GET THE GUYS THAT DID THIS. I'LL CLEAN UP HERE.
BUT DO ME A FAVOR. REMEMBER THAT THESE CREATURES—THEY'RE NOT THE ENEMY. THEY'RE *VICTIMS...*
...JUST LIKE ME.
WE'LL TAKE CARE OF 'EM, SCI-FI. WE JUST NEED TO FIND THEM FIRST.
I THINK I CAN FIND THEM FOR YOU.

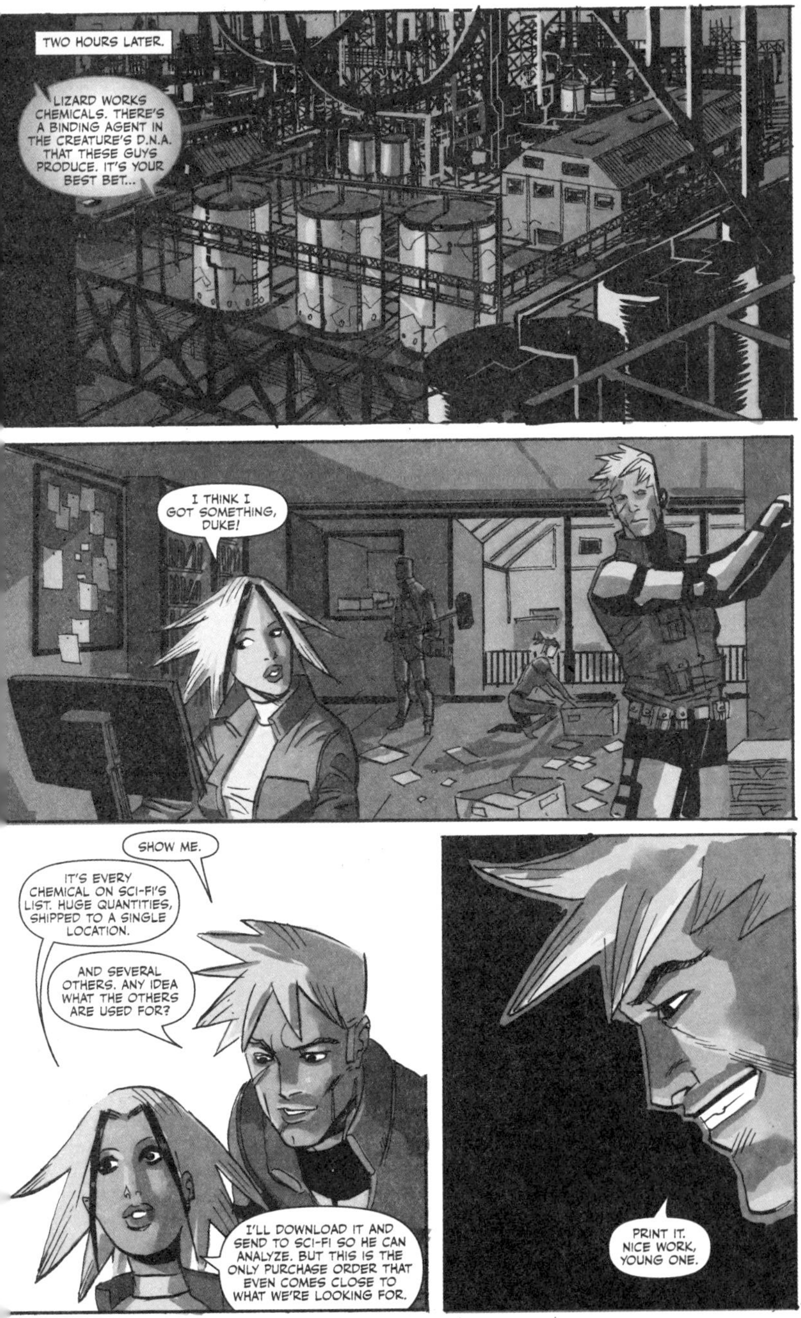
TWO HOURS LATER.
LIZARD WORKS CHEMICALS. THERE'S A BINDING AGENT IN THE CREATURE'S D.N.A. THAT THESE GUYS PRODUCE. IT'S YOUR BEST BET...
I THINK I GOT SOMETHING, DUKE!
SHOW ME.
IT'S EVERY CHEMICAL ON SCI-FI'S LIST. HUGE QUANTITIES, SHIPPED TO A SINGLE LOCATION.
AND SEVERAL OTHERS. ANY IDEA WHAT THE OTHERS ARE USED FOR?
I'LL DOWNLOAD IT AND SEND TO SCI-FI SO HE CAN ANALYZE. BUT THIS IS THE ONLY PURCHASE ORDER THAT EVEN COMES CLOSE TO WHAT WE'RE LOOKING FOR.
PRINT IT. NICE WORK, YOUNG ONE.

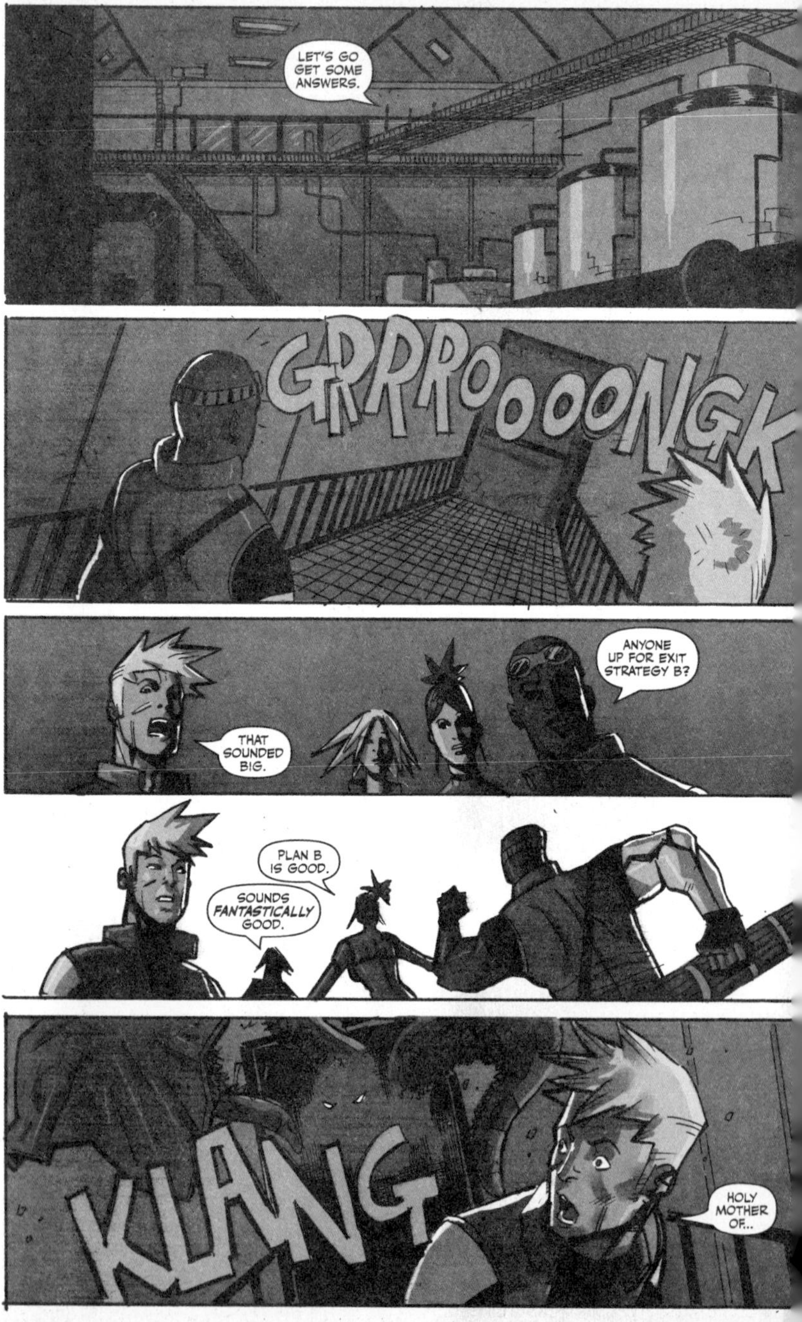
LET'S GO GET SOME ANSWERS.
GRRROOOONGK
ANYONE UP FOR EXIT STRATEGY B?
THAT SOUNDED BIG.
PLAN B IS GOOD.
SOUNDS *FANTASTICALLY* GOOD.
KLANG
HOLY MOTHER OF...

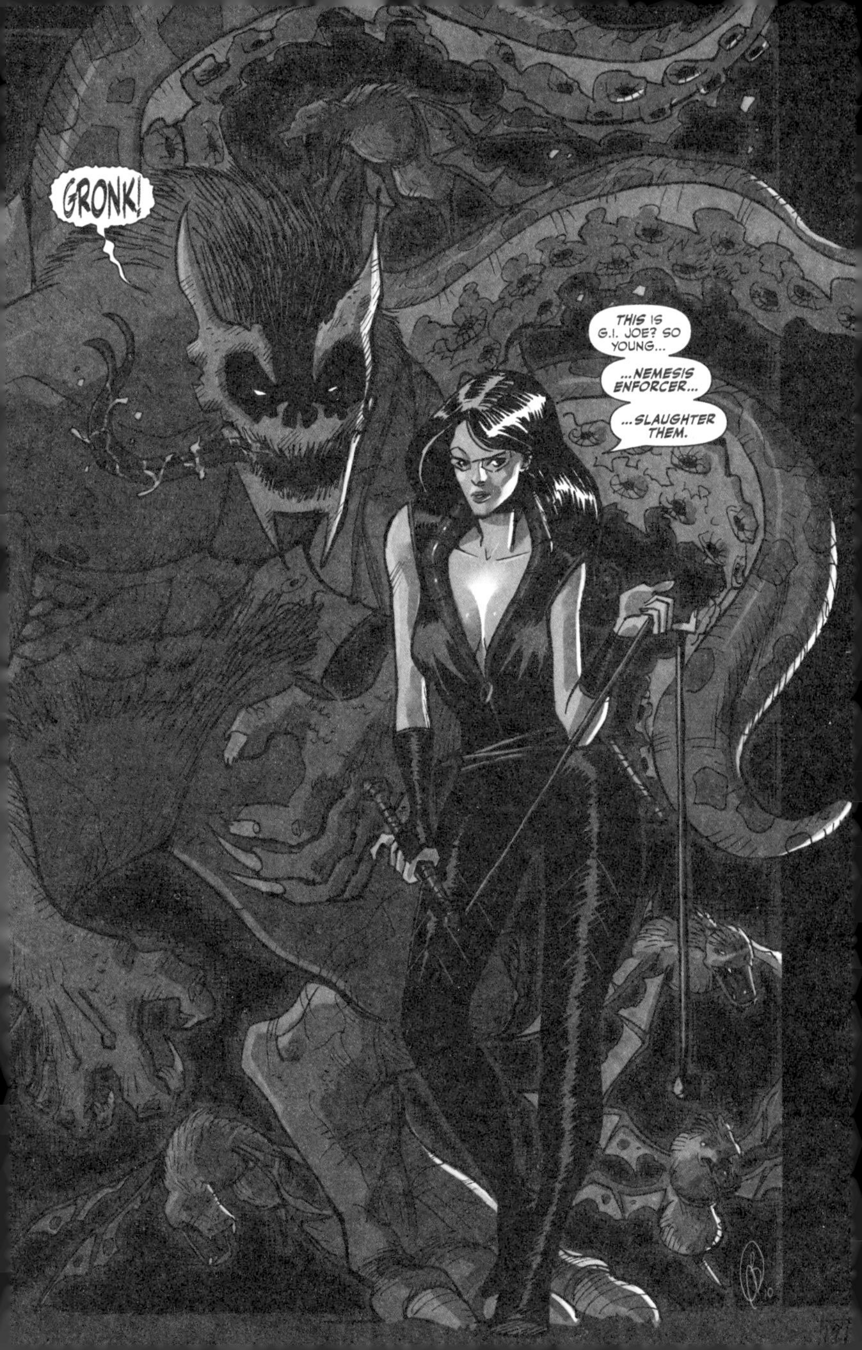
GRONK!
THIS IS G.I. JOE? SO YOUNG...
...NEMESIS ENFORCER...
...SLAUGHTER THEM.

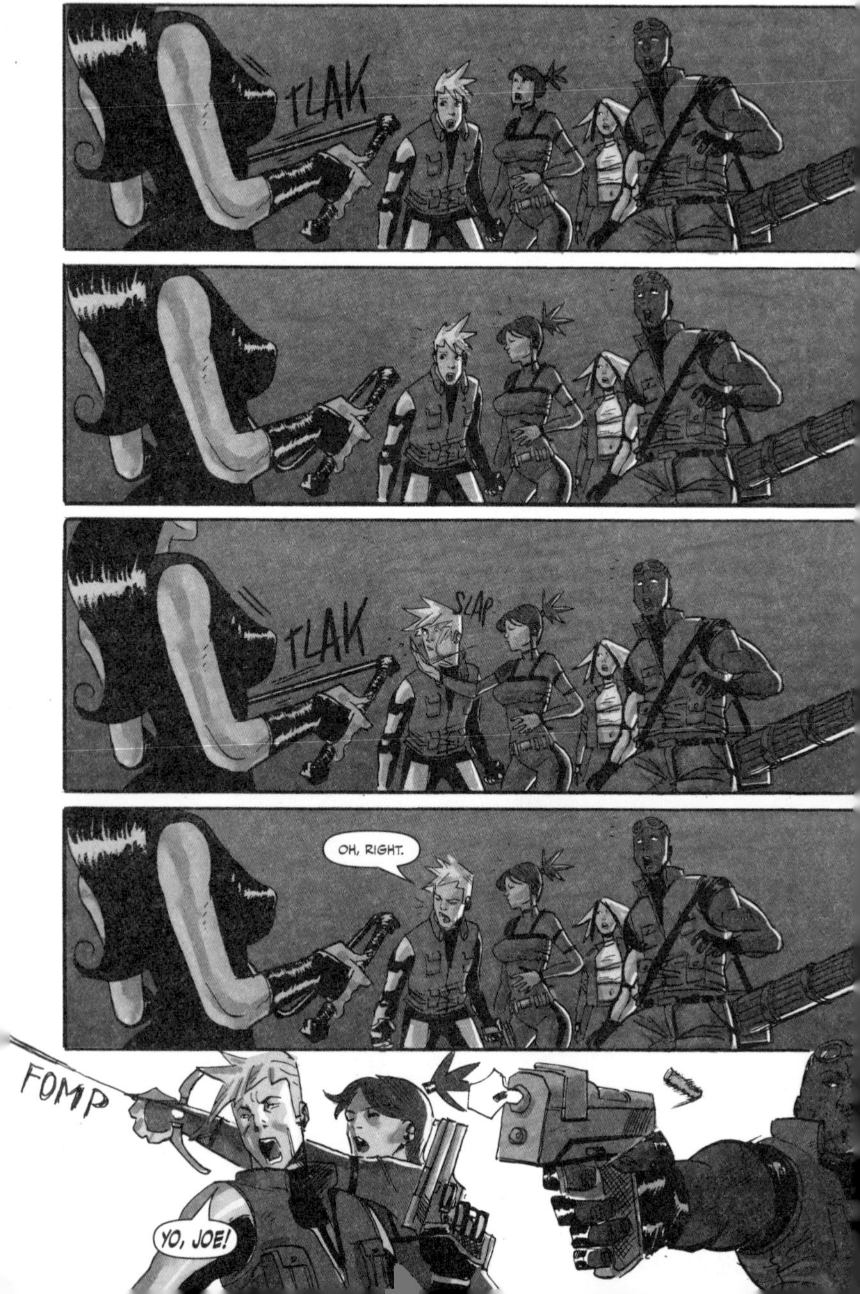
TLAK
TLAK
SLAP
OH, RIGHT.
FOMP
YO, JOE!

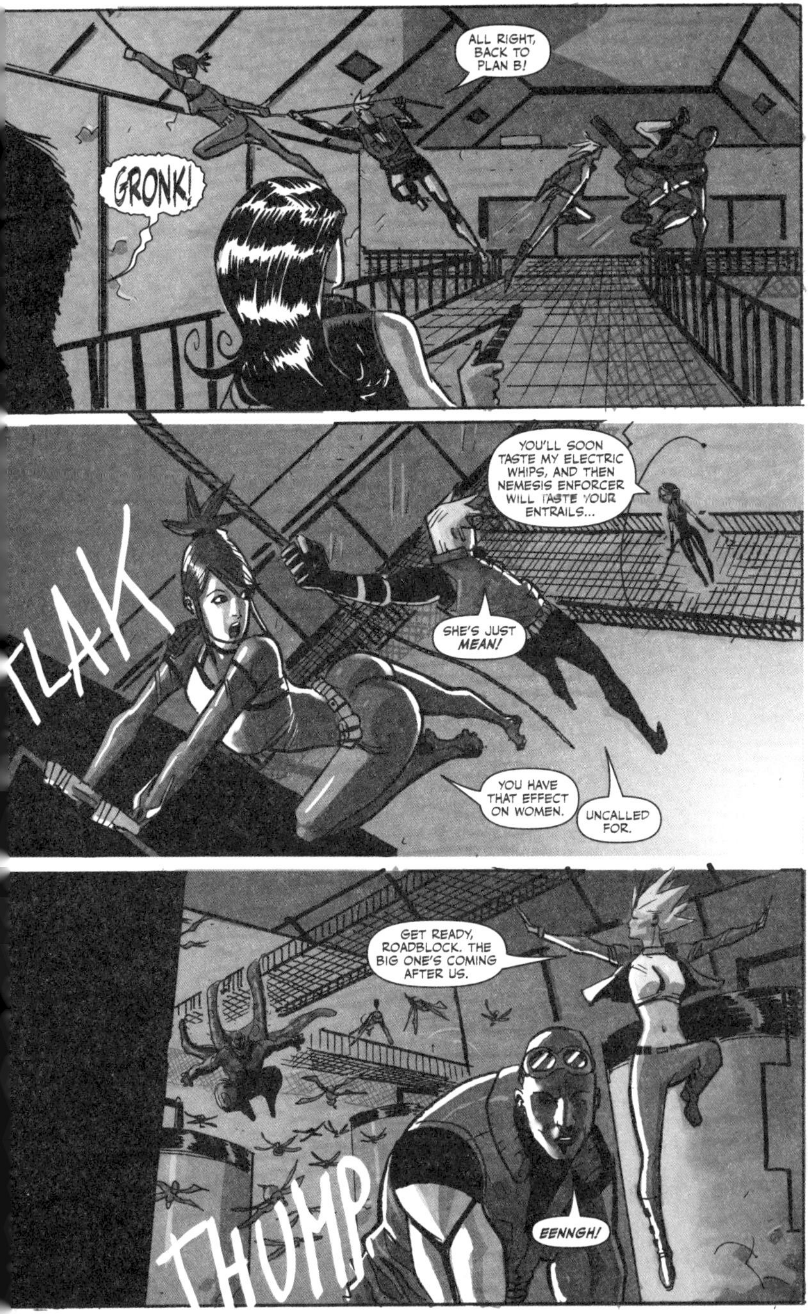
ALL RIGHT, BACK TO PLAN B!
GRONK!
YOU'LL SOON TASTE MY ELECTRIC WHIPS, AND THEN NEMESIS ENFORCER WILL TASTE YOUR ENTRAILS...
TLAK
SHE'S JUST MEAN!
YOU HAVE THAT EFFECT ON WOMEN.
UNCALLED FOR.
GET READY, ROADBLOCK. THE BIG ONE'S COMING AFTER US.
THUMP
EENNGH!

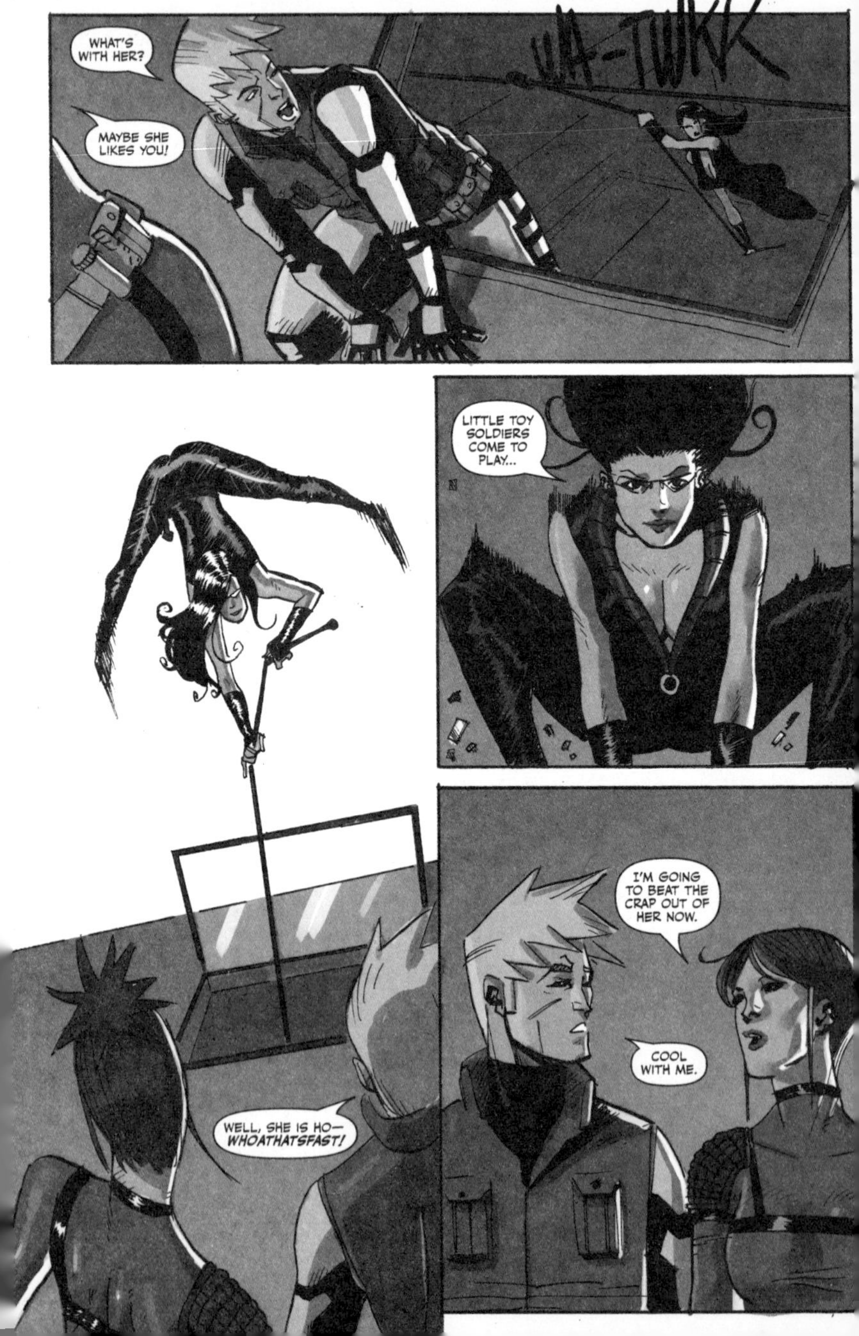
WHAT'S WITH HER?
WA-TWKK
MAYBE SHE LIKES YOU!
LITTLE TOY SOLDIERS COME TO PLAY...
WELL, SHE IS HO— WHOATHATSFAST!
I'M GOING TO BEAT THE CRAP OUT OF HER NOW.
COOL WITH ME.

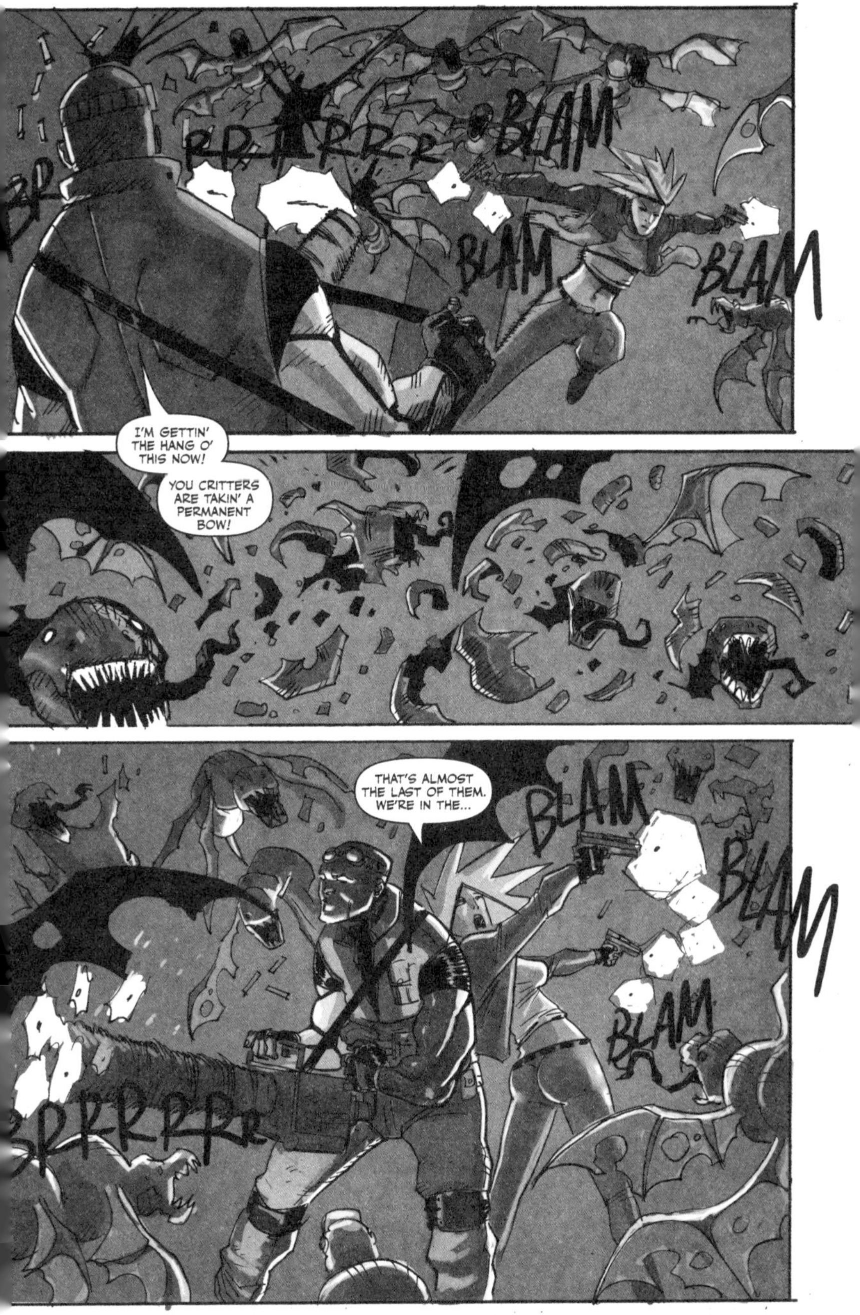
BRRRRR
BLAM
BLAM
BLAM
I'M GETTIN' THE HANG O' THIS NOW!
YOU CRITTERS ARE TAKIN' A PERMANENT BOW!
THAT'S ALMOST THE LAST OF THEM. WE'RE IN THE...
BLAM
BLAM
BLAM
BRRRRRRR

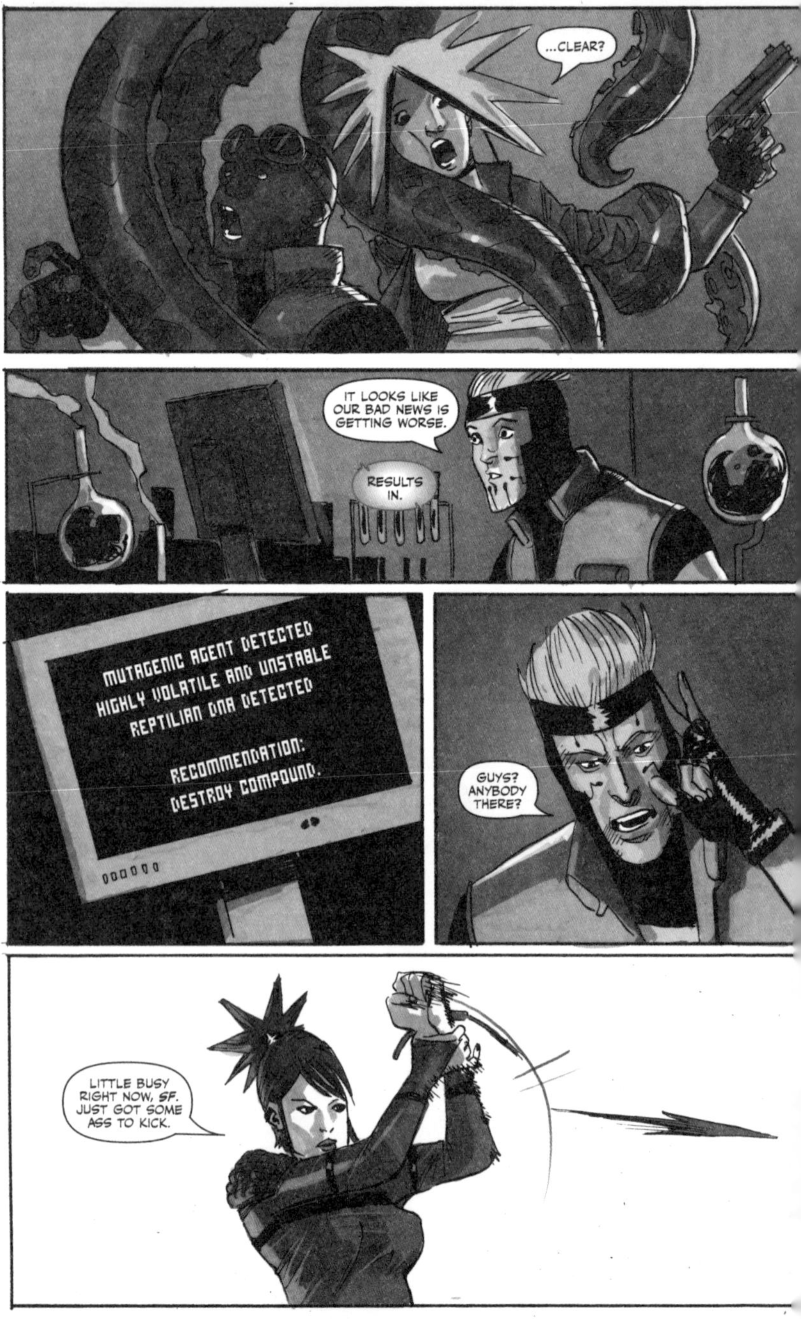
...CLEAR?
IT LOOKS LIKE OUR BAD NEWS IS GETTING WORSE.
RESULTS IN.
MUTAGENIC AGENT DETECTED
HIGHLY VOLATILE AND UNSTABLE
REPTILIAN DNA DETECTED
RECOMMENDATION:
DESTROY COMPOUND.
GUYS? ANYBODY THERE?
LITTLE BUSY RIGHT NOW, SF. JUST GOT SOME ASS TO KICK.

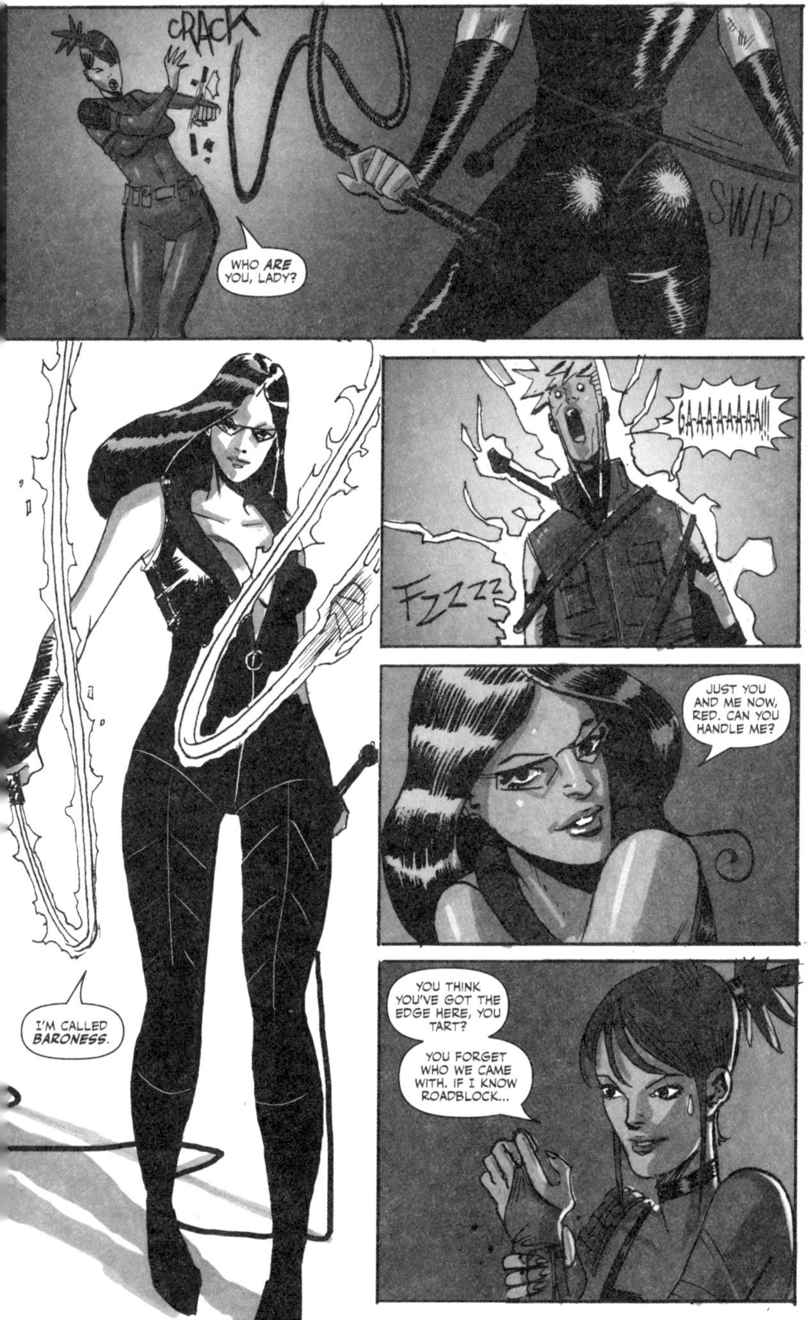
CRACK
SWIP
WHO ARE YOU, LADY?
I'M CALLED BARONESS.
GAAAAAAAA!!!
FZZZZ
JUST YOU AND ME NOW, RED. CAN YOU HANDLE ME?
YOU THINK YOU'VE GOT THE EDGE HERE, YOU TART?
YOU FORGET WHO WE CAME WITH. IF I KNOW ROADBLOCK...

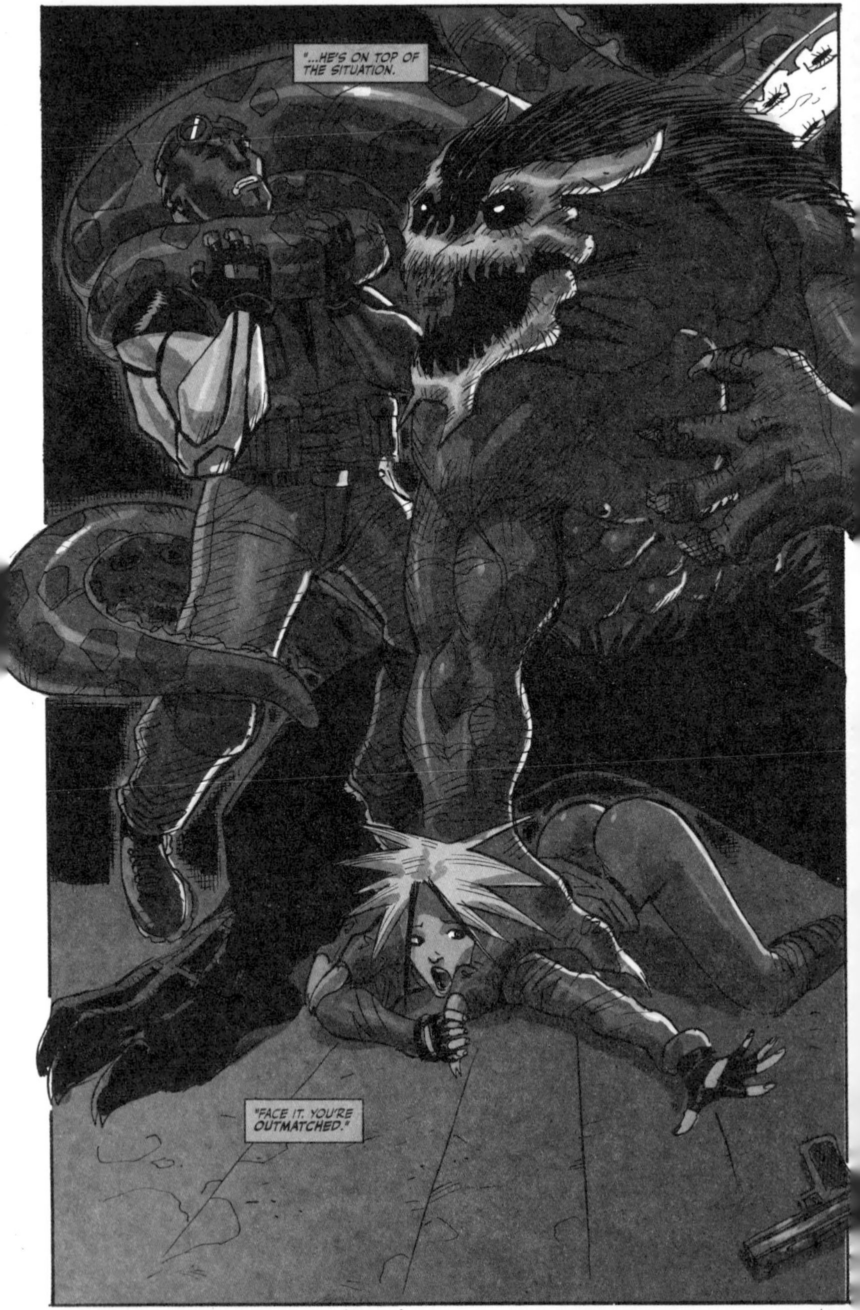
"...HE'S ON TOP OF THE SITUATION.
"FACE IT. YOU'RE OUTMATCHED."

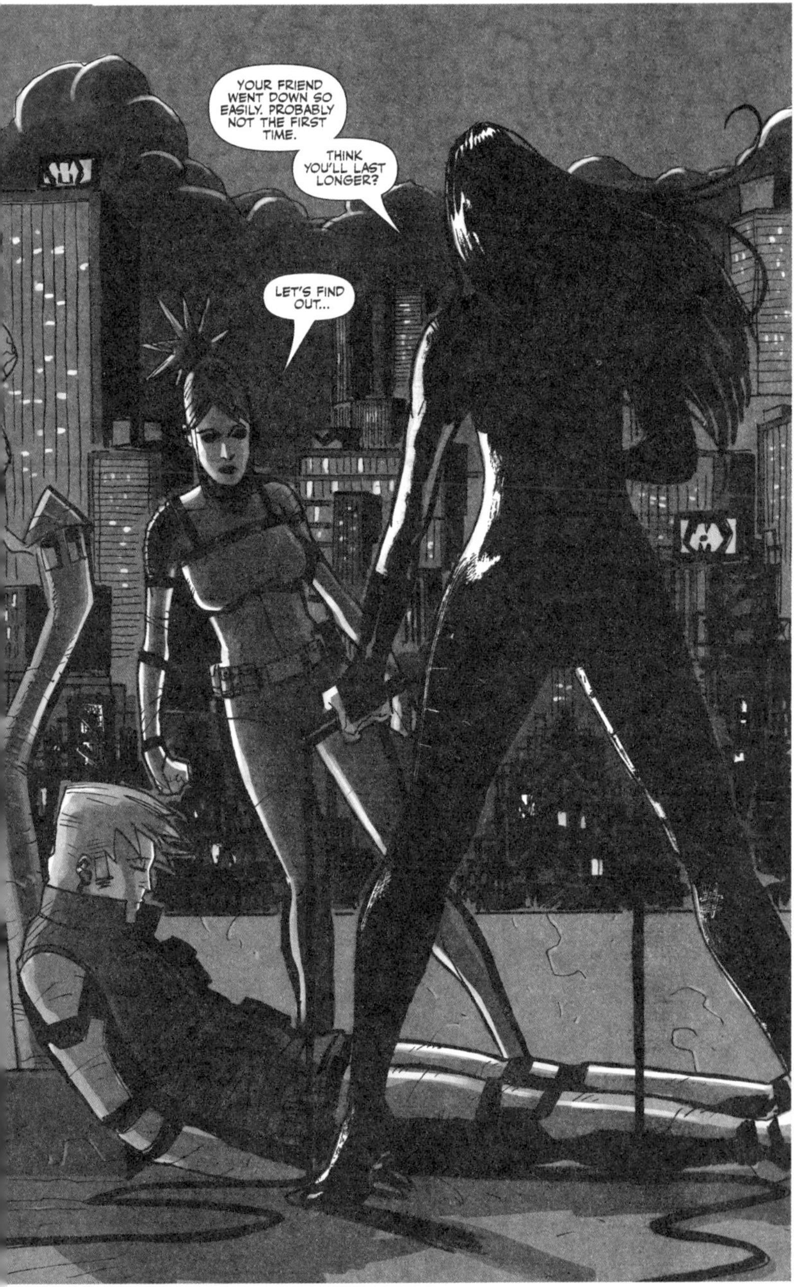
YOUR FRIEND WENT DOWN SO EASILY. PROBABLY NOT THE FIRST TIME.
THINK YOU'LL LAST LONGER?
LET'S FIND OUT...

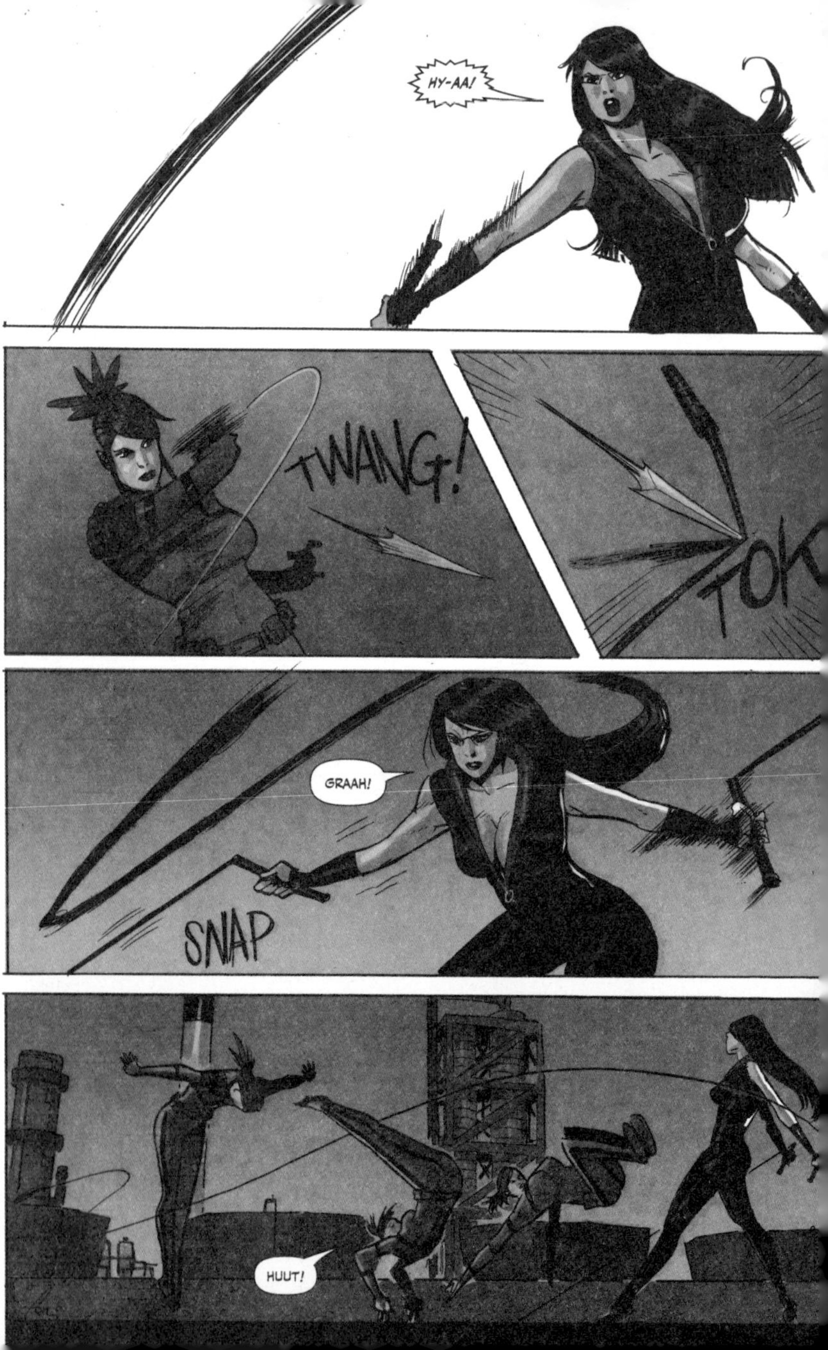
HY-AA!
TWANG!
TOK
GRAAH!
SNAP
HUUT!

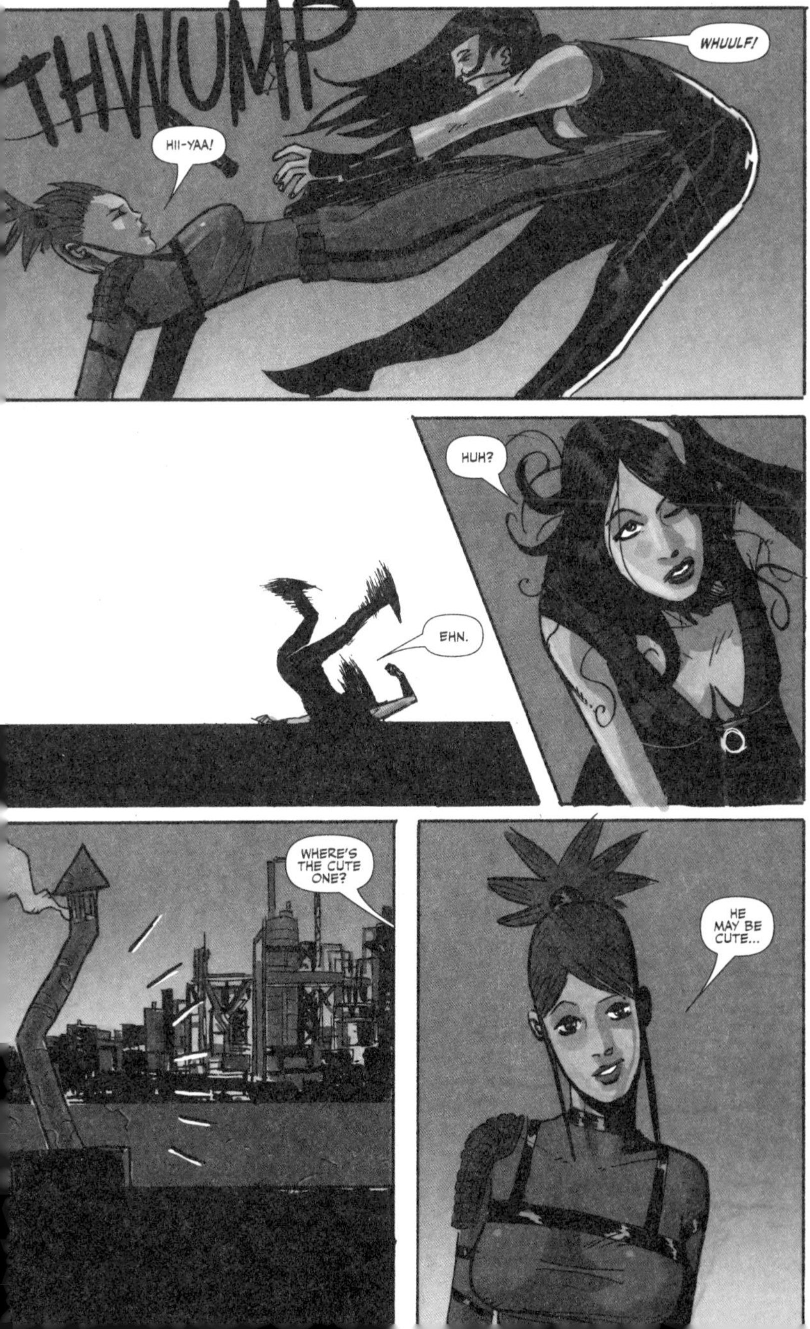
THWUMP
WHUULF!
HII-YAA!
HUH?
EHN.
WHERE'S THE CUTE ONE?
HE MAY BE CUTE...

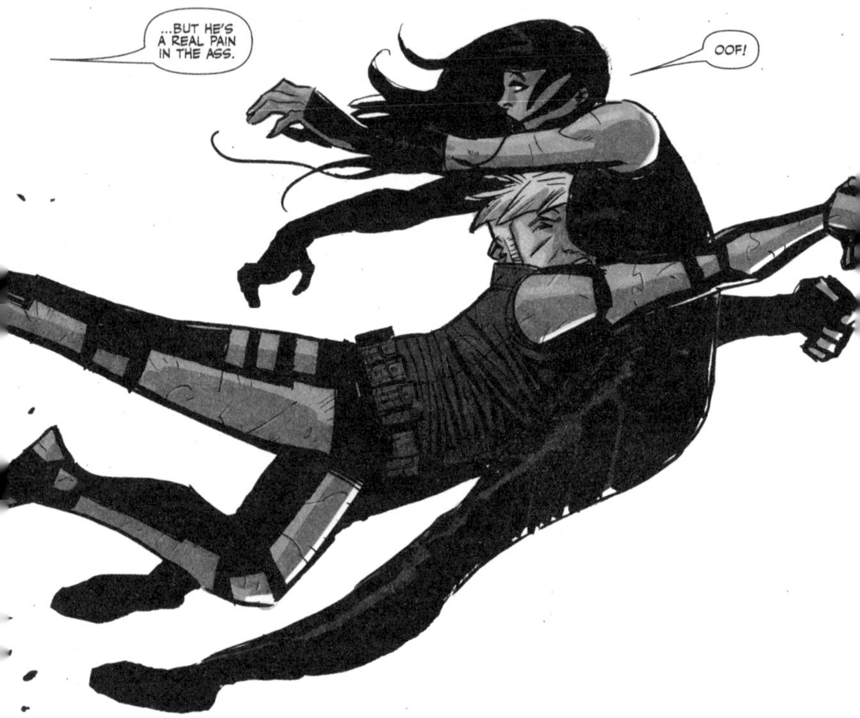
...BUT HE'S A REAL PAIN IN THE ASS.
OOF!

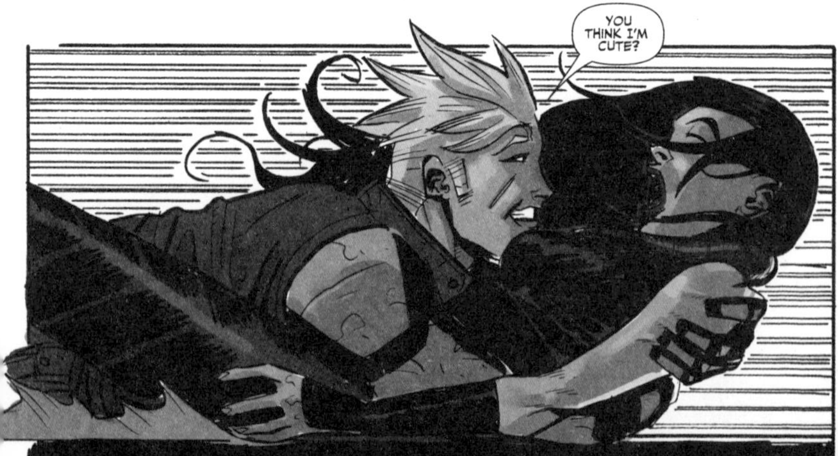
YOU THINK I'M CUTE?

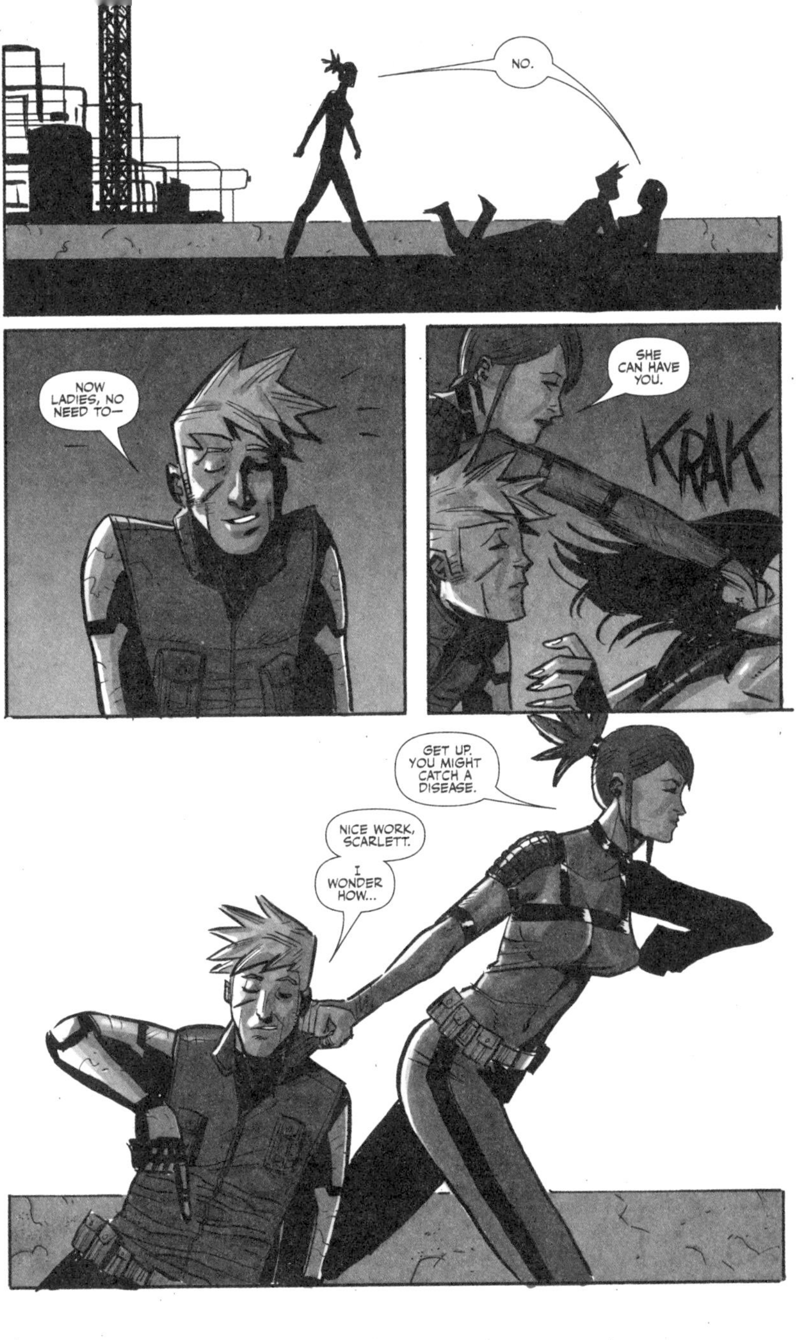
NO.
NOW LADIES, NO NEED TO—
SHE CAN HAVE YOU.
KRAK
GET UP. YOU MIGHT CATCH A DISEASE.
NICE WORK, SCARLETT.
I WONDER HOW...

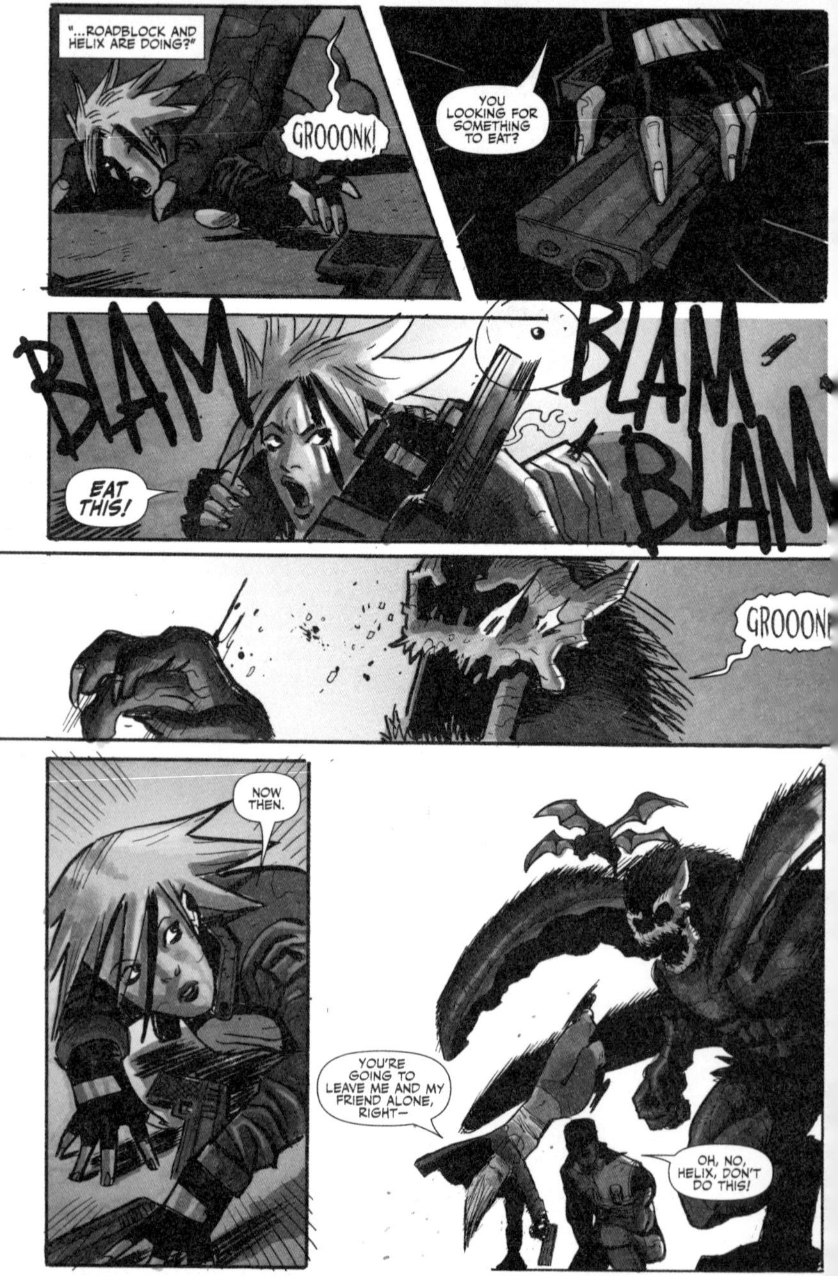
"...ROADBLOCK AND HELIX ARE DOING?"
GROOONK!
YOU LOOKING FOR SOMETHING TO EAT?
BLAM
BLAM
BLAM
BLAM
EAT THIS!
GROOON
NOW THEN.
YOU'RE GOING TO LEAVE ME AND MY FRIEND ALONE, RIGHT—
OH, NO, HELIX, DON'T DO THIS!

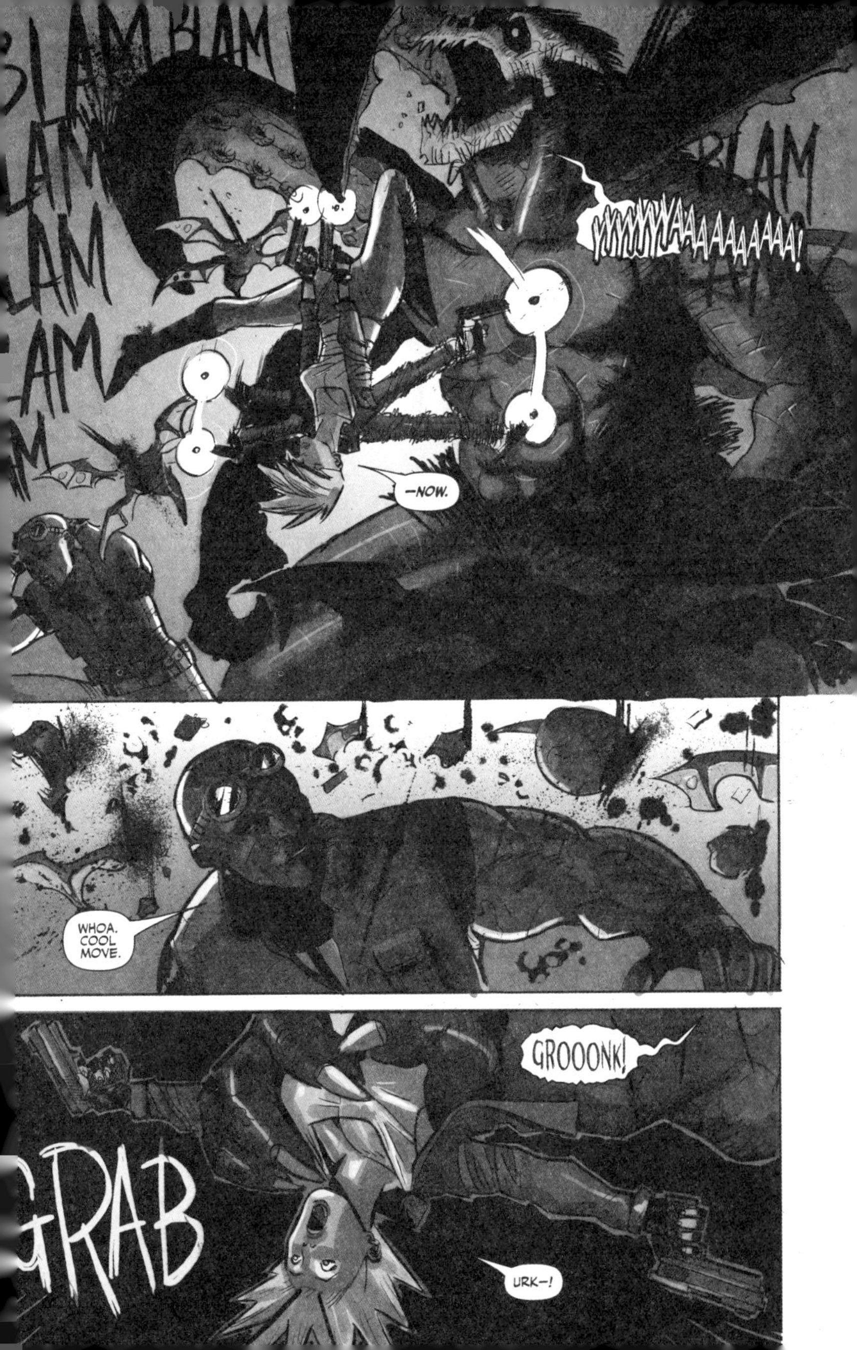
BLAM BLAM
BLAM
BLAM
BLAM
BLAM
BLAM
BLAM
BLAM
YYYYYYAAAAAAAAAA!
—NOW.
WHOA. COOL MOVE.
GROOONK!
GRAB
URK—!

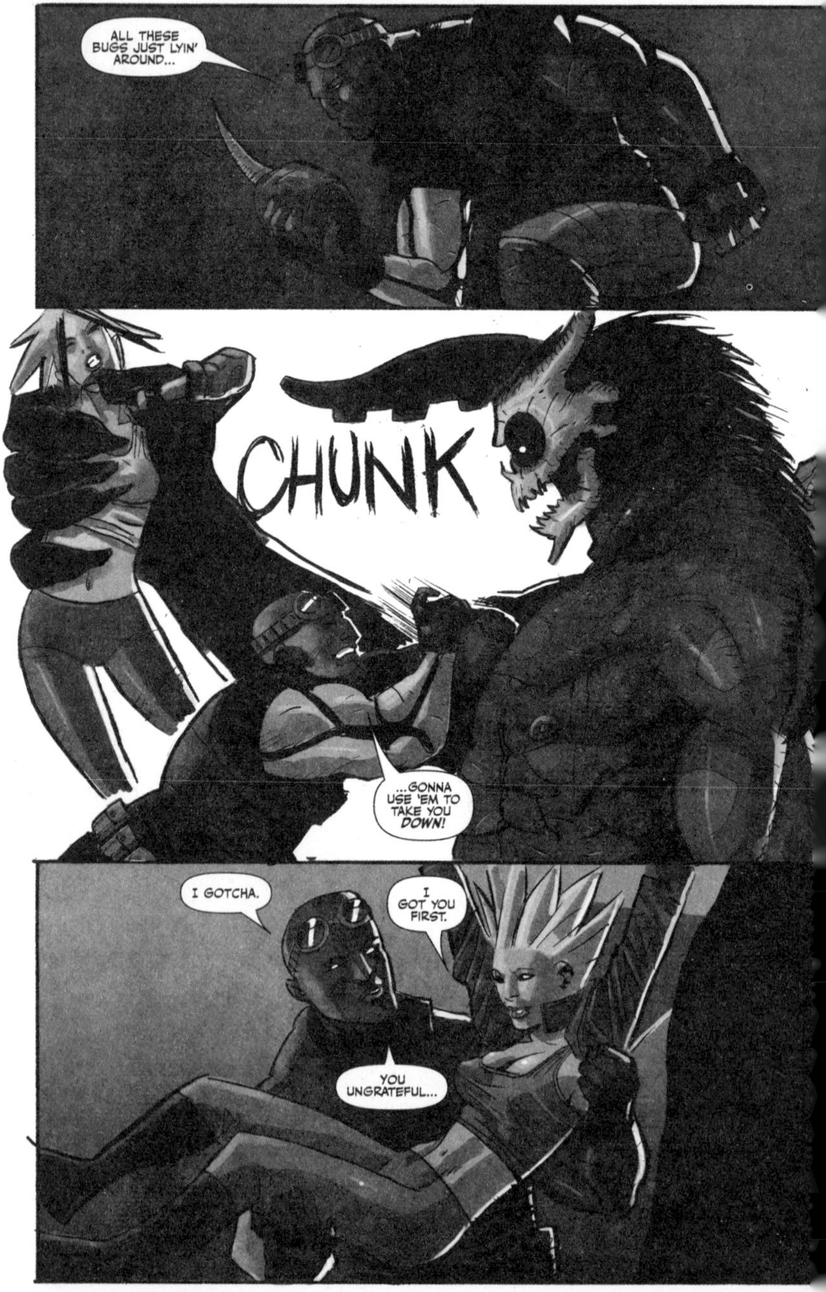

ALL THESE BUGS JUST LYIN' AROUND...
CHUNK
...GONNA USE 'EM TO TAKE YOU *DOWN!*
I GOTCHA.
I GOT YOU FIRST.
YOU UNGRATEFUL...

HURK!

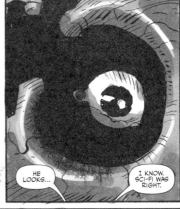

HE LOOKS...

I KNOW. SCI-FI WAS RIGHT.

HE'S A VICTIM JUST AS MUCH AS WE WOULD HAVE BEEN.

HMM...

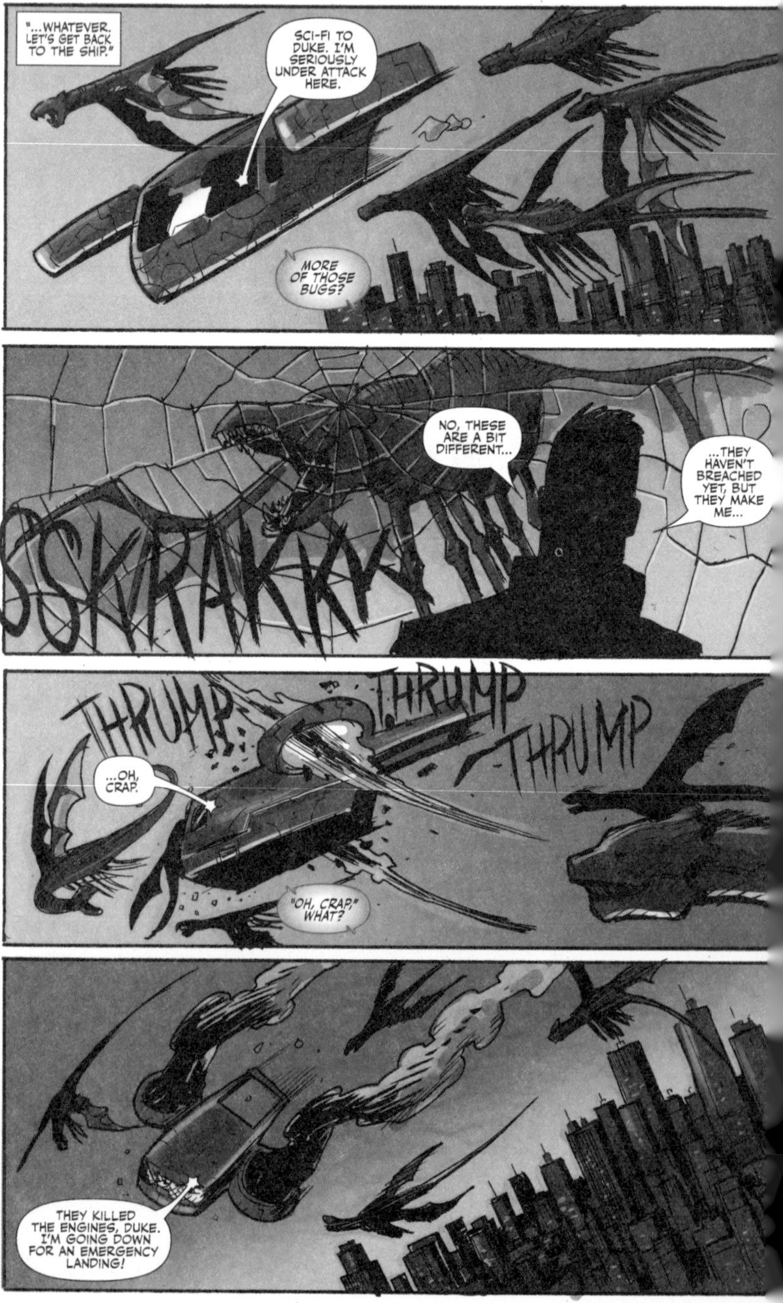
"...WHATEVER. LET'S GET BACK TO THE SHIP."
SCI-FI TO DUKE. I'M SERIOUSLY UNDER ATTACK HERE.
MORE OF THOSE BUGS?
NO, THESE ARE A BIT DIFFERENT...
SSKRAKKK
...THEY HAVEN'T BREACHED YET, BUT THEY MAKE ME...
THRUMP THRUMP THRUMP
...OH, CRAP.
"OH, CRAP," WHAT?
THEY KILLED THE ENGINES, DUKE. I'M GOING DOWN FOR AN EMERGENCY LANDING!

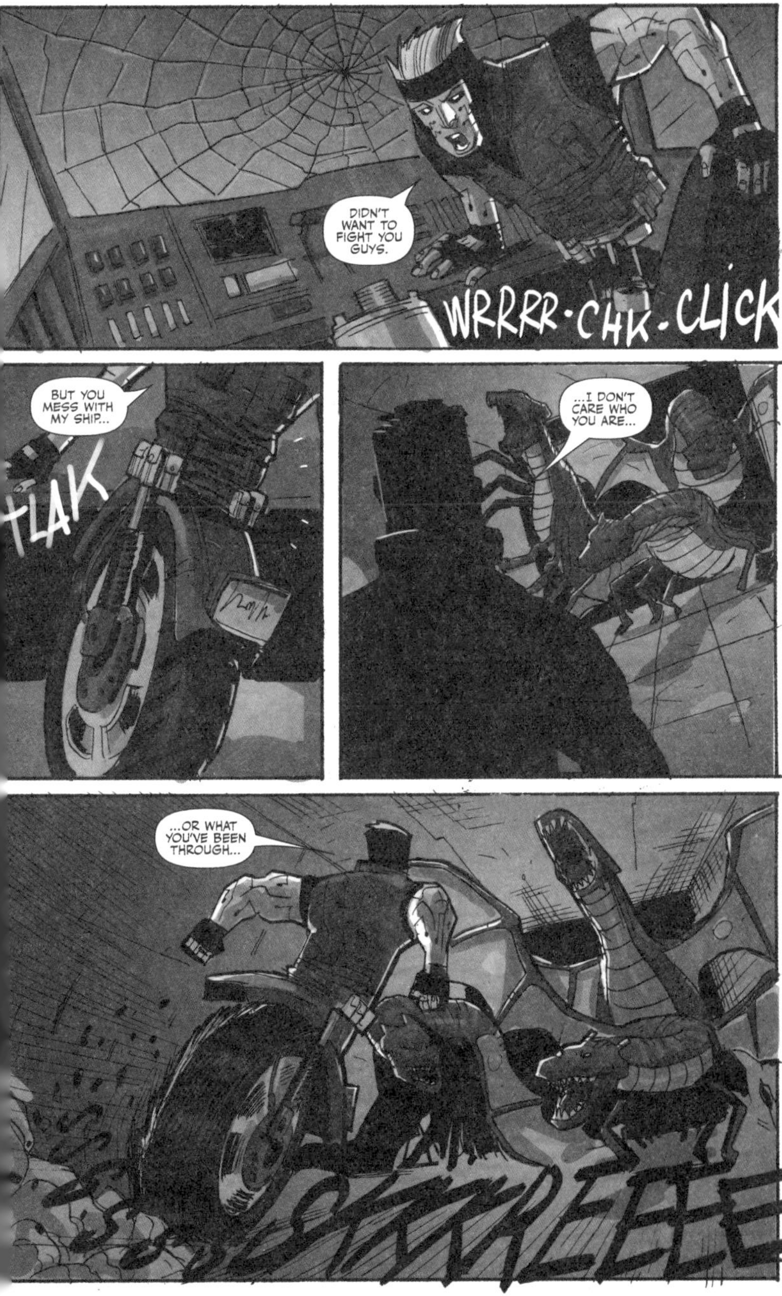
DIDN'T WANT TO FIGHT YOU GUYS.
WRRRR-CHK-CLICK
BUT YOU MESS WITH MY SHIP...
TLAK
...I DON'T CARE WHO YOU ARE...
...OR WHAT YOU'VE BEEN THROUGH...
SKRREEE

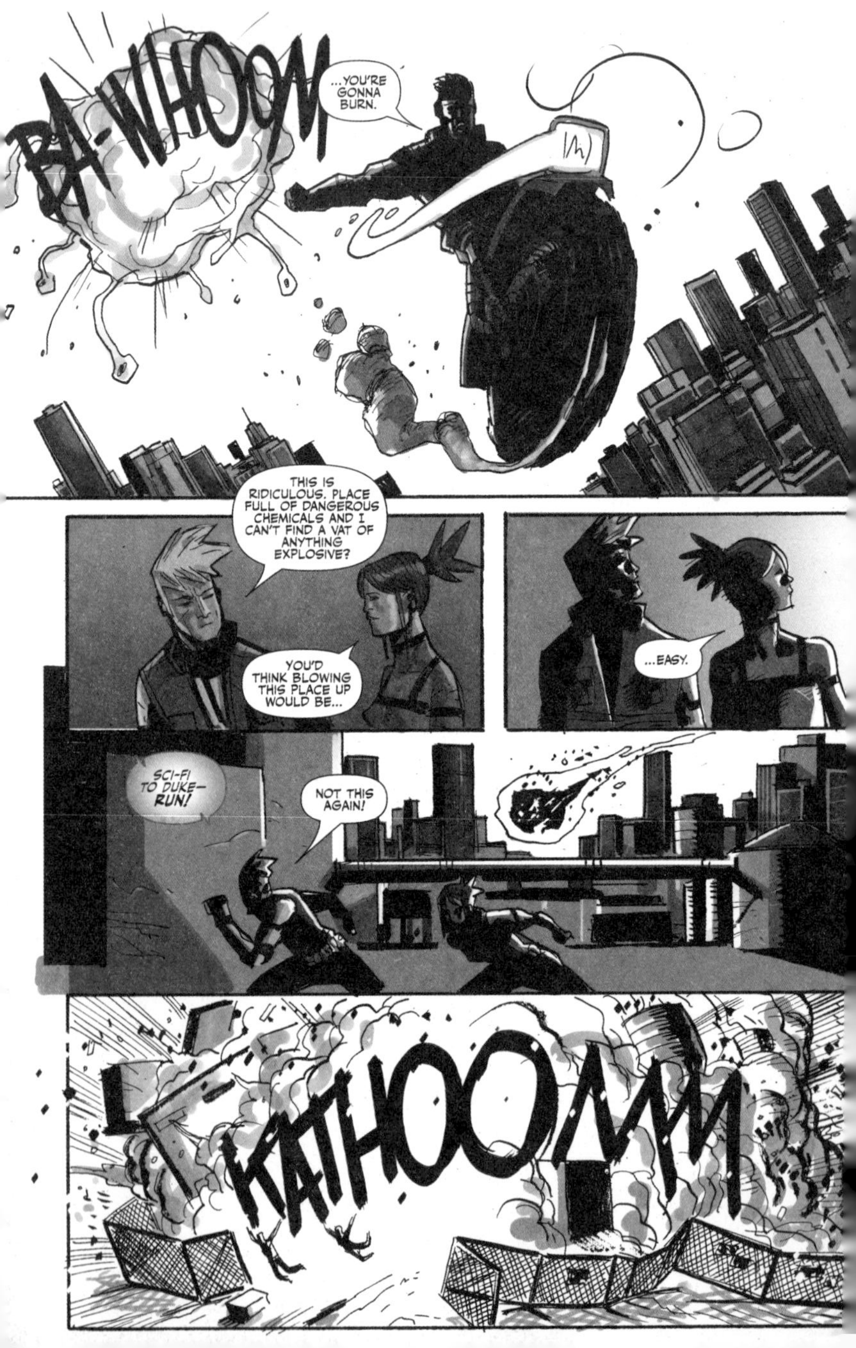
BA-WHOOM
...YOU'RE GONNA BURN.
THIS IS RIDICULOUS. PLACE FULL OF DANGEROUS CHEMICALS AND I CAN'T FIND A VAT OF ANYTHING EXPLOSIVE?
YOU'D THINK BLOWING THIS PLACE UP WOULD BE...
...EASY.
SCI-FI TO DUKE— RUN!
NOT THIS AGAIN!
KATHOOMM

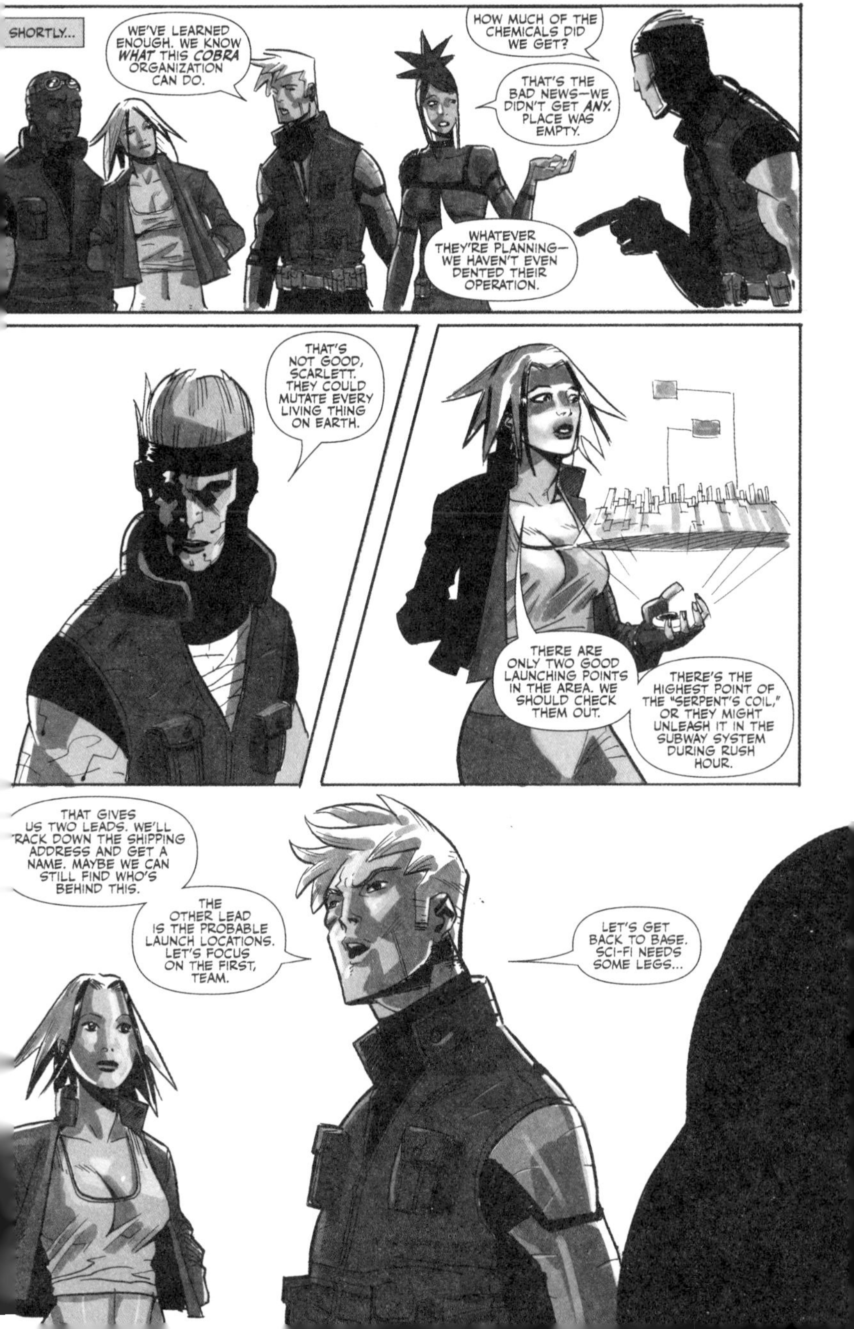
SHORTLY...
WE'VE LEARNED ENOUGH. WE KNOW *WHAT* THIS *COBRA* ORGANIZATION CAN DO.
HOW MUCH OF THE CHEMICALS DID WE GET?
THAT'S THE BAD NEWS—WE DIDN'T GET *ANY*. PLACE WAS EMPTY.
WHATEVER THEY'RE PLANNING— WE HAVEN'T EVEN DENTED THEIR OPERATION.
THAT'S NOT GOOD, SCARLETT. THEY COULD MUTATE EVERY LIVING THING ON EARTH.
THERE ARE ONLY TWO GOOD LAUNCHING POINTS IN THE AREA. WE SHOULD CHECK THEM OUT.
THERE'S THE HIGHEST POINT OF THE "SERPENT'S COIL," OR THEY MIGHT UNLEASH IT IN THE SUBWAY SYSTEM DURING RUSH HOUR.
THAT GIVES US TWO LEADS. WE'LL RACK DOWN THE SHIPPING ADDRESS AND GET A NAME. MAYBE WE CAN STILL FIND WHO'S BEHIND THIS.
THE OTHER LEAD IS THE PROBABLE LAUNCH LOCATIONS. LET'S FOCUS ON THE FIRST, TEAM.
LET'S GET BACK TO BASE. SCI-FI NEEDS SOME LEGS...

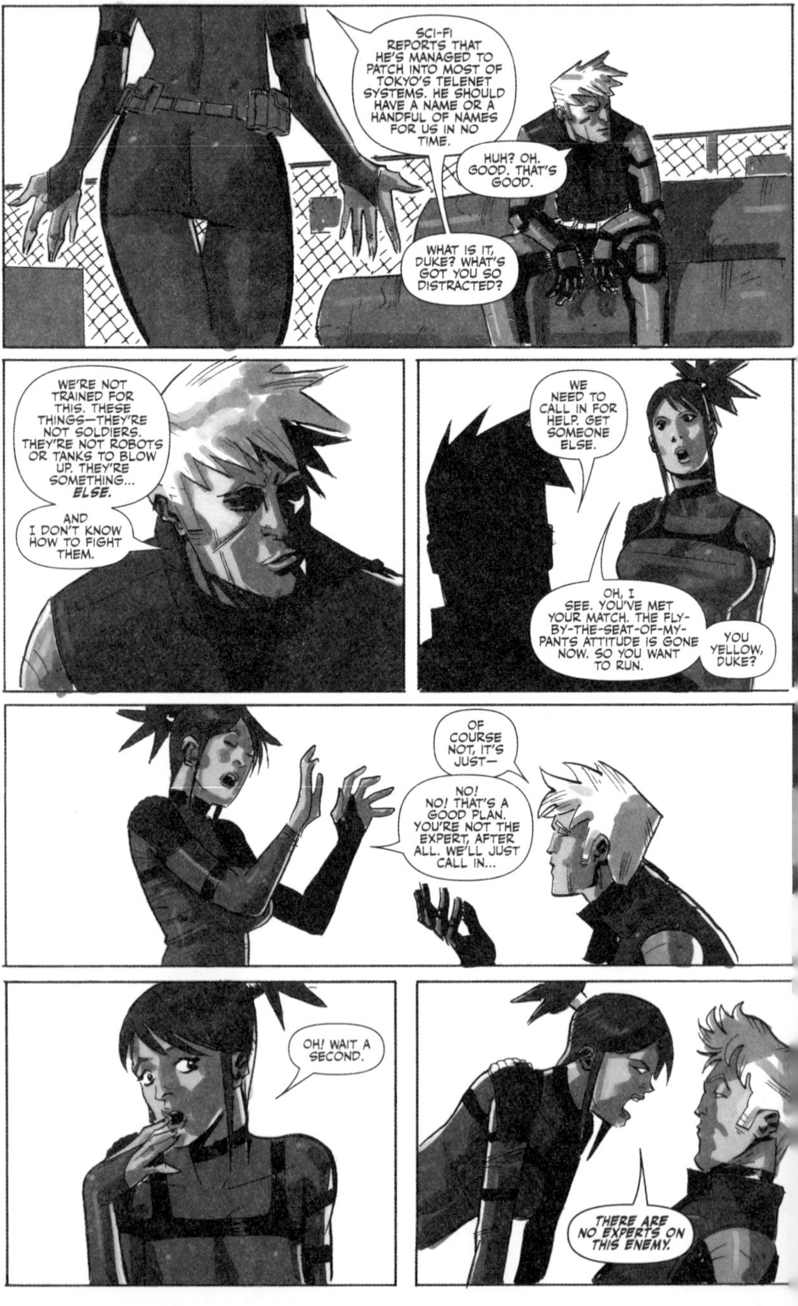
SCI-FI REPORTS THAT HE'S MANAGED TO PATCH INTO MOST OF TOKYO'S TELENET SYSTEMS. HE SHOULD HAVE A NAME OR A HANDFUL OF NAMES FOR US IN NO TIME.
HUH? OH. GOOD. THAT'S GOOD.
WHAT IS IT, DUKE? WHAT'S GOT YOU SO DISTRACTED?
WE'RE NOT TRAINED FOR THIS. THESE THINGS—THEY'RE NOT SOLDIERS. THEY'RE NOT ROBOTS OR TANKS TO BLOW UP. THEY'RE SOMETHING... *ELSE.*
AND I DON'T KNOW HOW TO FIGHT THEM.
WE NEED TO CALL IN FOR HELP. GET SOMEONE ELSE.
OH, I SEE. YOU'VE MET YOUR MATCH. THE FLY-BY-THE-SEAT-OF-MY-PANTS ATTITUDE IS GONE NOW. SO YOU WANT TO RUN.
YOU YELLOW, DUKE?
OF COURSE NOT, IT'S JUST—
NO! *NO!* THAT'S A GOOD PLAN. YOU'RE NOT THE EXPERT, AFTER ALL. WE'LL JUST CALL IN...
OH! WAIT A SECOND.
THERE ARE NO EXPERTS ON THIS ENEMY.

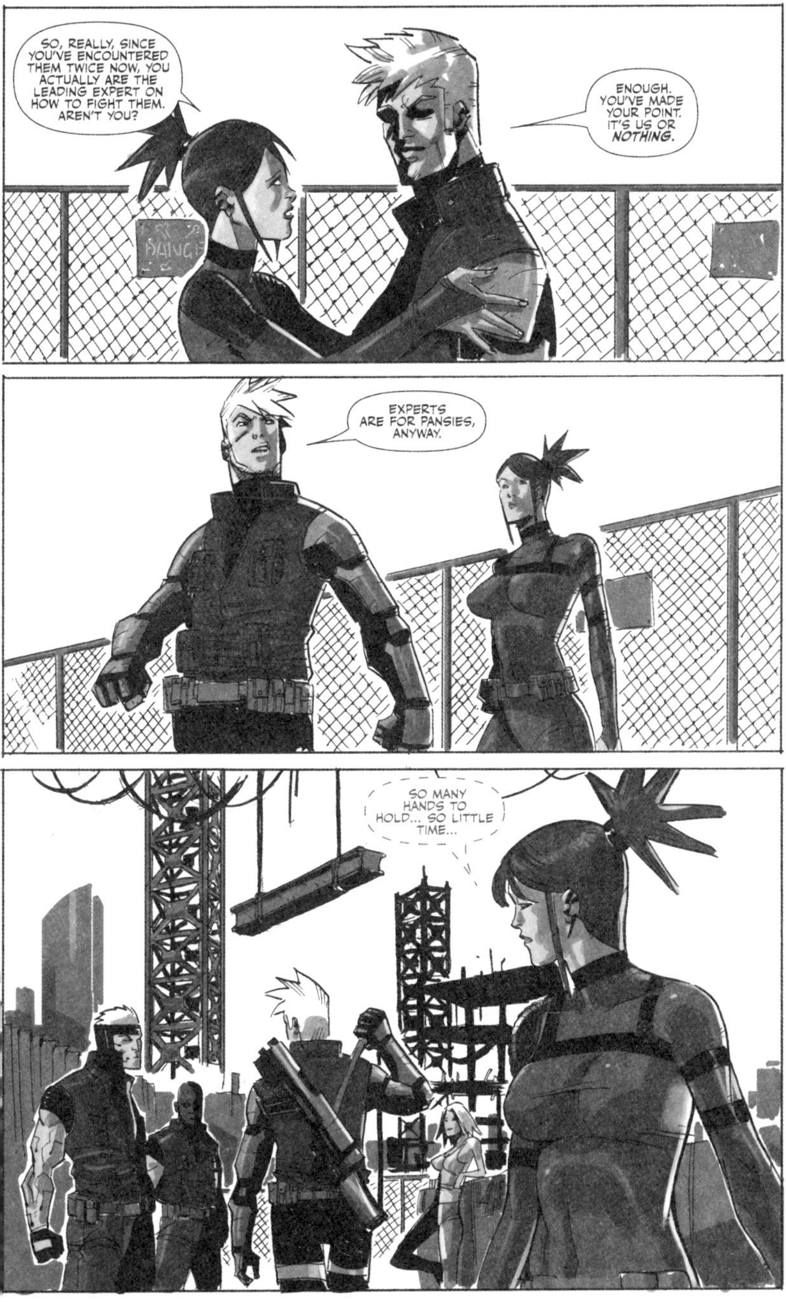
SO, REALLY, SINCE YOU'VE ENCOUNTERED THEM TWICE NOW, YOU ACTUALLY ARE THE LEADING EXPERT ON HOW TO FIGHT THEM. AREN'T YOU?
ENOUGH. YOU'VE MADE YOUR POINT. IT'S US OR *NOTHING.*
EXPERTS ARE FOR PANSIES, ANYWAY.
SO MANY HANDS TO HOLD... SO LITTLE TIME...

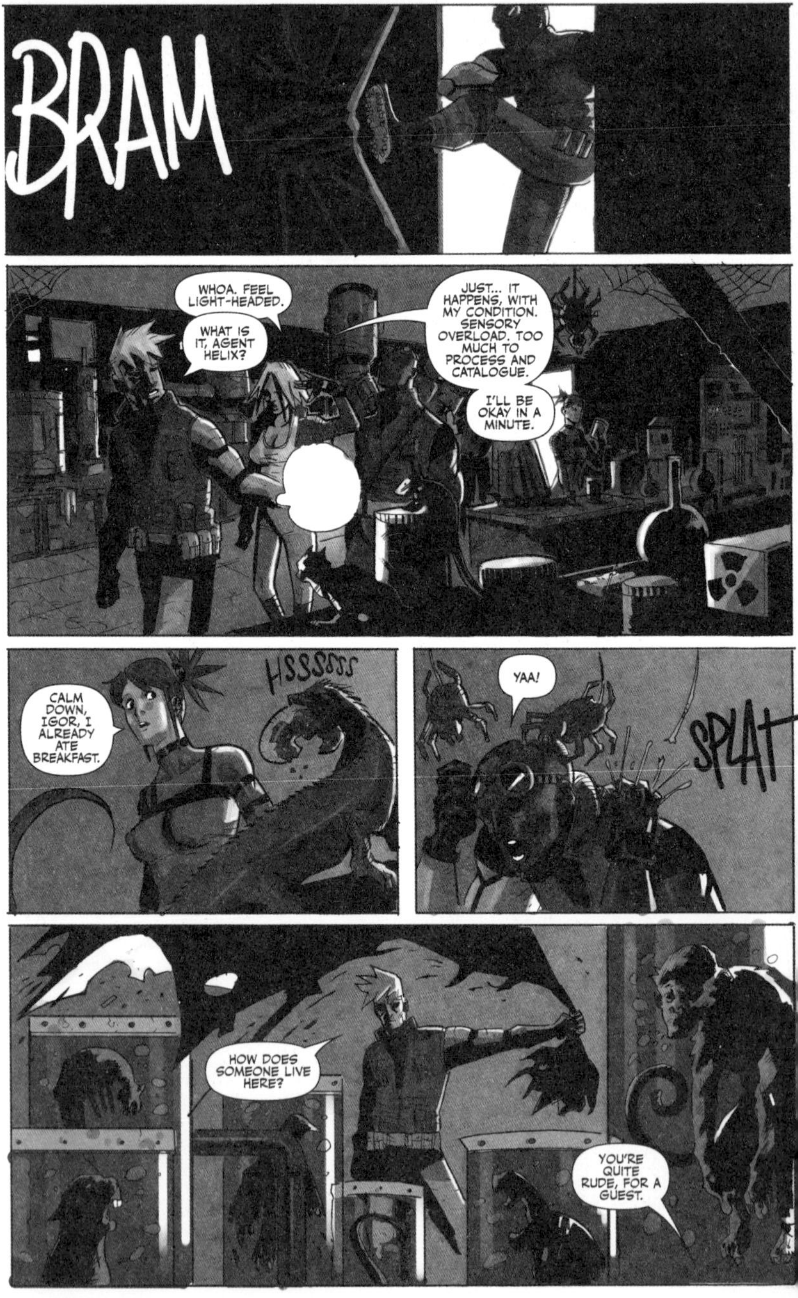
BRAM
WHOA. FEEL LIGHT-HEADED.
WHAT IS IT, AGENT HELIX?
JUST... IT HAPPENS, WITH MY CONDITION. SENSORY OVERLOAD. TOO MUCH TO PROCESS AND CATALOGUE.
I'LL BE OKAY IN A MINUTE.
HSSSSSS
CALM DOWN, IGOR, I ALREADY ATE BREAKFAST.
YAA!
SPLAT
HOW DOES SOMEONE LIVE HERE?
YOU'RE QUITE RUDE, FOR A GUEST.

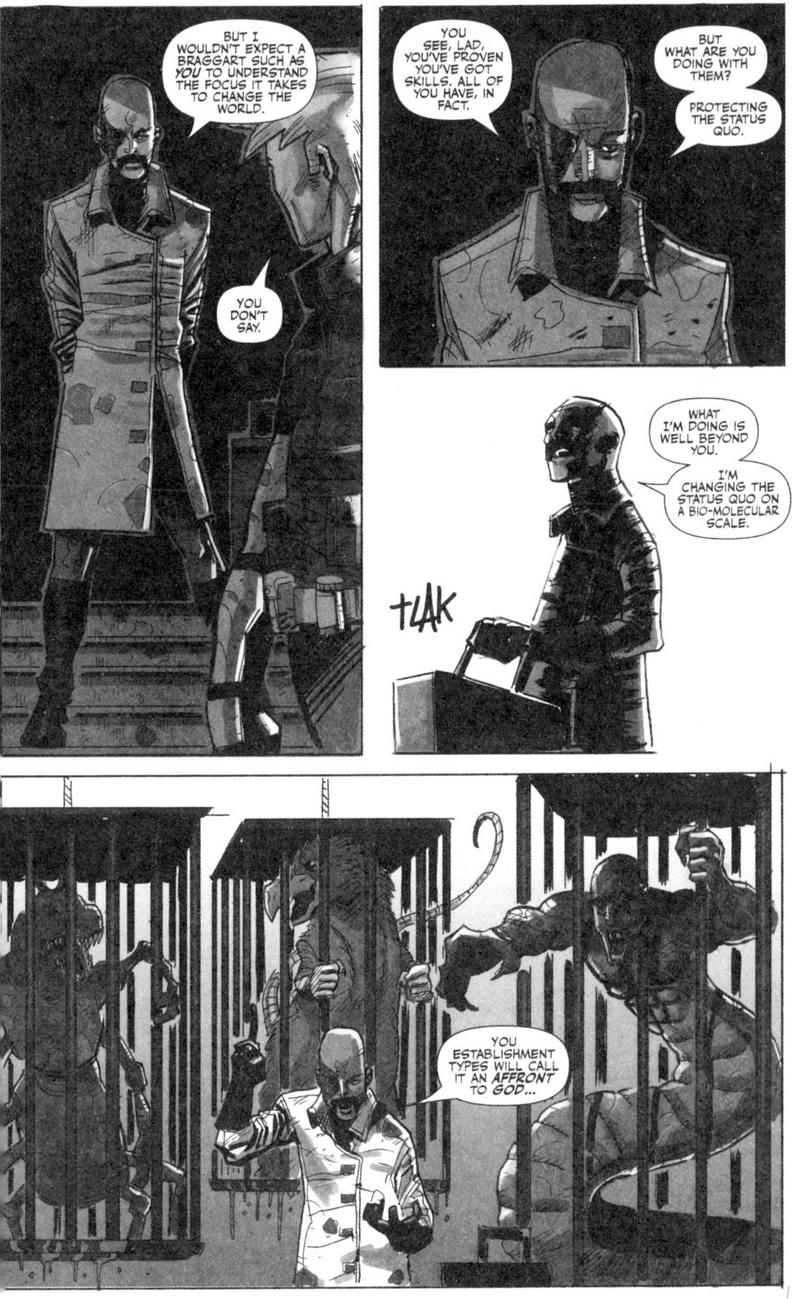
BUT I WOULDN'T EXPECT A BRAGGART SUCH AS *YOU* TO UNDERSTAND THE FOCUS IT TAKES TO CHANGE THE WORLD.
YOU DON'T SAY.
YOU SEE, LAD, YOU'VE PROVEN YOU'VE GOT SKILLS. ALL OF YOU HAVE, IN FACT.
BUT WHAT ARE YOU DOING WITH THEM?
PROTECTING THE STATUS QUO.
WHAT I'M DOING IS WELL BEYOND YOU.
I'M CHANGING THE STATUS QUO ON A BIO-MOLECULAR SCALE.
TLAK
YOU ESTABLISHMENT TYPES WILL CALL IT AN *AFFRONT* TO *GOD*...

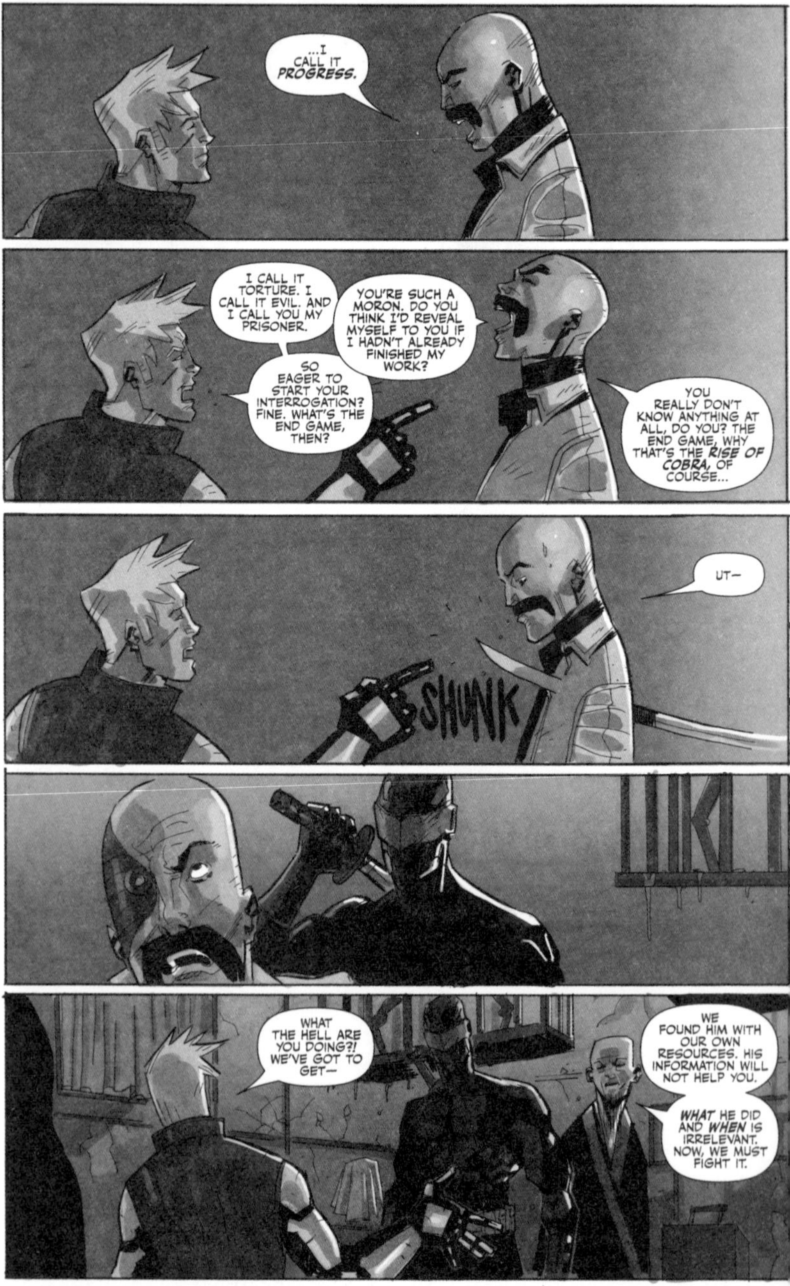
...I CALL IT PROGRESS.
I CALL IT TORTURE. I CALL IT EVIL. AND I CALL YOU MY PRISONER.
YOU'RE SUCH A MORON. DO YOU THINK I'D REVEAL MYSELF TO YOU IF I HADN'T ALREADY FINISHED MY WORK?
SO EAGER TO START YOUR INTERROGATION? FINE. WHAT'S THE END GAME, THEN?
YOU REALLY DON'T KNOW ANYTHING AT ALL, DO YOU? THE END GAME, WHY THAT'S THE RISE OF COBRA, OF COURSE...
UT—
SHUNK
WHAT THE HELL ARE YOU DOING?! WE'VE GOT TO GET—
WE FOUND HIM WITH OUR OWN RESOURCES. HIS INFORMATION WILL NOT HELP YOU.
WHAT HE DID AND WHEN IS IRRELEVANT. NOW, WE MUST FIGHT IT.

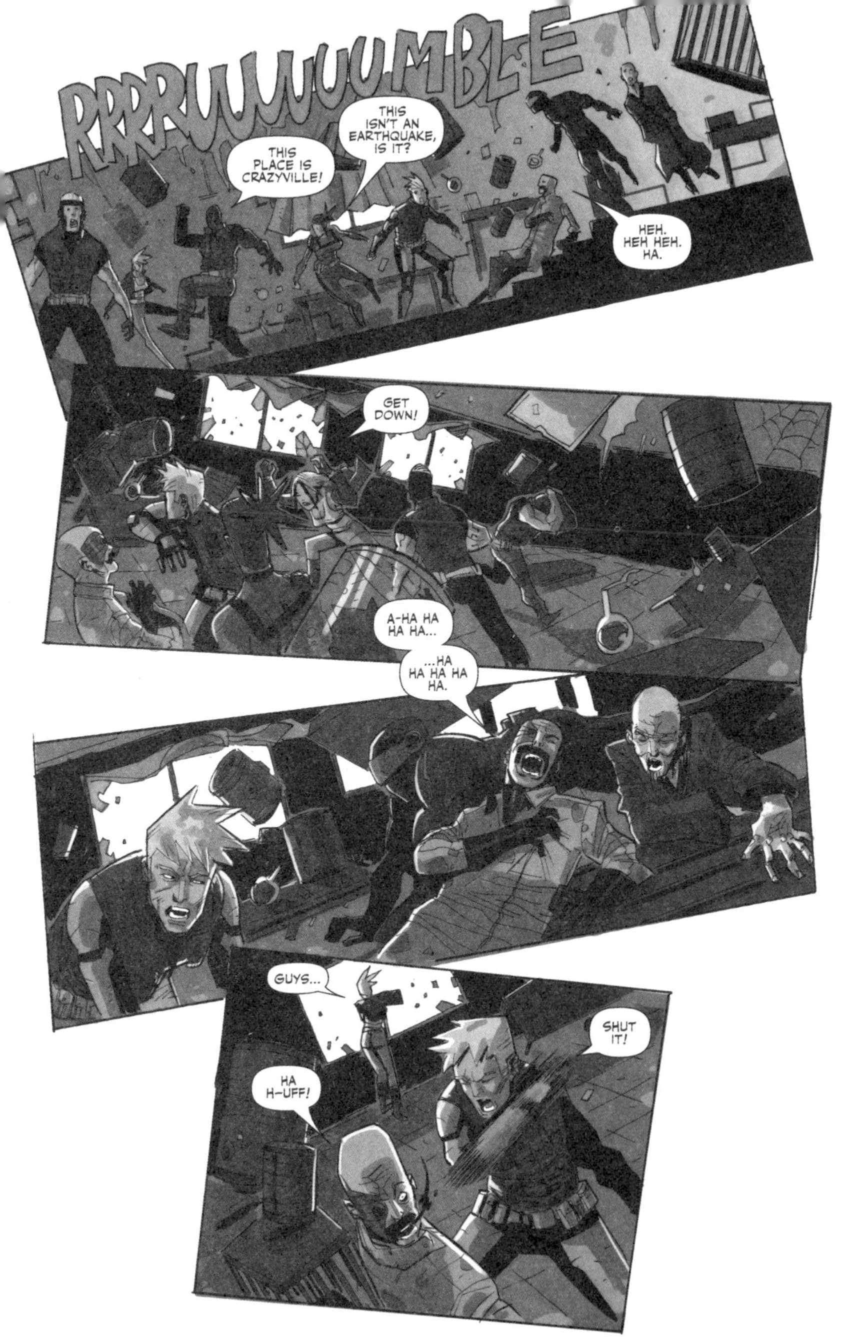
RRRRUUUUUUMBLE
THIS PLACE IS CRAZYVILLE!
THIS ISN'T AN EARTHQUAKE, IS IT?
HEH. HEH HEH. HA.
GET DOWN!
A-HA HA HA HA...
...HA HA HA HA HA.
GUYS...
SHUT IT!
HA H-UFF!

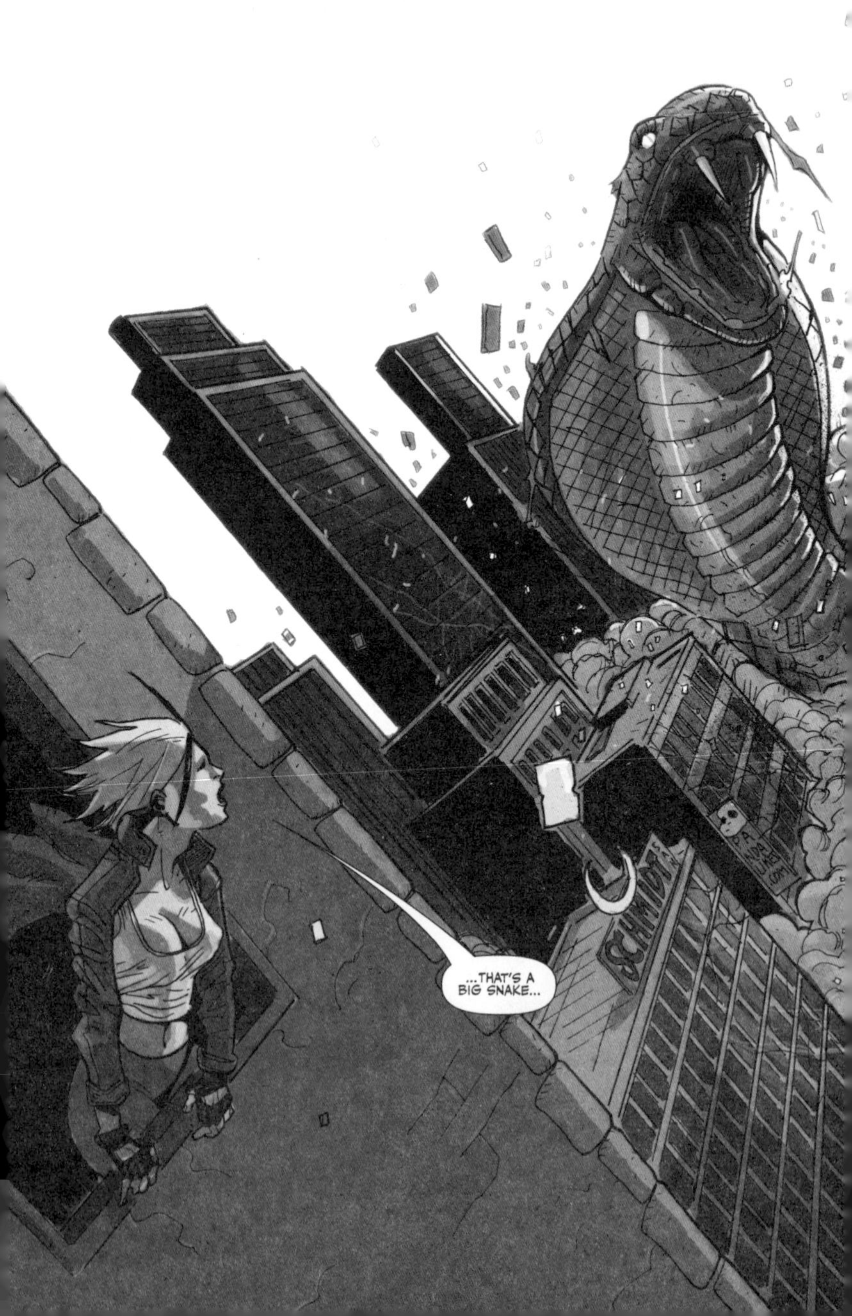
...THAT'S A BIG SNAKE...

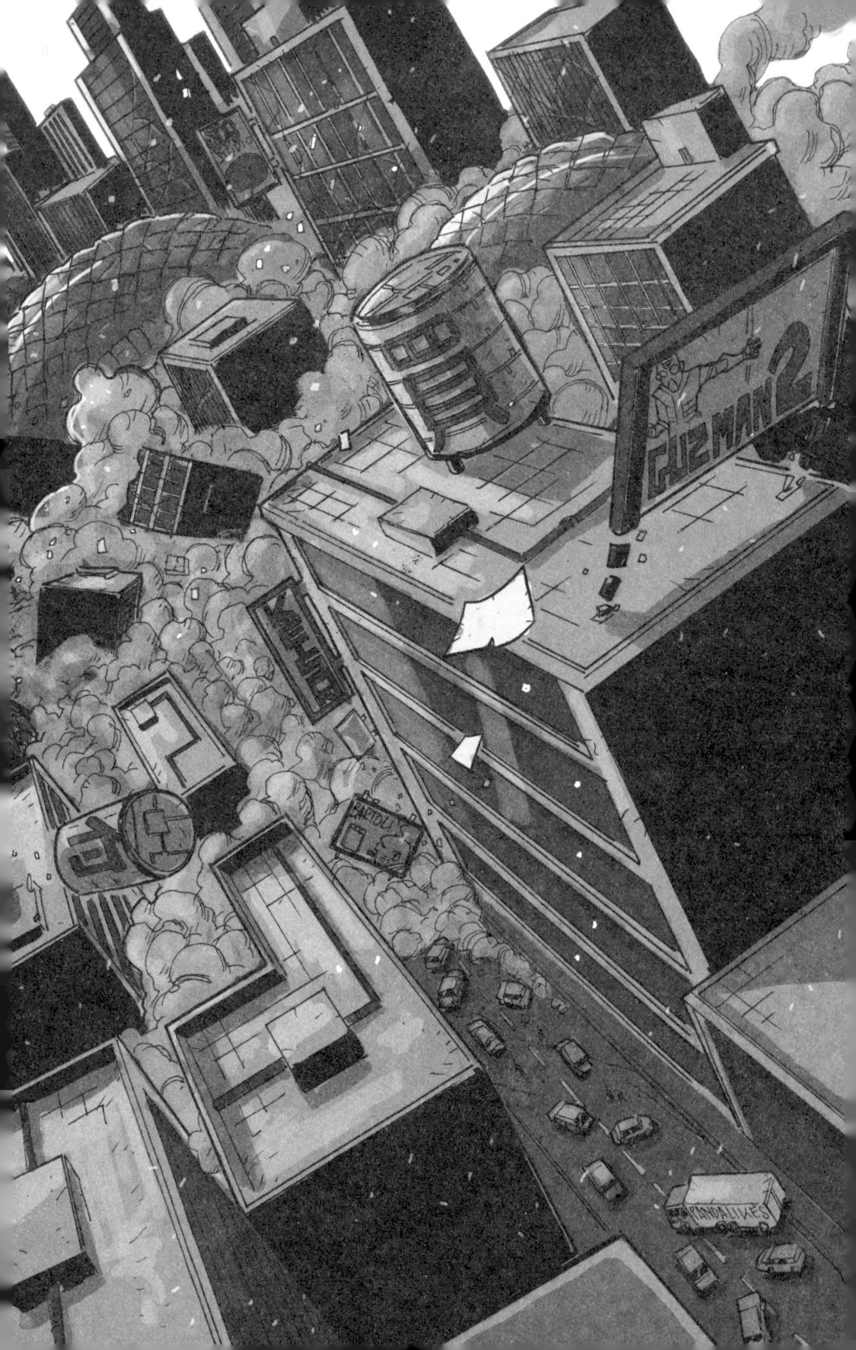
GUZMAN 2
BARTOLI
PANDA LIVES

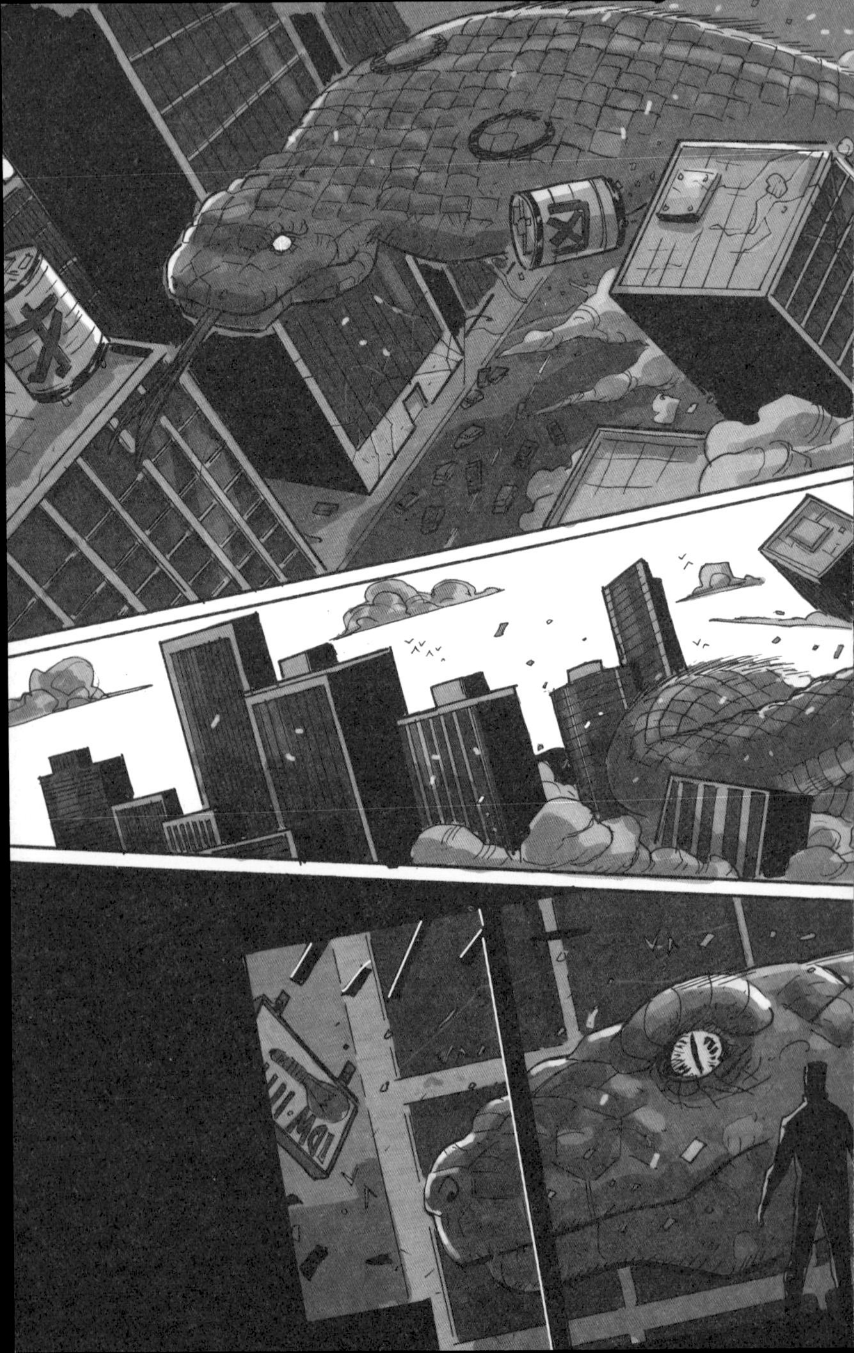

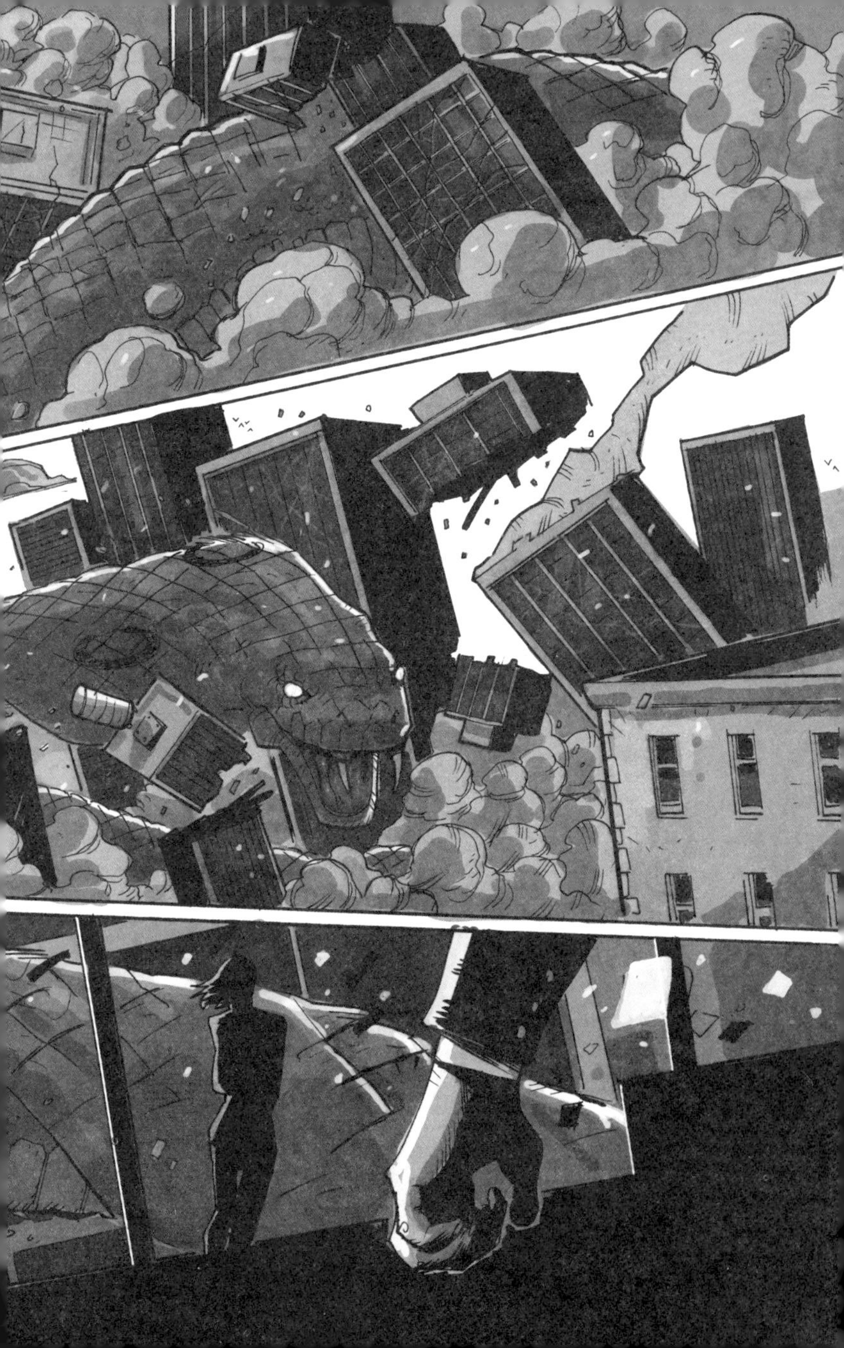

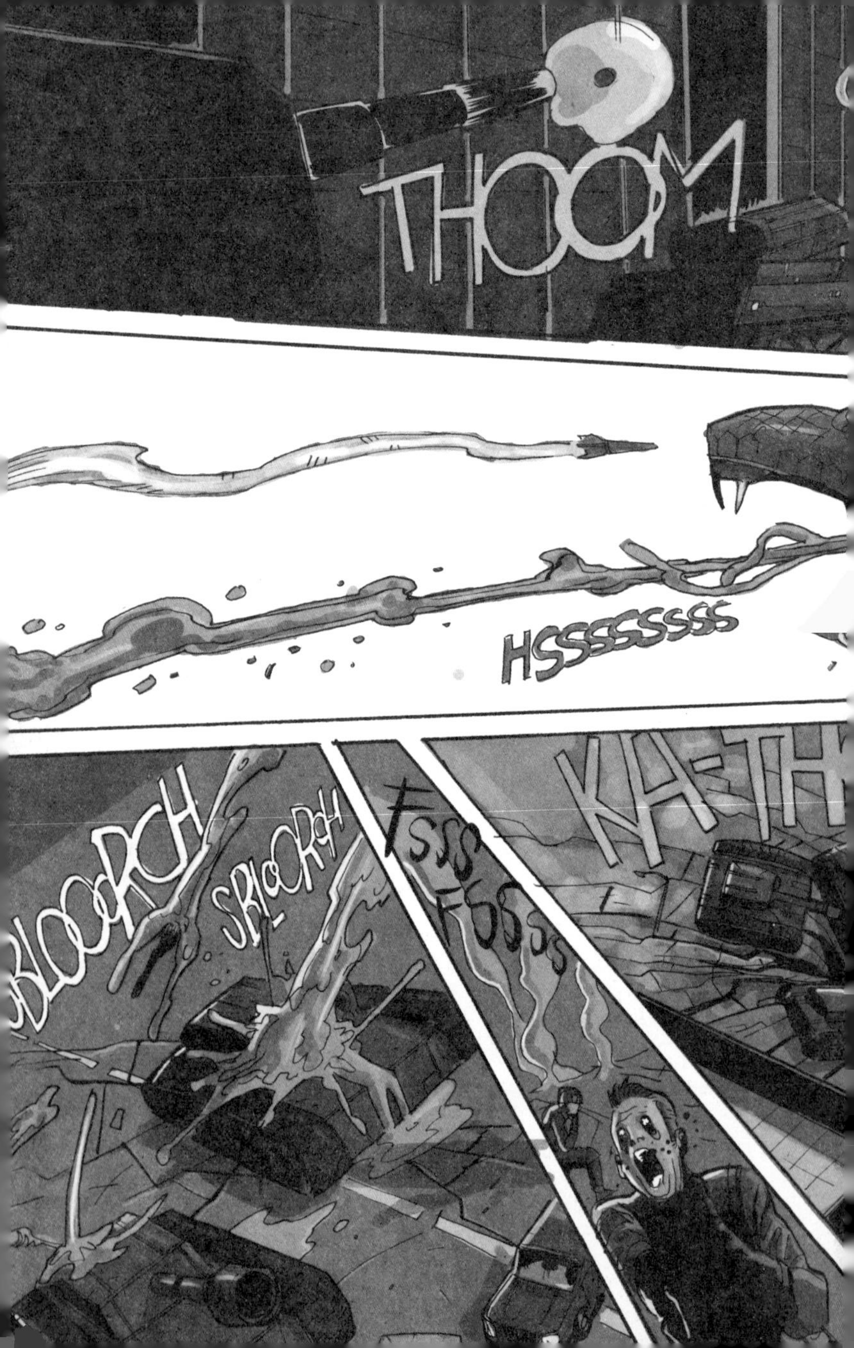
THOOM
HSSSSSSSS
BLOOORCH
SPLOORCH
TSSS
FSSSSS
KA-TH

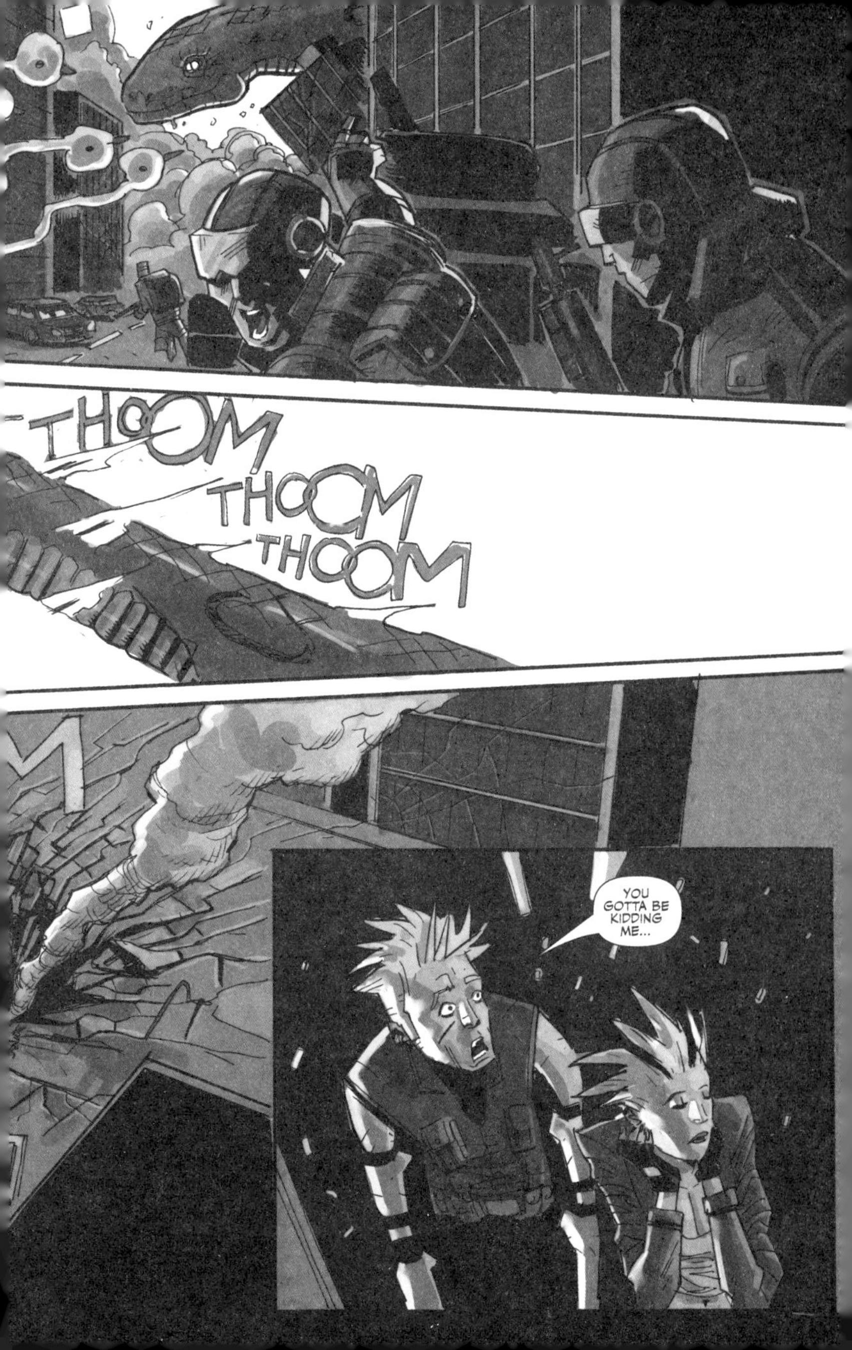
THOOM
THOOM
THOOM
YOU GOTTA BE KIDDING ME...

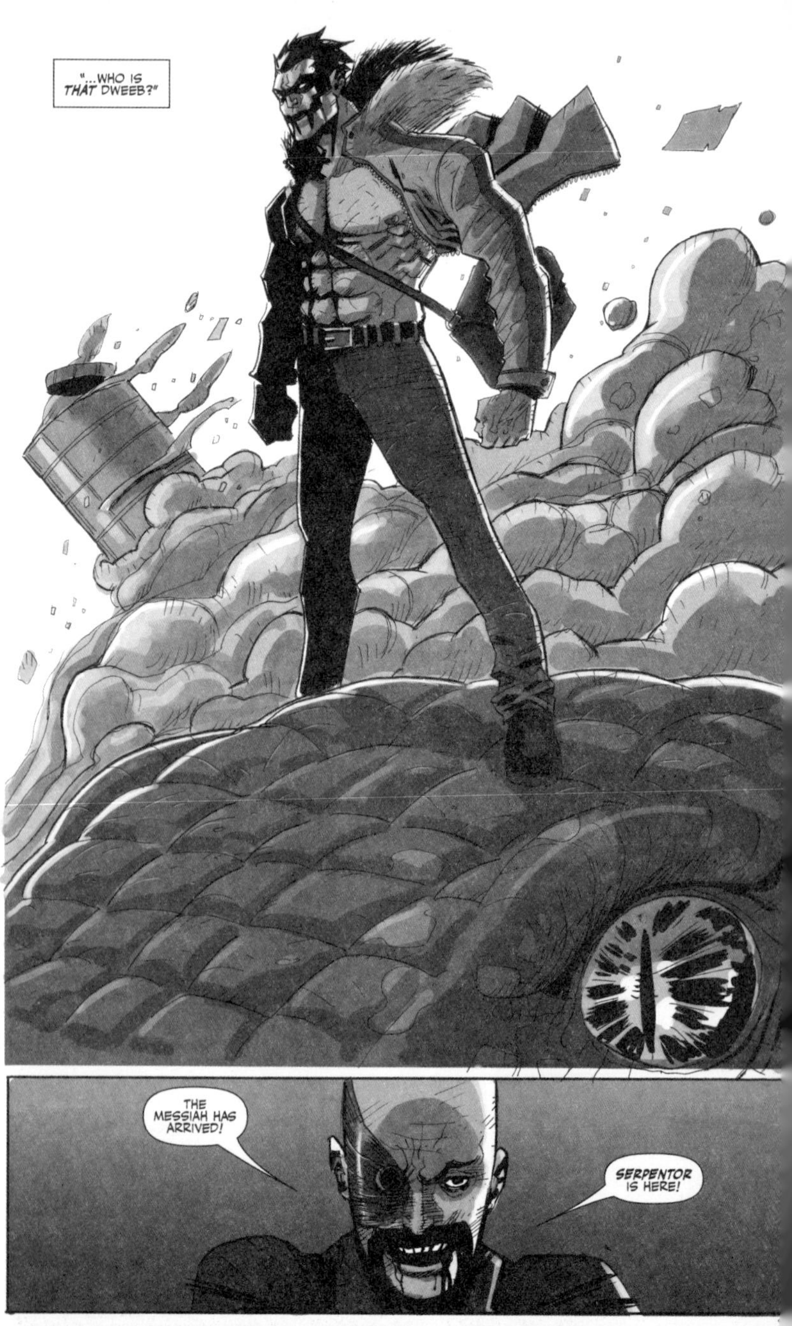
"...WHO IS *THAT* DWEEB?"
THE MESSIAH HAS ARRIVED!
SERPENTOR IS HERE!

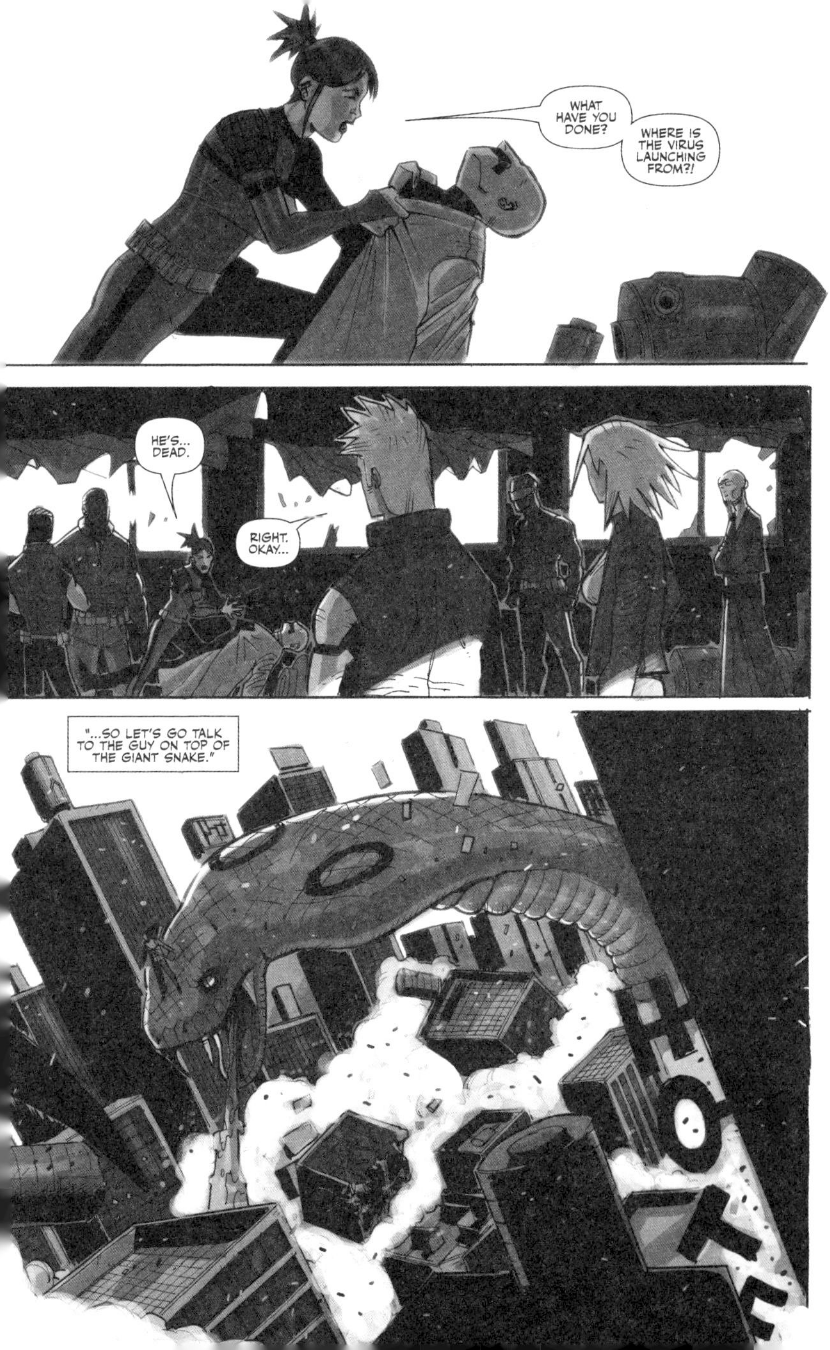
WHAT HAVE YOU DONE?
WHERE IS THE VIRUS LAUNCHING FROM?!
HE'S... DEAD.
RIGHT. OKAY...
"...SO LET'S GO TALK TO THE GUY ON TOP OF THE GIANT SNAKE."

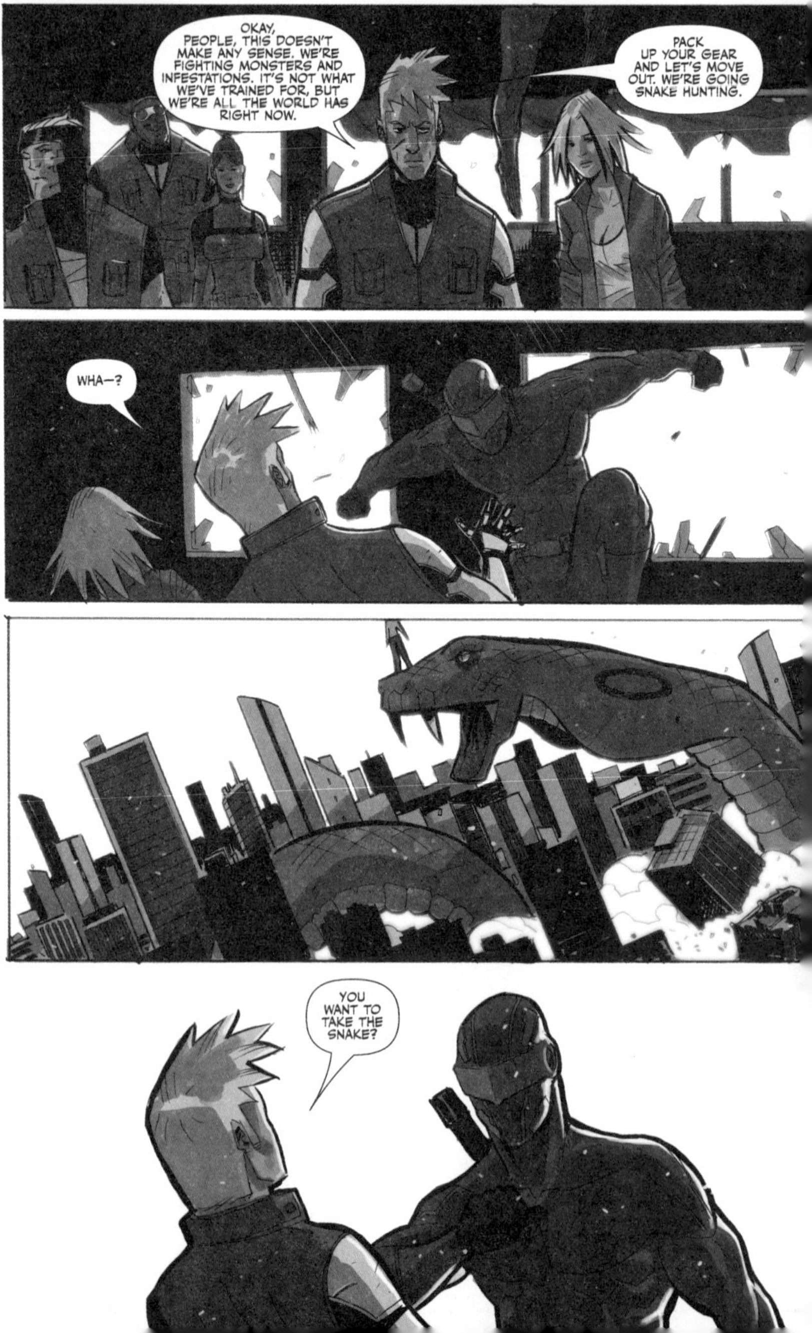
OKAY, PEOPLE, THIS DOESN'T MAKE ANY SENSE. WE'RE FIGHTING MONSTERS AND INFESTATIONS. IT'S NOT WHAT WE'VE TRAINED FOR, BUT WE'RE ALL THE WORLD HAS RIGHT NOW.
PACK UP YOUR GEAR AND LET'S MOVE OUT. WE'RE GOING SNAKE HUNTING.
WHA--?
YOU WANT TO TAKE THE SNAKE?

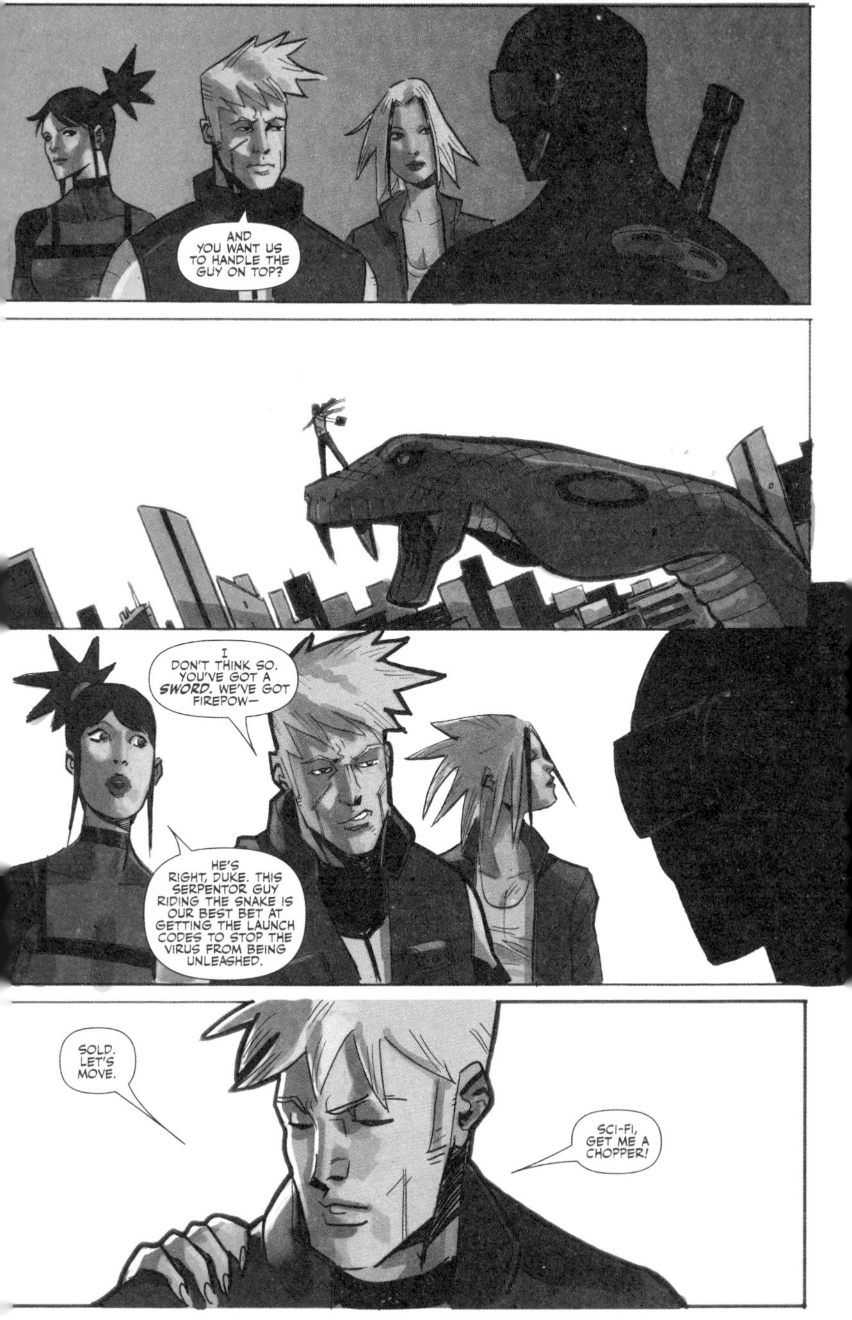
AND YOU WANT US TO HANDLE THE GUY ON TOP?
I DON'T THINK SO. YOU'VE GOT A SWORD. WE'VE GOT FIREPOW—
HE'S RIGHT, DUKE. THIS SERPENTOR GUY RIDING THE SNAKE IS OUR BEST BET AT GETTING THE LAUNCH CODES TO STOP THE VIRUS FROM BEING UNLEASHED.
SOLD. LET'S MOVE.
SCI-FI, GET ME A CHOPPER!

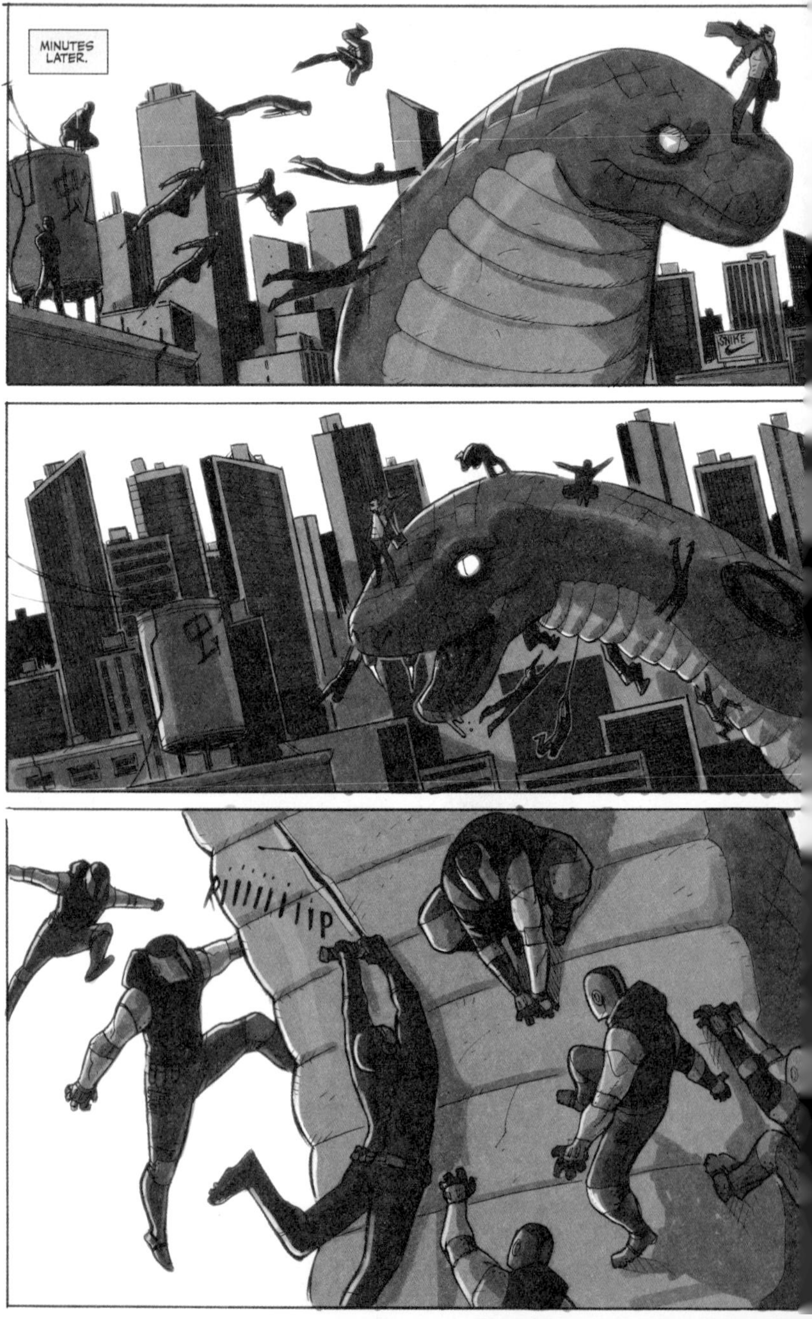
MINUTES LATER.
SNIKE
RIIIIIIIIP

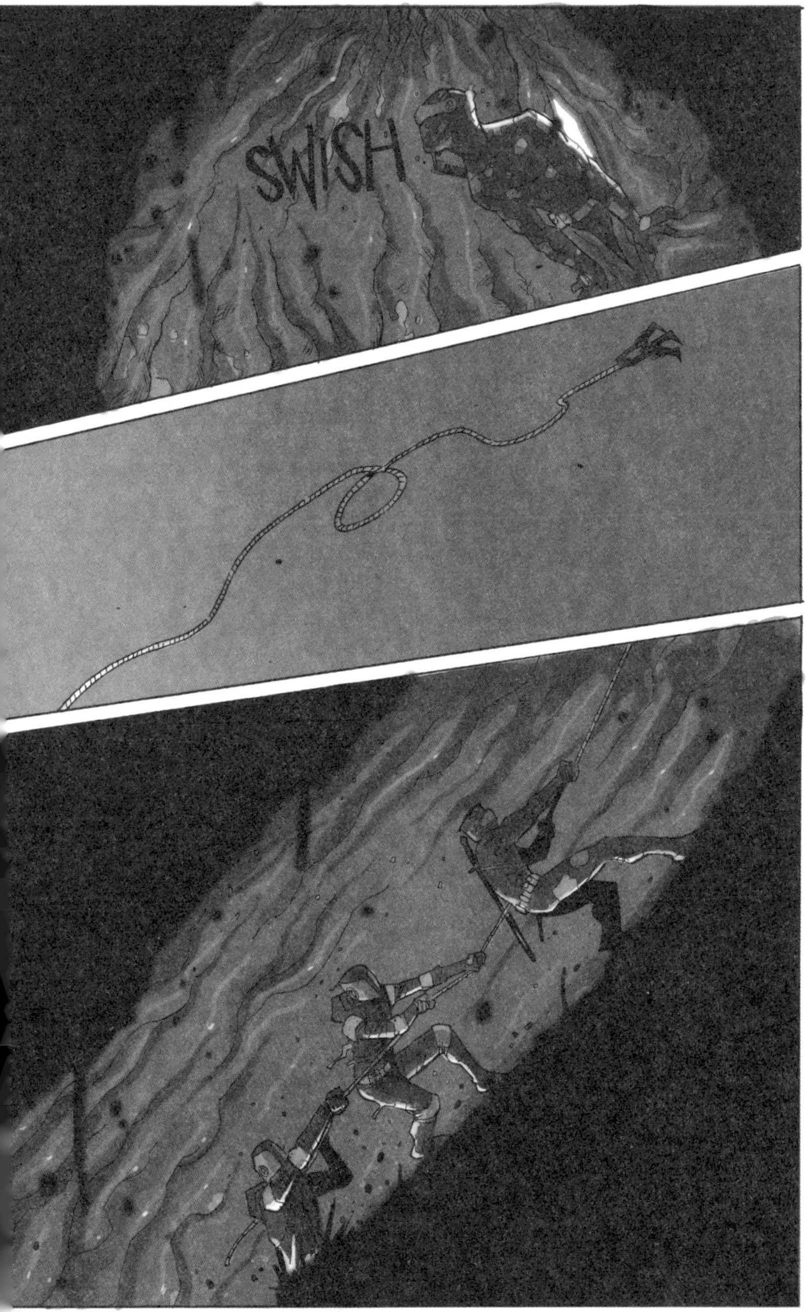
SWISH

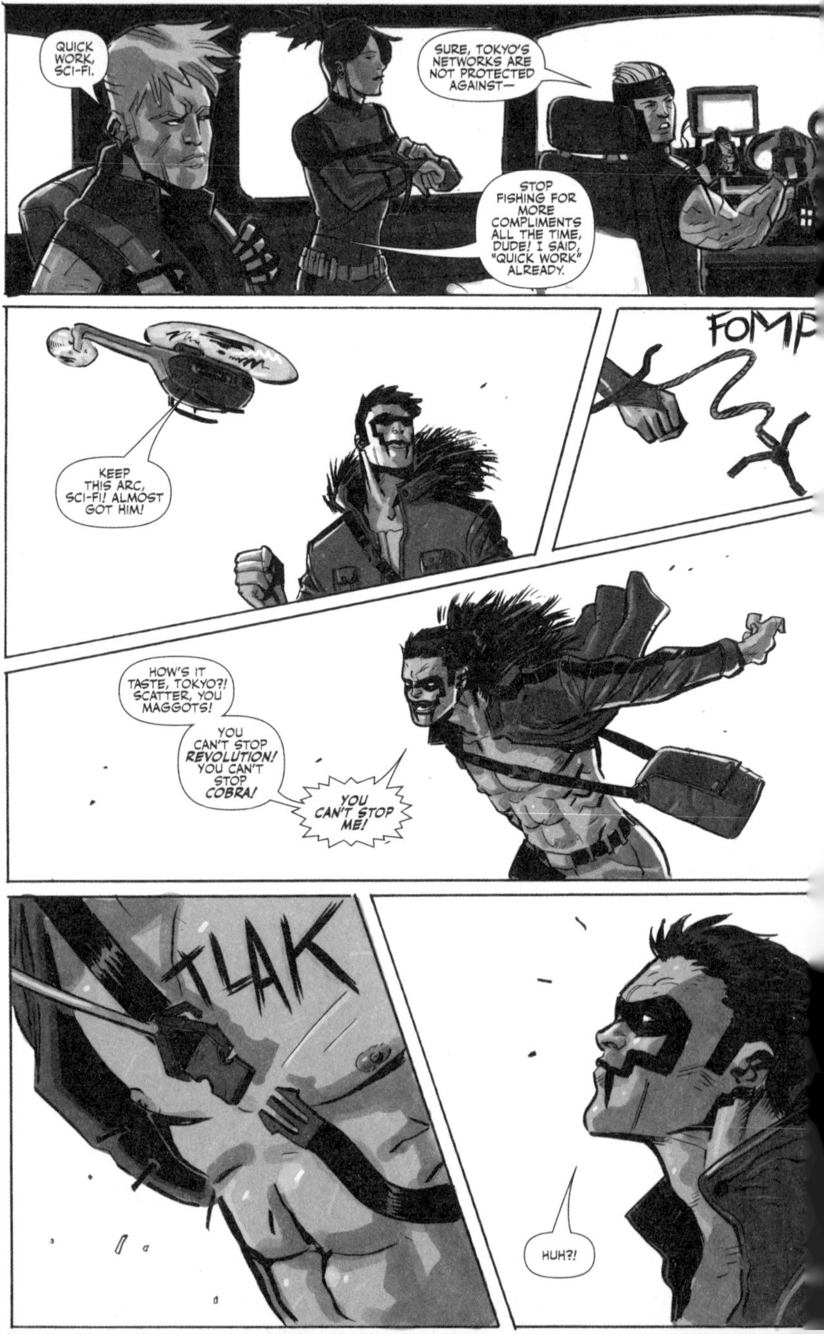
QUICK WORK, SCI-FI.
SURE, TOKYO'S NETWORKS ARE NOT PROTECTED AGAINST—
STOP FISHING FOR MORE COMPLIMENTS ALL THE TIME, DUDE! I SAID, "QUICK WORK" ALREADY.
KEEP THIS ARC, SCI-FI! ALMOST GOT HIM!
FOMP
HOW'S IT TASTE, TOKYO?! SCATTER, YOU MAGGOTS!
YOU CAN'T STOP REVOLUTION! YOU CAN'T STOP COBRA!
YOU CAN'T STOP ME!
TLAK
HUH?!

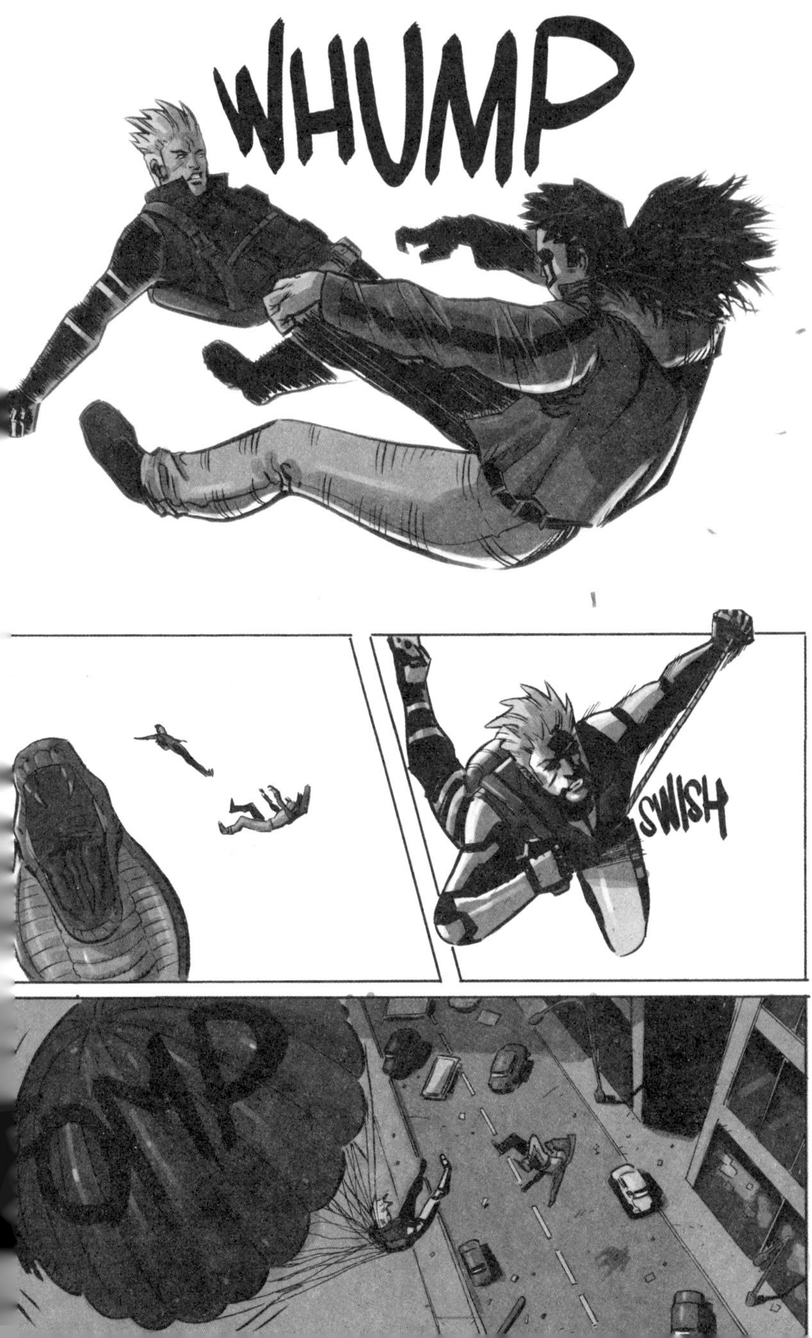
WHUMP
SWISH
OMP

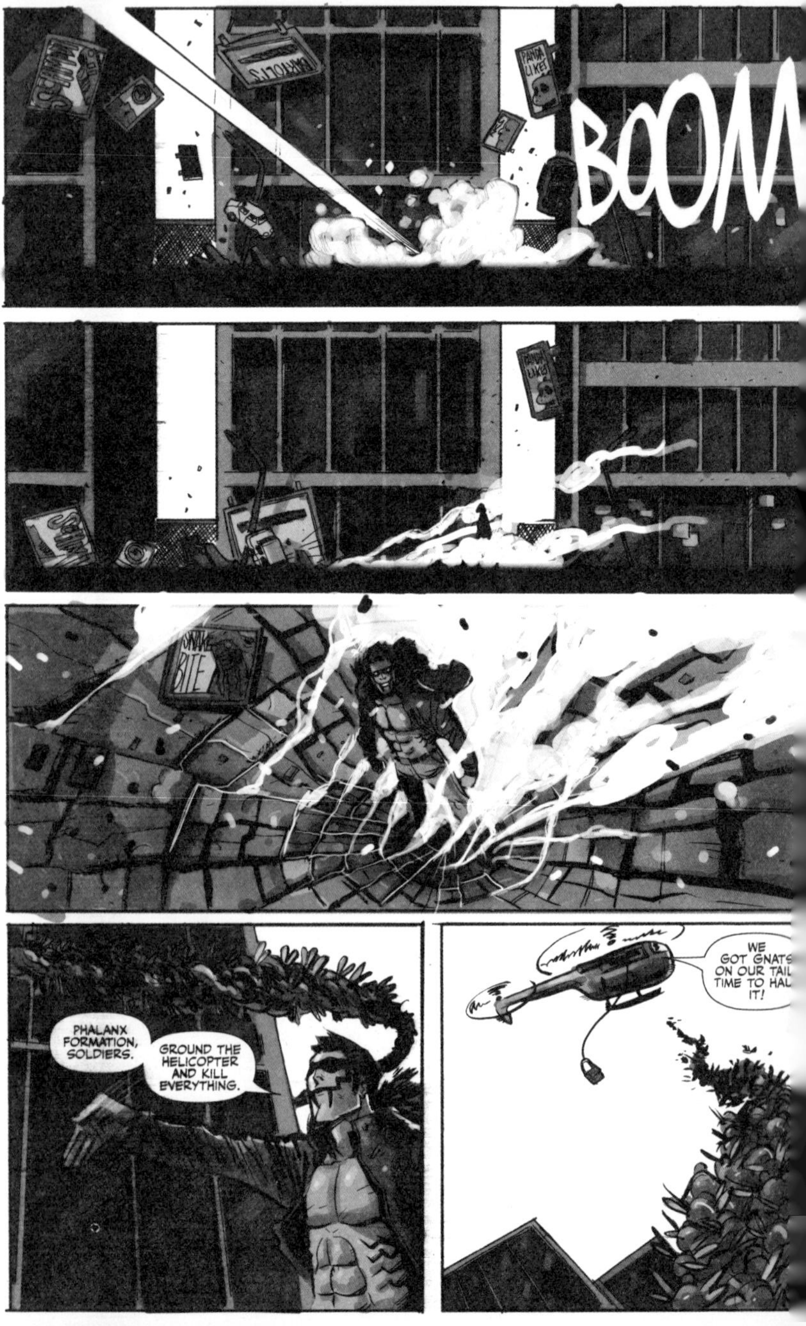
BOOM
PANDA LIKES
SNAKE BITE
PHALANX FORMATION, SOLDIERS.
GROUND THE HELICOPTER AND KILL EVERYTHING.
WE GOT GNATS ON OUR TAIL TIME TO HAL IT!

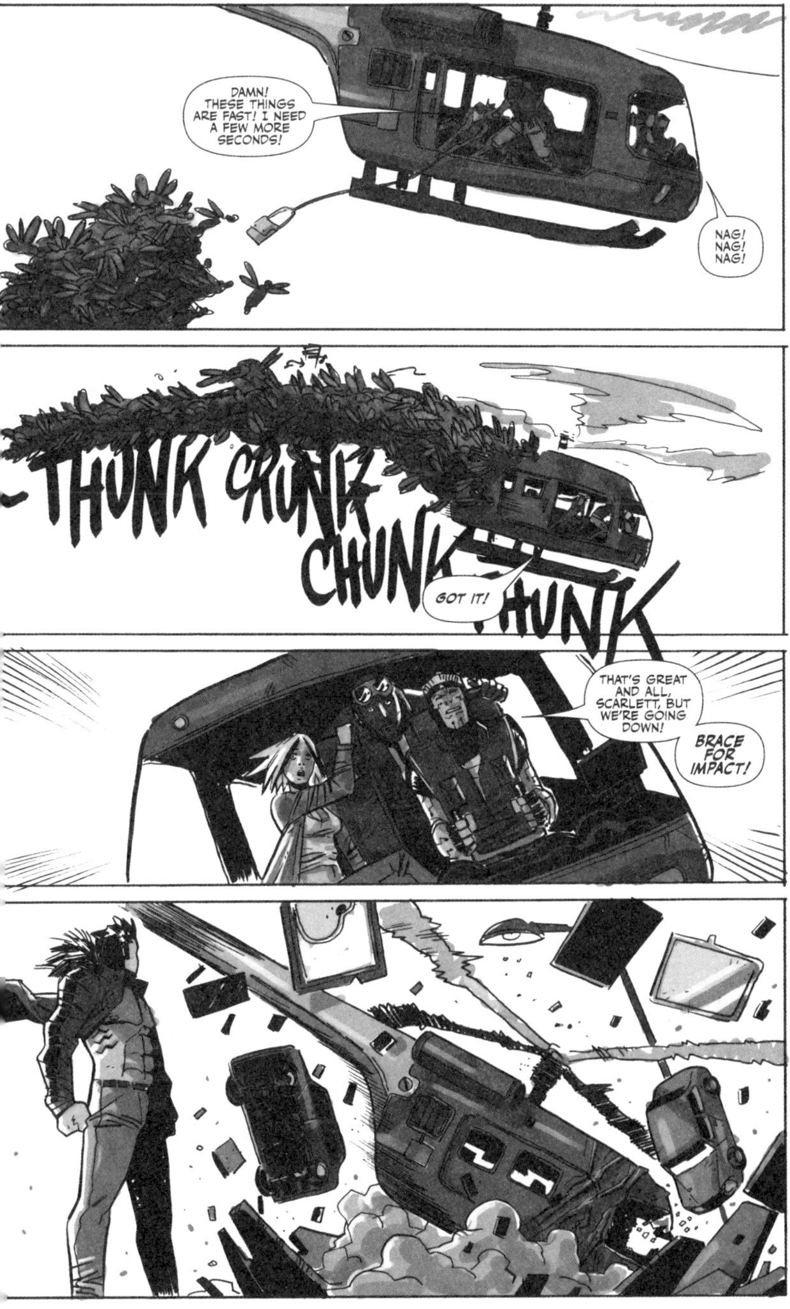
DAMN! THESE THINGS ARE FAST! I NEED A FEW MORE SECONDS!
NAG! NAG! NAG!
THUNK CRUNK
CHUNK
GOT IT!
THUNK
THAT'S GREAT AND ALL, SCARLETT, BUT WE'RE GOING DOWN!
BRACE FOR IMPACT!

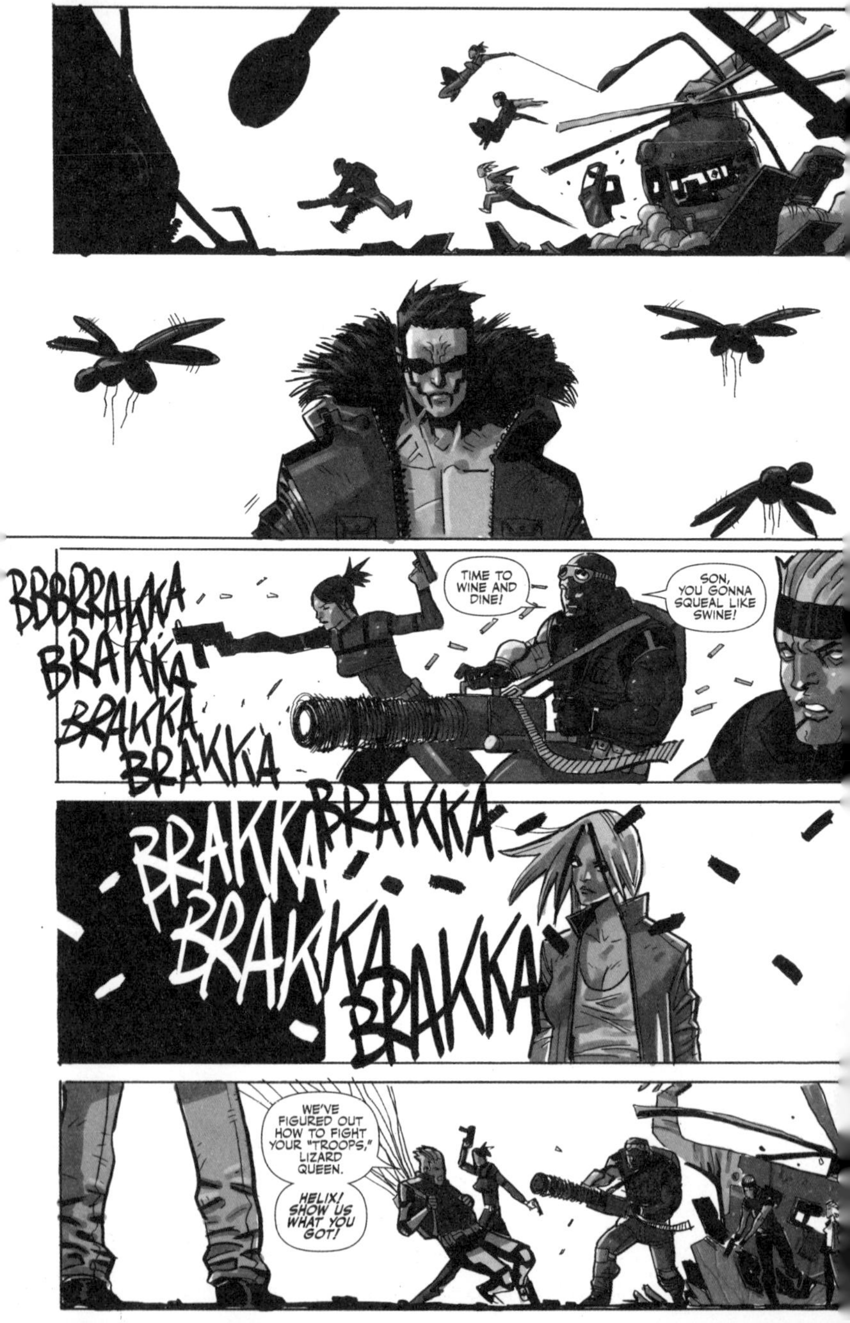
BBBRRAKKA BRAKKA BRAKKA BRAKKA
TIME TO WINE AND DINE!
SON, YOU GONNA SQUEAL LIKE SWINE!
BRAKKA BRAKKA BRAKKA BRAKKA BRAKKA
WE'VE FIGURED OUT HOW TO FIGHT YOUR "TROOPS," LIZARD QUEEN.
HELIX! SHOW US WHAT YOU GOT!

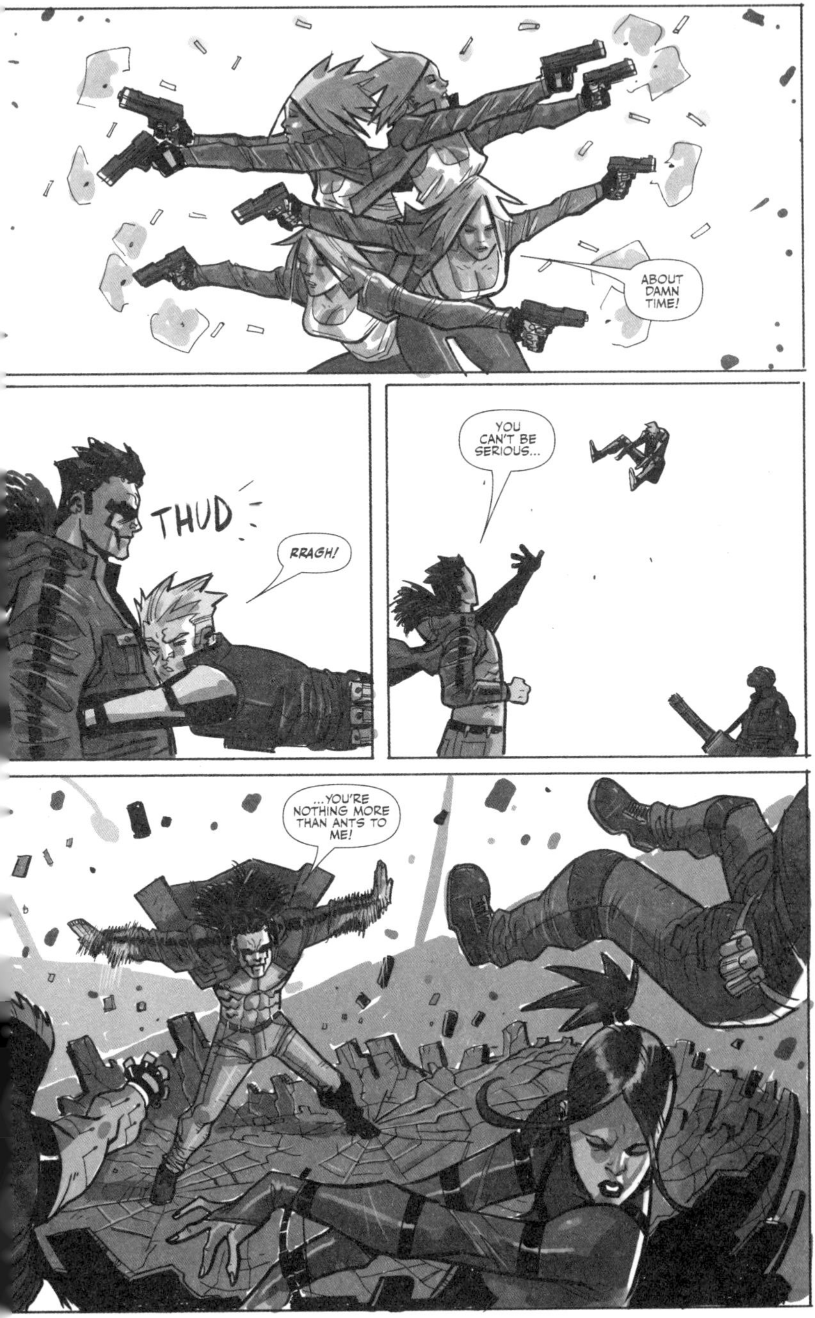
ABOUT DAMN TIME!
THUD
RRAGH!
YOU CAN'T BE SERIOUS...
...YOU'RE NOTHING MORE THAN ANTS TO ME!

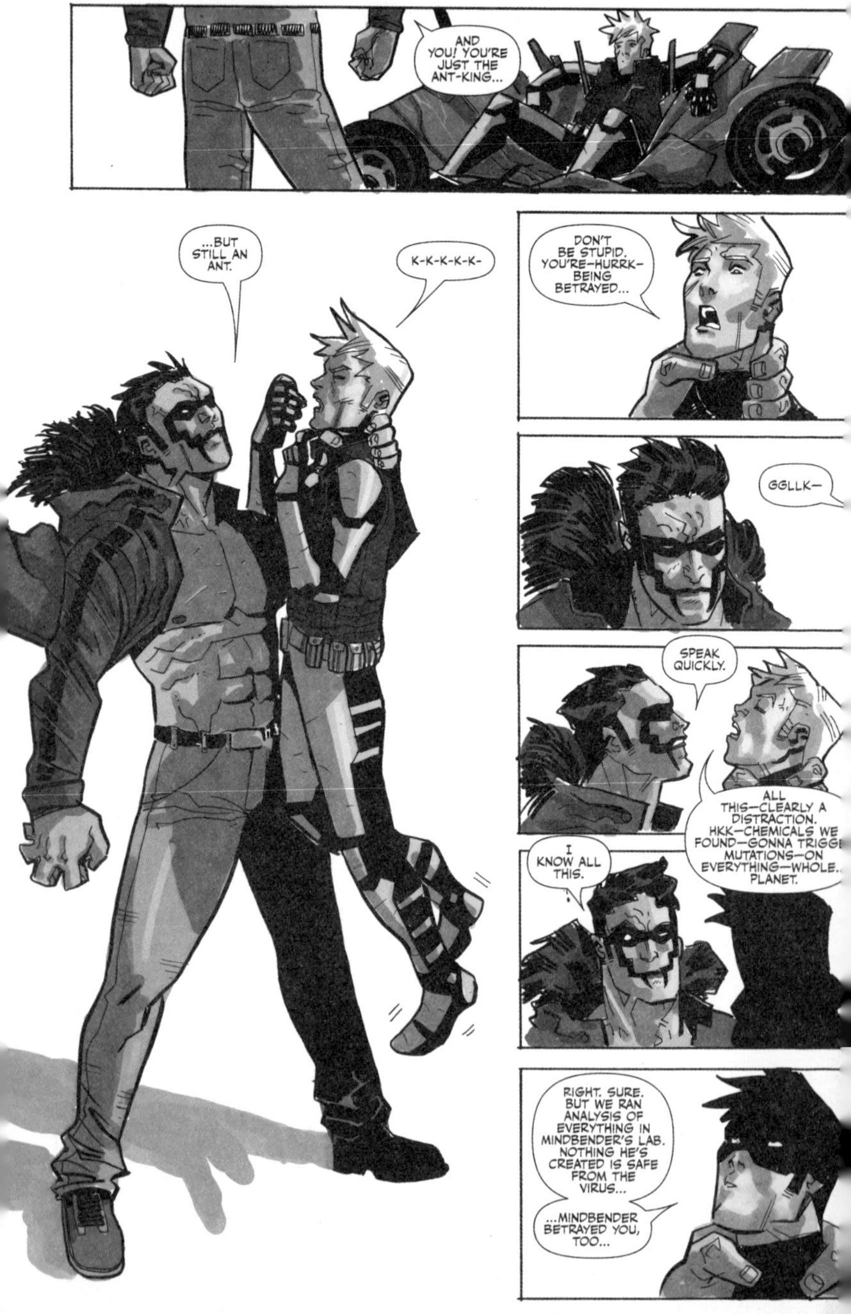
AND YOU! YOU'RE JUST THE ANT-KING...
...BUT STILL AN ANT.
K-K-K-K-K-
DON'T BE STUPID. YOU'RE—HURRK— BEING BETRAYED...
GGLLK—
SPEAK QUICKLY.
ALL THIS—CLEARLY A DISTRACTION. HKK—CHEMICALS WE FOUND—GONNA TRIGGE MUTATIONS—ON EVERYTHING—WHOLE... PLANET.
I KNOW ALL THIS.
RIGHT. SURE. BUT WE RAN ANALYSIS OF EVERYTHING IN MINDBENDER'S LAB. NOTHING HE'S CREATED IS SAFE FROM THE VIRUS...
...MINDBENDER BETRAYED YOU, TOO...

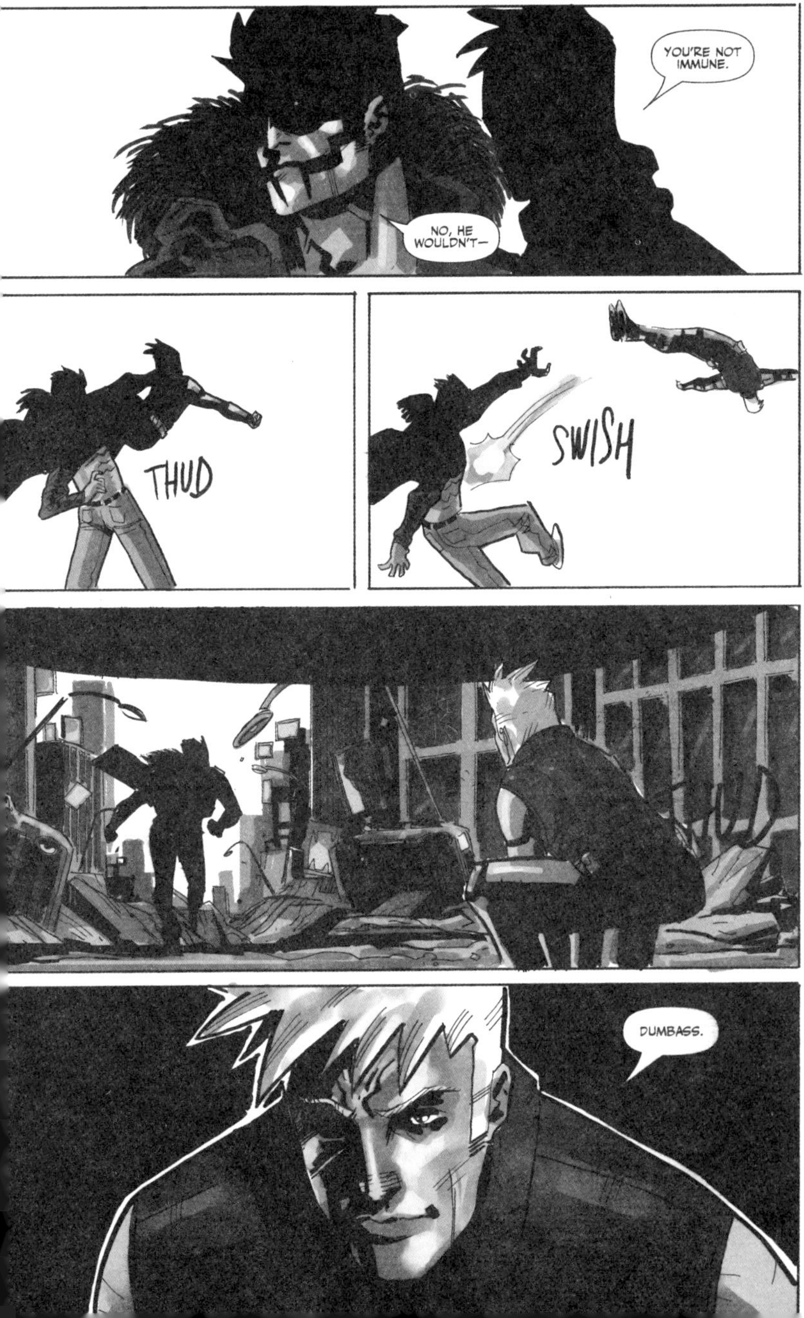
YOU'RE NOT IMMUNE.
NO, HE WOULDN'T—
THUD
SWISH
THUD
DUMBASS.

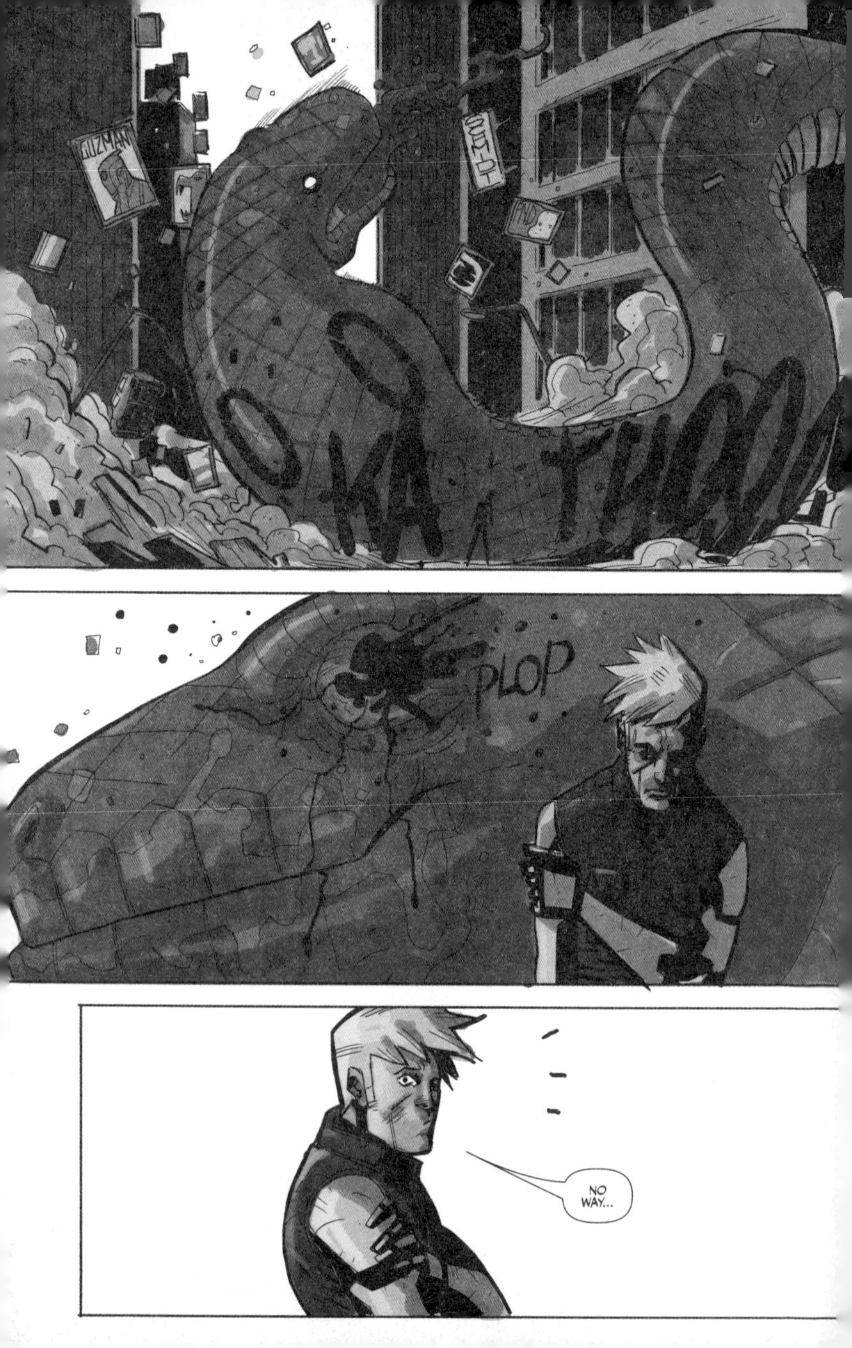
GUZMAN
PLOP
NO WAY...

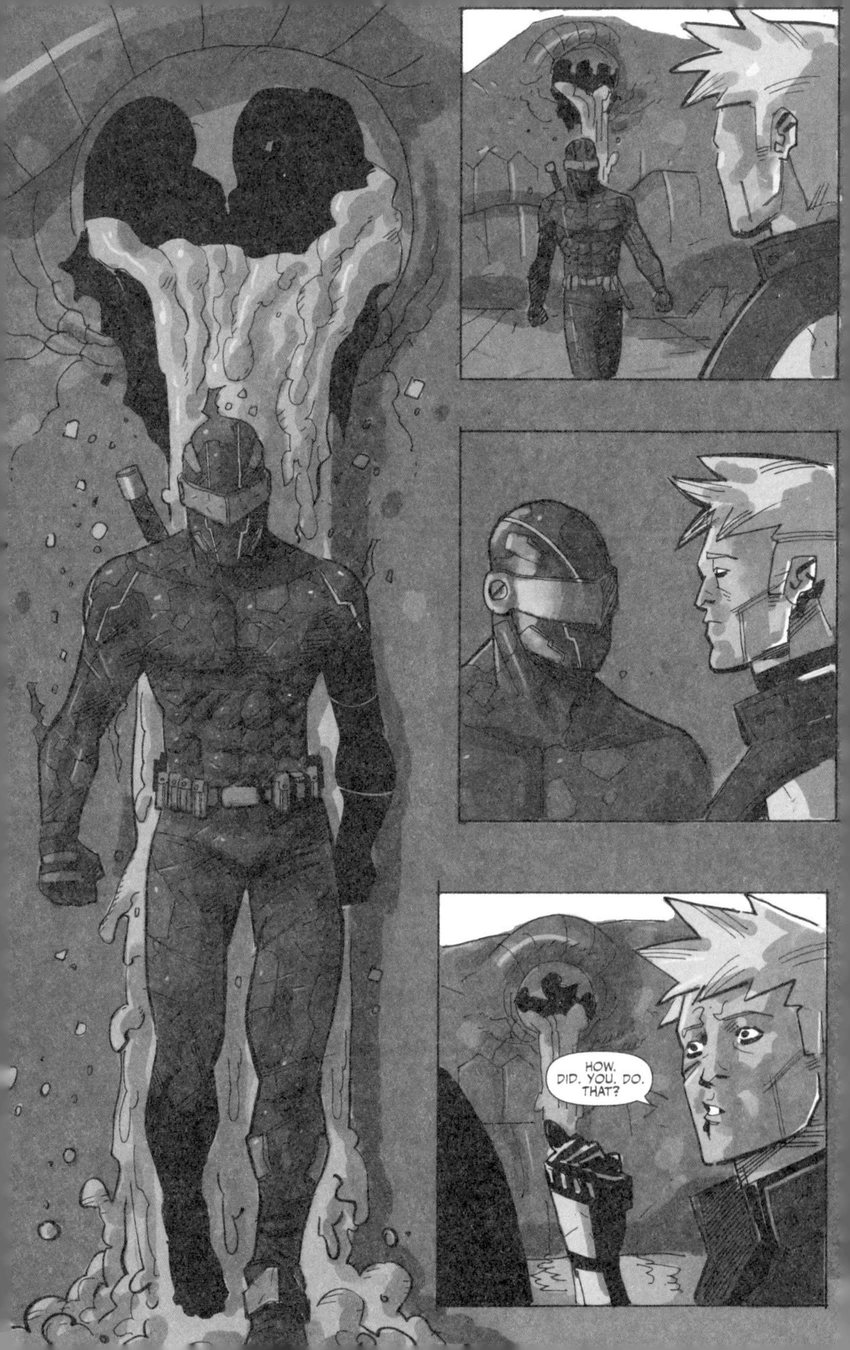
HOW. DID. YOU. DO. THAT?

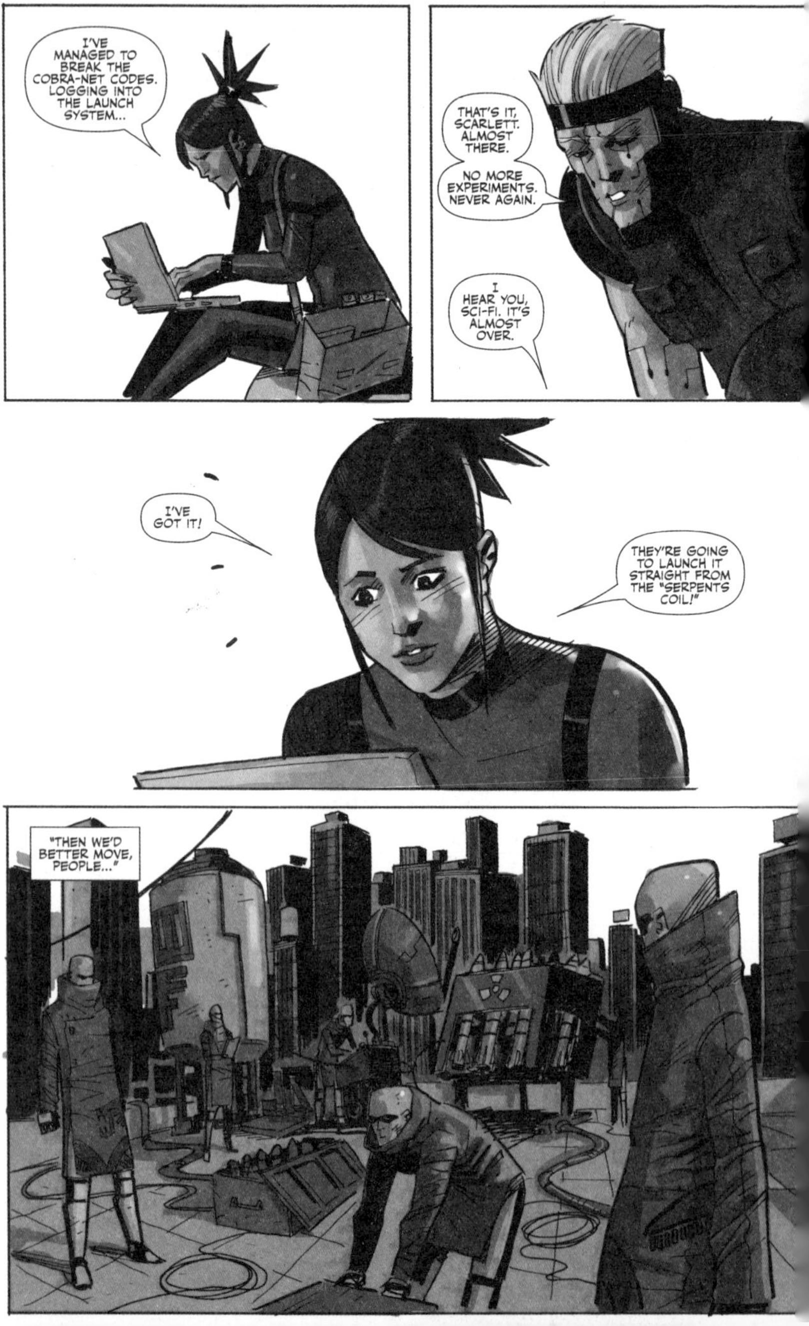
I'VE MANAGED TO BREAK THE COBRA-NET CODES. LOGGING INTO THE LAUNCH SYSTEM...
THAT'S IT, SCARLETT. ALMOST THERE.
NO MORE EXPERIMENTS. NEVER AGAIN.
I HEAR YOU, SCI-FI. IT'S ALMOST OVER.
I'VE GOT IT!
THEY'RE GOING TO LAUNCH IT STRAIGHT FROM THE "SERPENTS COIL!"
"THEN WE'D BETTER MOVE, PEOPLE..."

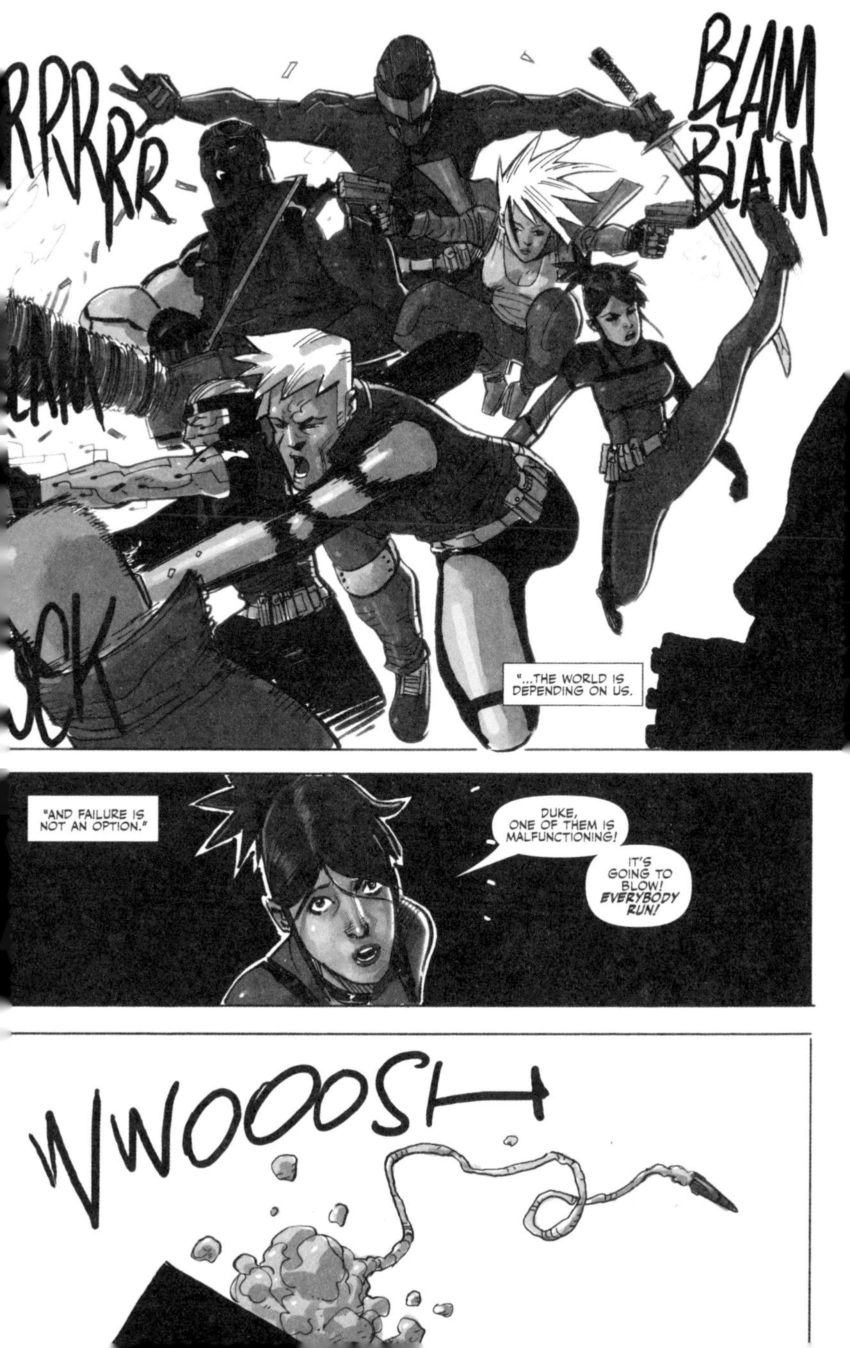
RRRRRR
BLAM BLAM
"...THE WORLD IS DEPENDING ON US.
"AND FAILURE IS NOT AN OPTION."
DUKE, ONE OF THEM IS MALFUNCTIONING!
IT'S GOING TO BLOW! *EVERYBODY RUN!*
WWOOOSH

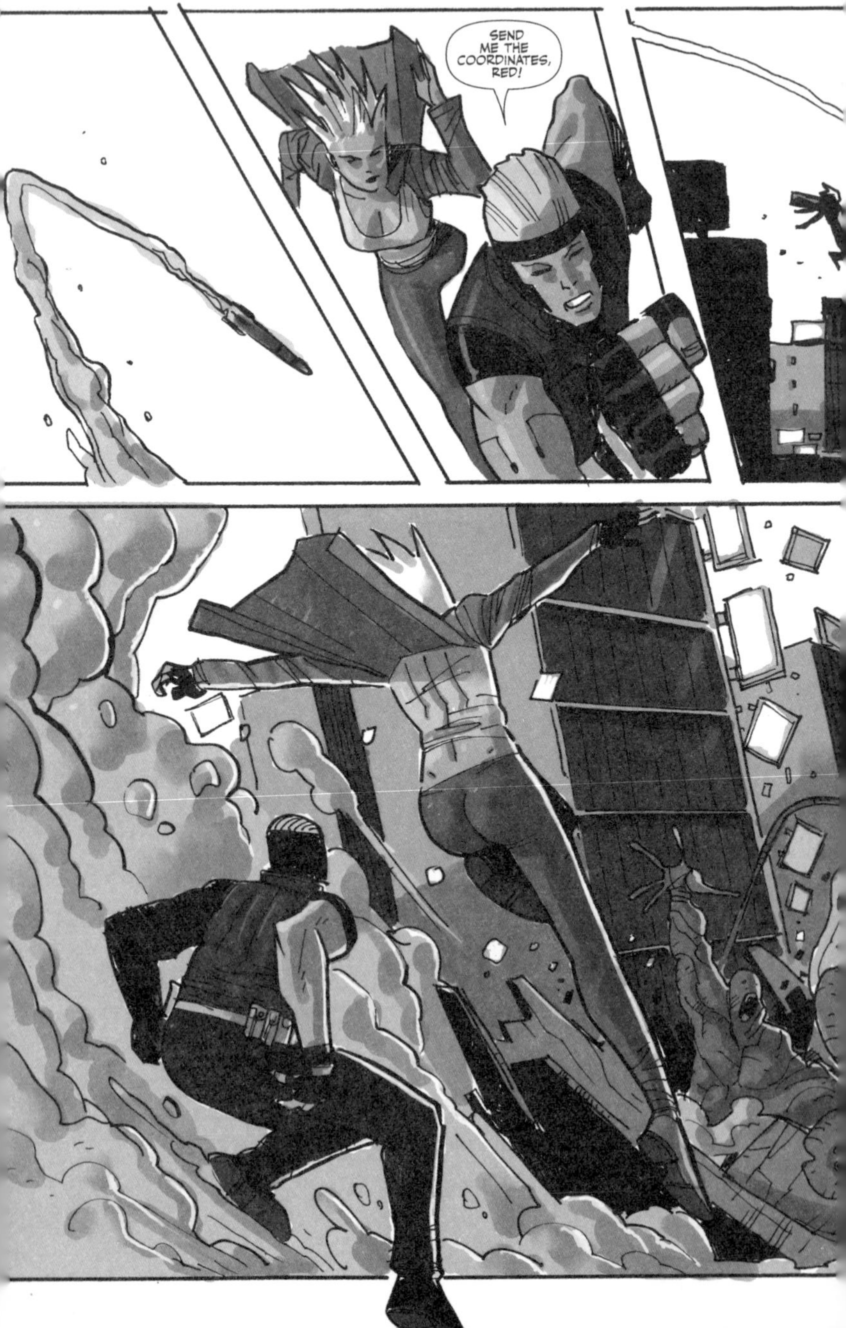
SEND ME THE COORDINATES, RED!

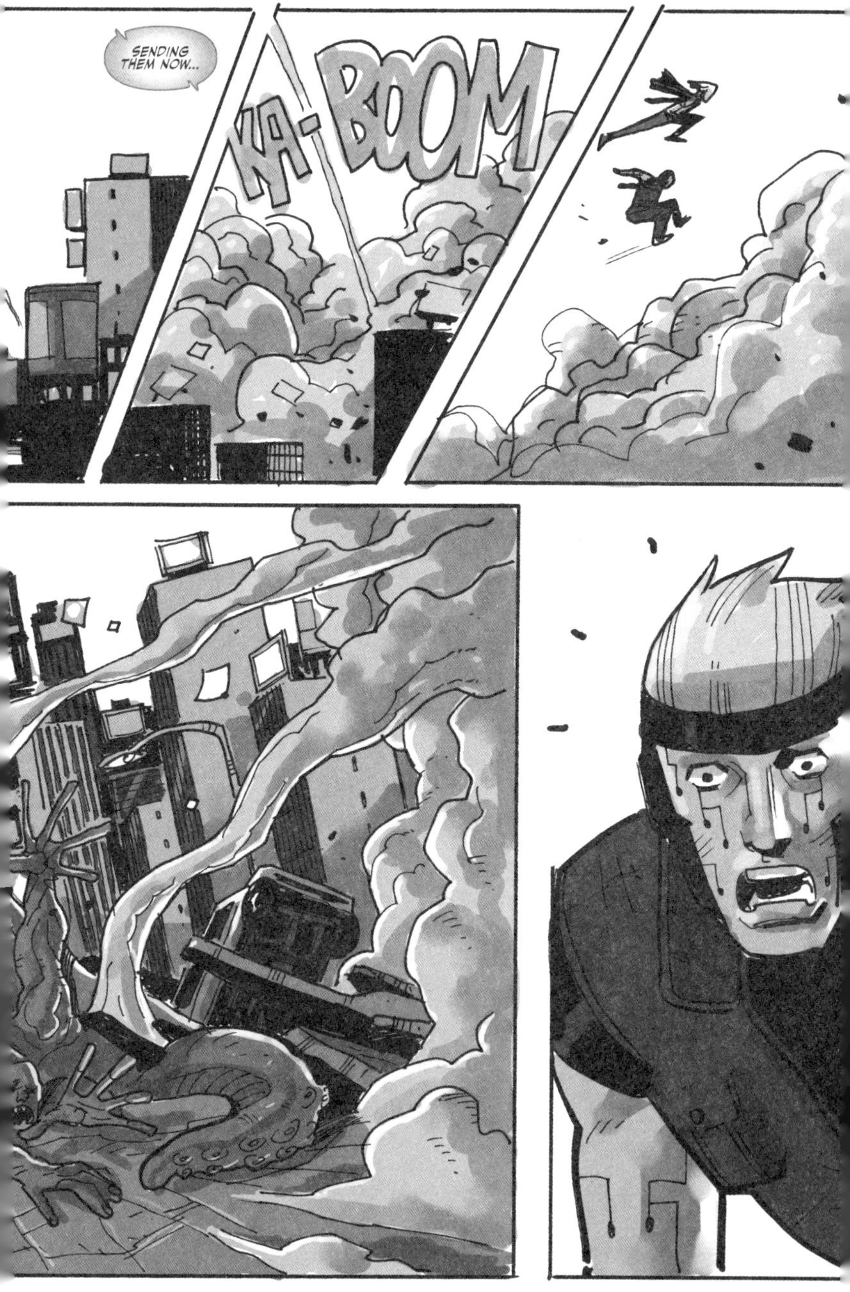
SENDING THEM NOW...
KA-BOOM

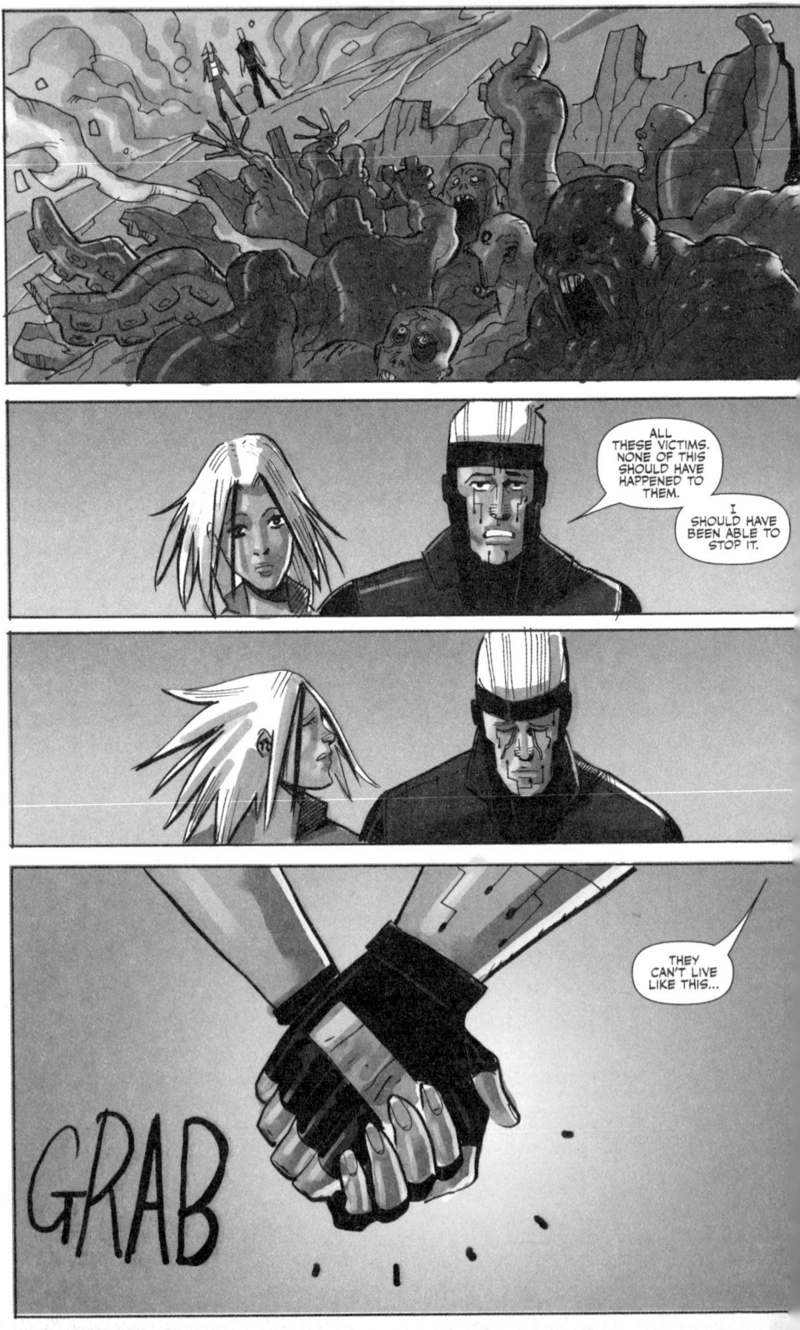
ALL THESE VICTIMS. NONE OF THIS SHOULD HAVE HAPPENED TO THEM.
I SHOULD HAVE BEEN ABLE TO STOP IT.
THEY CAN'T LIVE LIKE THIS...
GRAB

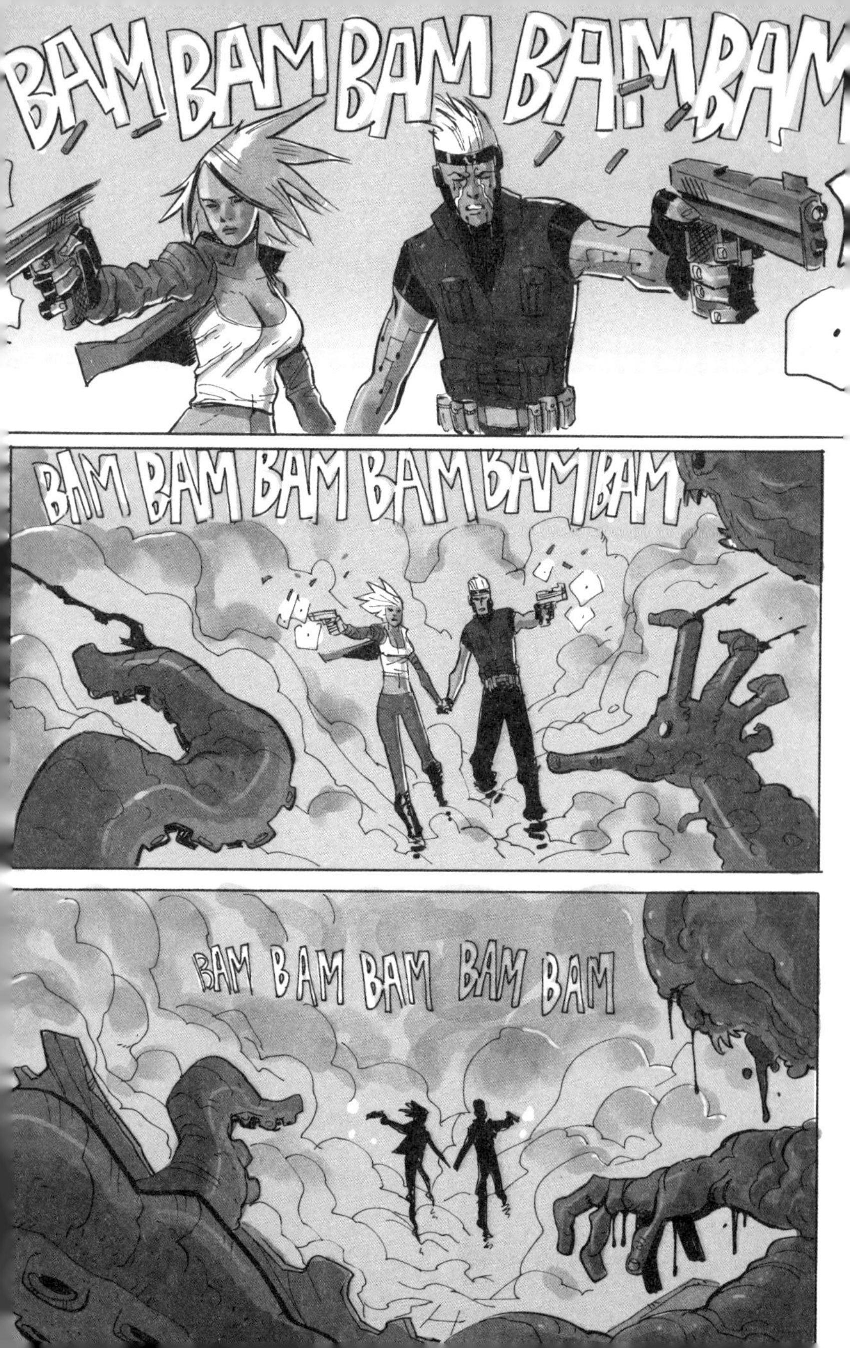
BAM BAM BAM BAM BAM
BAM BAM BAM BAM BAM BAM
BAM BAM BAM BAM BAM

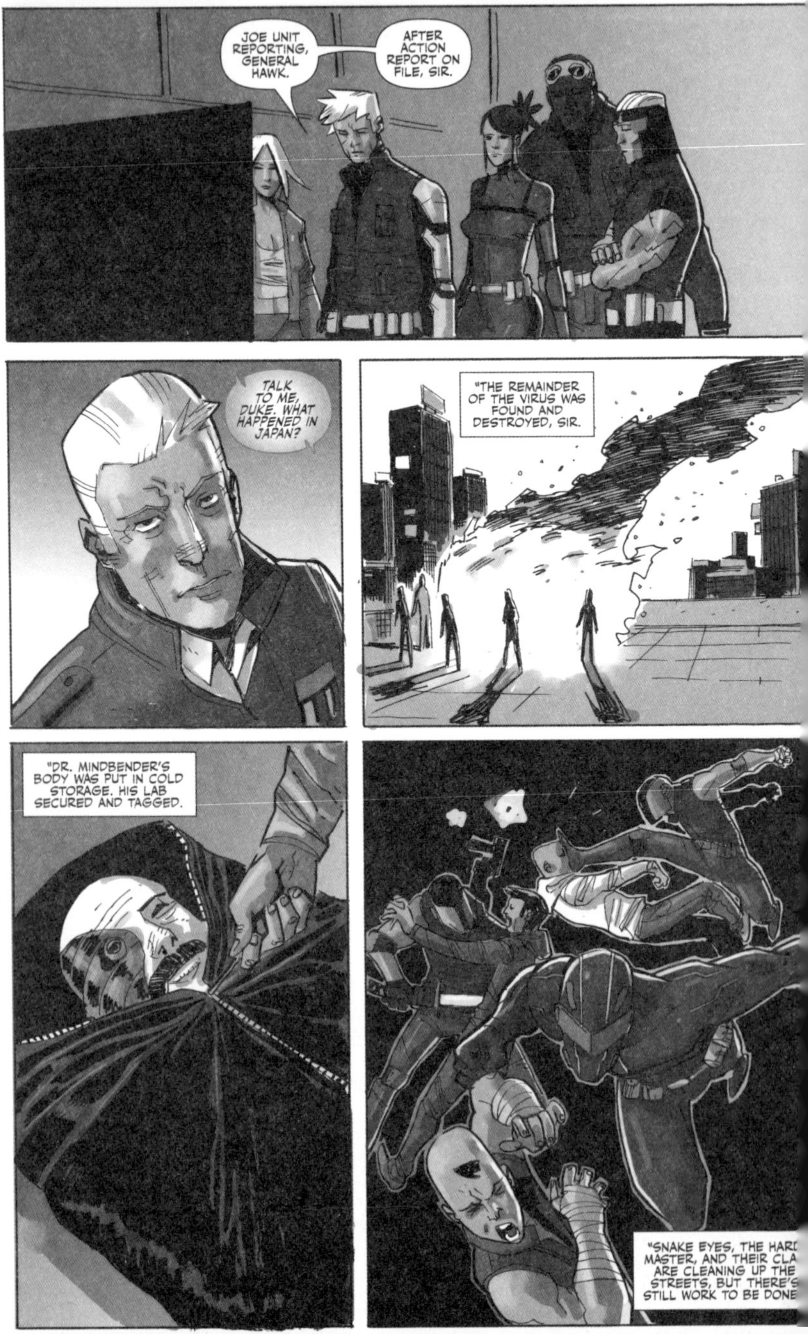
JOE UNIT REPORTING, GENERAL HAWK.
AFTER ACTION REPORT ON FILE, SIR.
TALK TO ME, DUKE. WHAT HAPPENED IN JAPAN?
"THE REMAINDER OF THE VIRUS WAS FOUND AND DESTROYED, SIR.
"DR. MINDBENDER'S BODY WAS PUT IN COLD STORAGE. HIS LAB SECURED AND TAGGED.
"SNAKE EYES, THE HARD MASTER, AND THEIR CLA ARE CLEANING UP THE STREETS, BUT THERE'S STILL WORK TO BE DONE

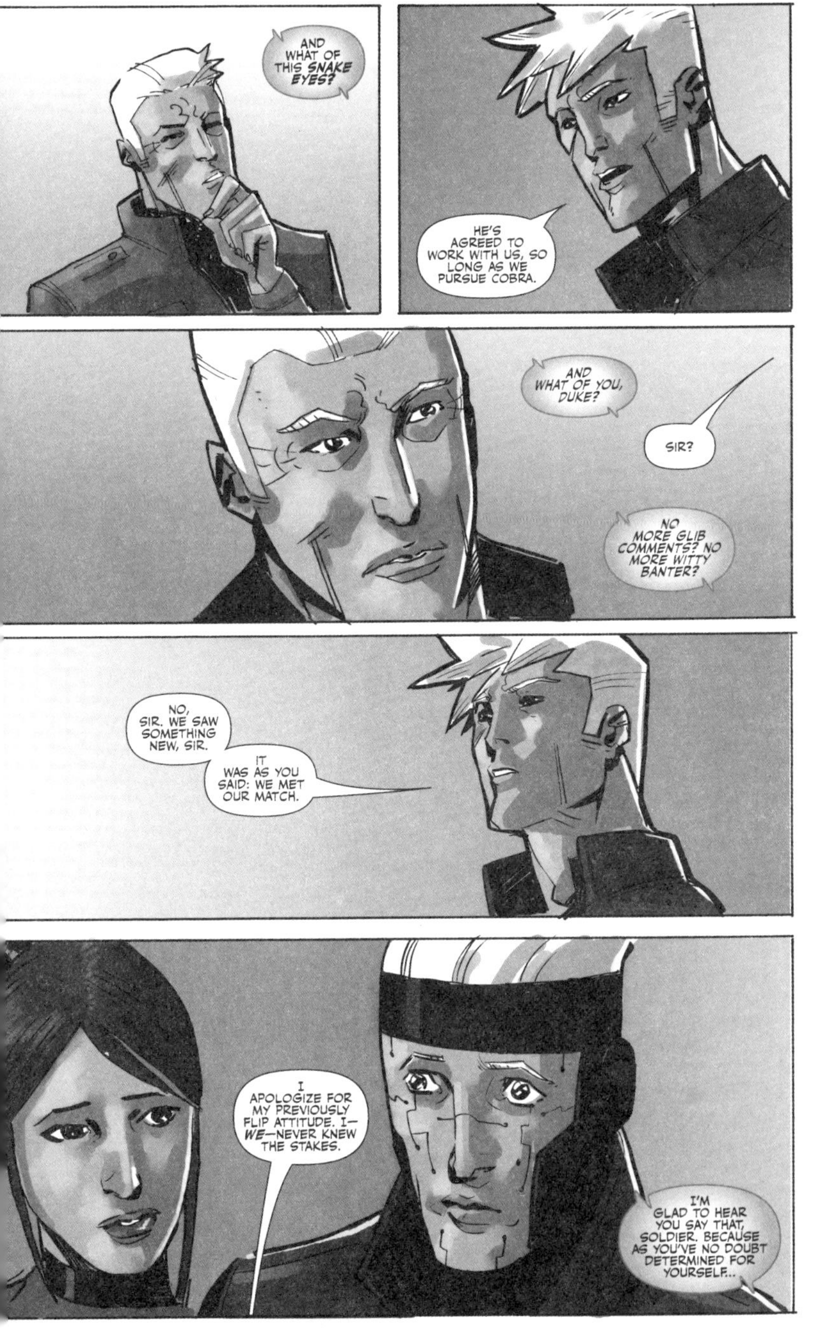
AND WHAT OF THIS SNAKE EYES?
HE'S AGREED TO WORK WITH US, SO LONG AS WE PURSUE COBRA.
AND WHAT OF YOU, DUKE?
SIR?
NO MORE GLIB COMMENTS? NO MORE WITTY BANTER?
NO, SIR. WE SAW SOMETHING NEW, SIR.
IT WAS AS YOU SAID: WE MET OUR MATCH.
I APOLOGIZE FOR MY PREVIOUSLY FLIP ATTITUDE. I—WE—NEVER KNEW THE STAKES.
I'M GLAD TO HEAR YOU SAY THAT, SOLDIER. BECAUSE AS YOU'VE NO DOUBT DETERMINED FOR YOURSELF...

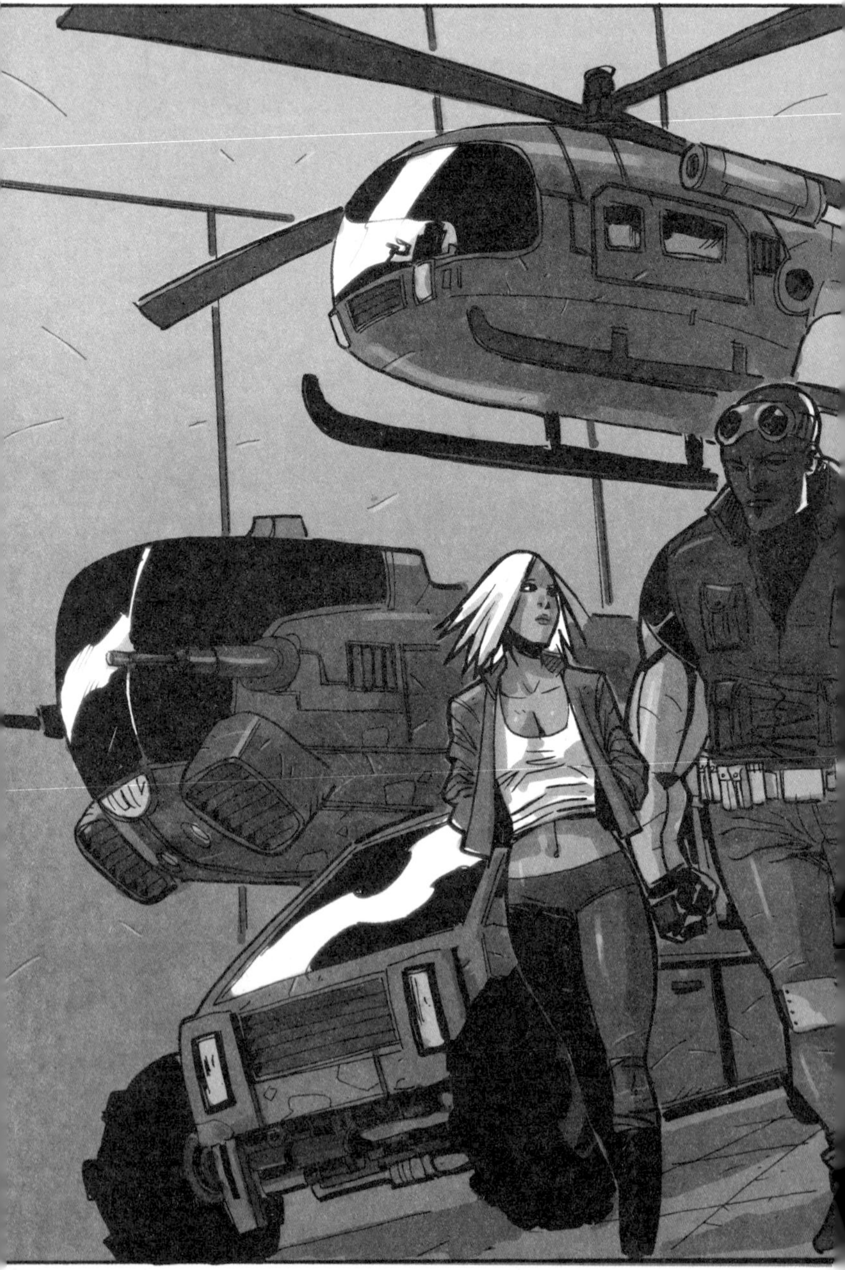

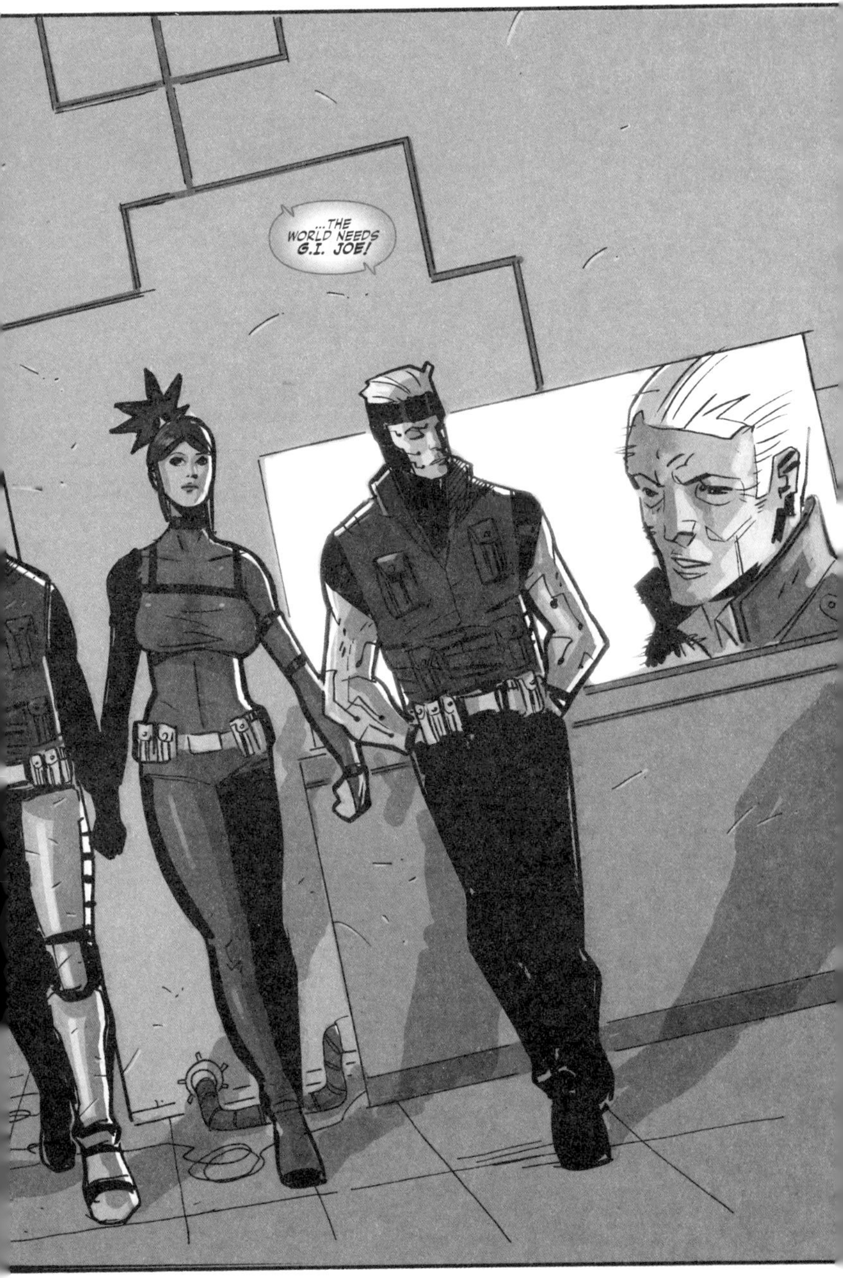
...THE WORLD NEEDS G.I. JOE!

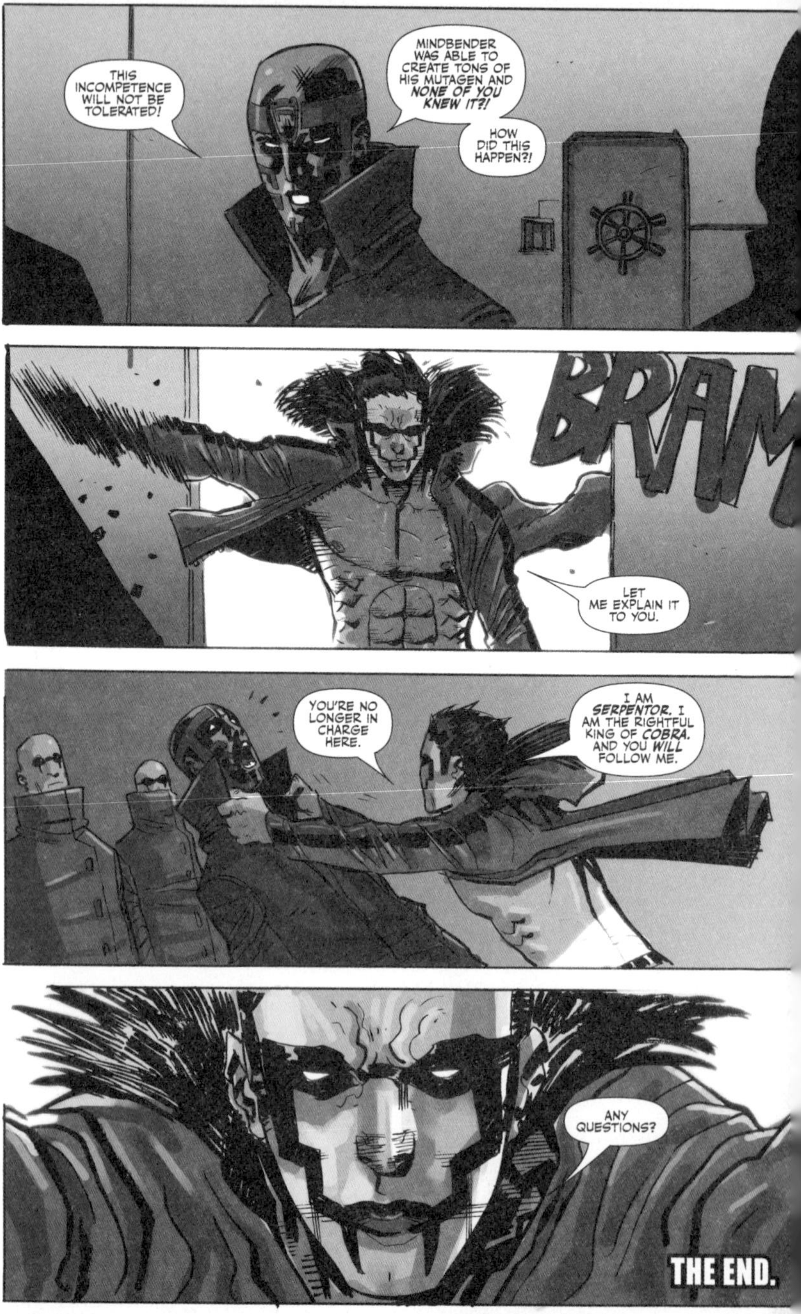
THIS INCOMPETENCE WILL NOT BE TOLERATED!
MINDBENDER WAS ABLE TO CREATE TONS OF HIS MUTAGEN AND NONE OF YOU KNEW IT?!
HOW DID THIS HAPPEN?!
BRAM
LET ME EXPLAIN IT TO YOU.
YOU'RE NO LONGER IN CHARGE HERE.
I AM SERPENTOR. I AM THE RIGHTFUL KING OF COBRA. AND YOU WILL FOLLOW ME.
ANY QUESTIONS?
THE END.

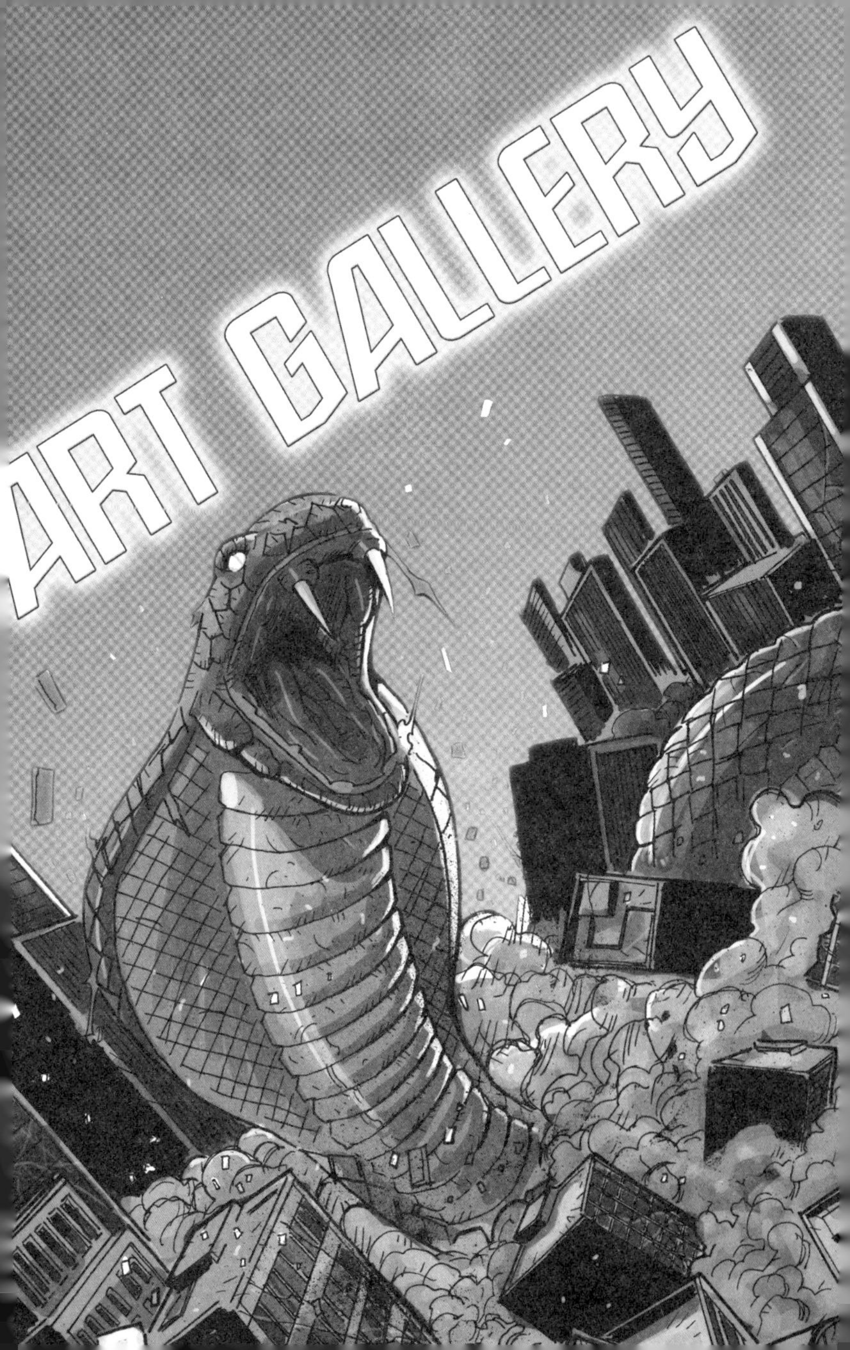
ART GALLERY

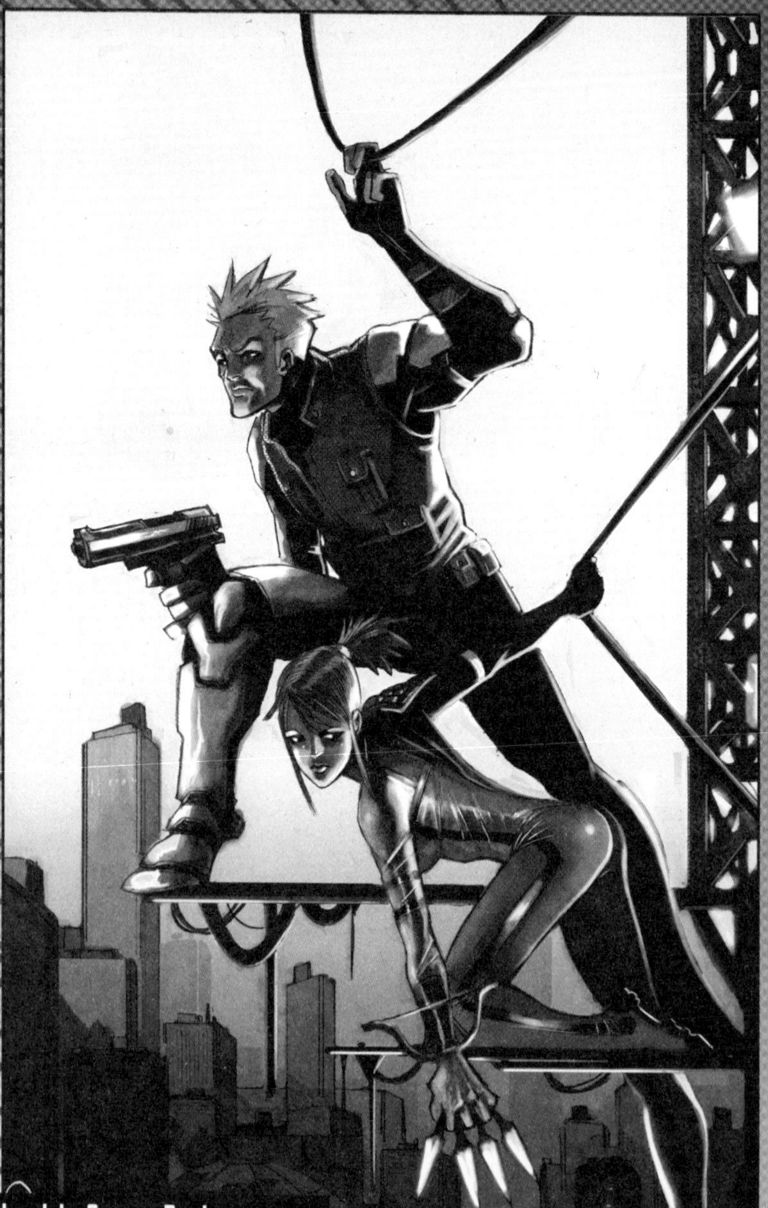

artwork by Giacomo Bevilacqua

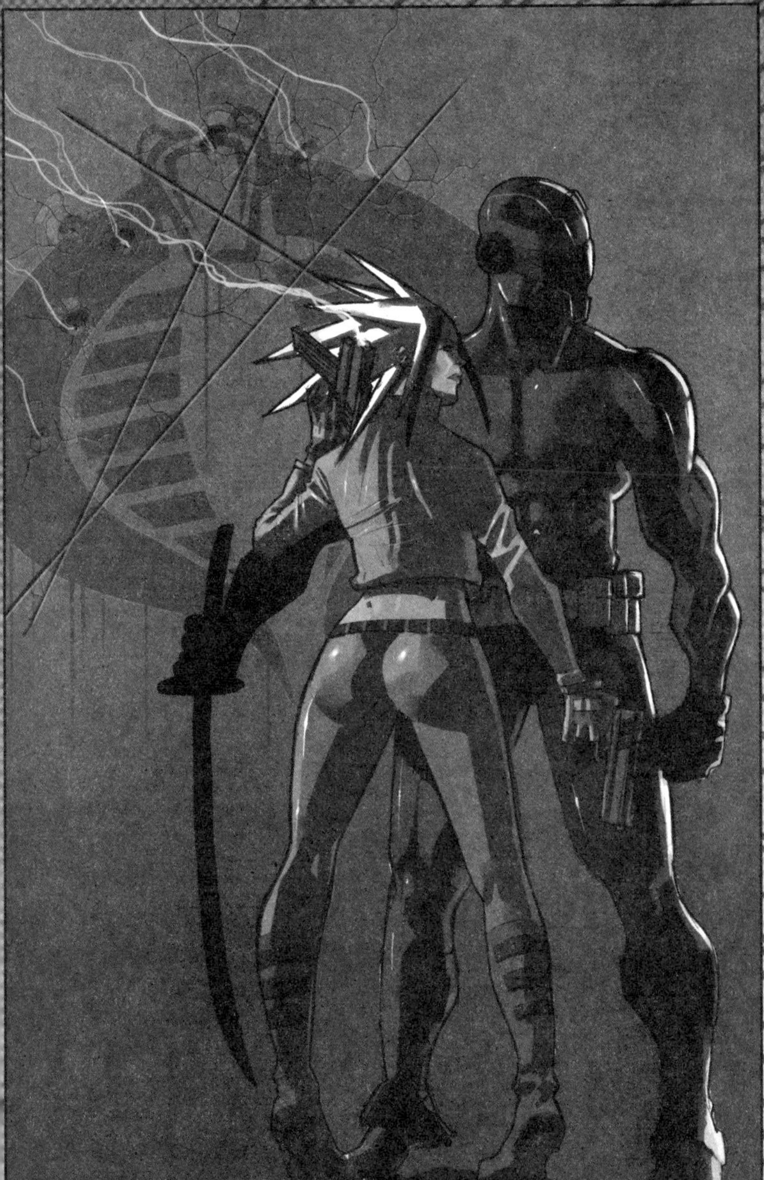

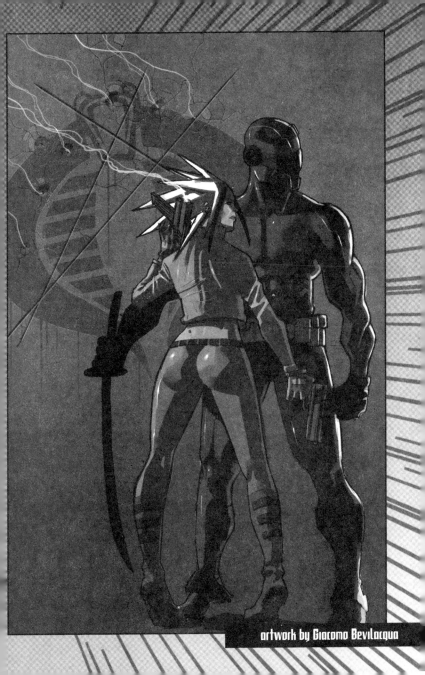

artwork by Giacomo Bevilacqua

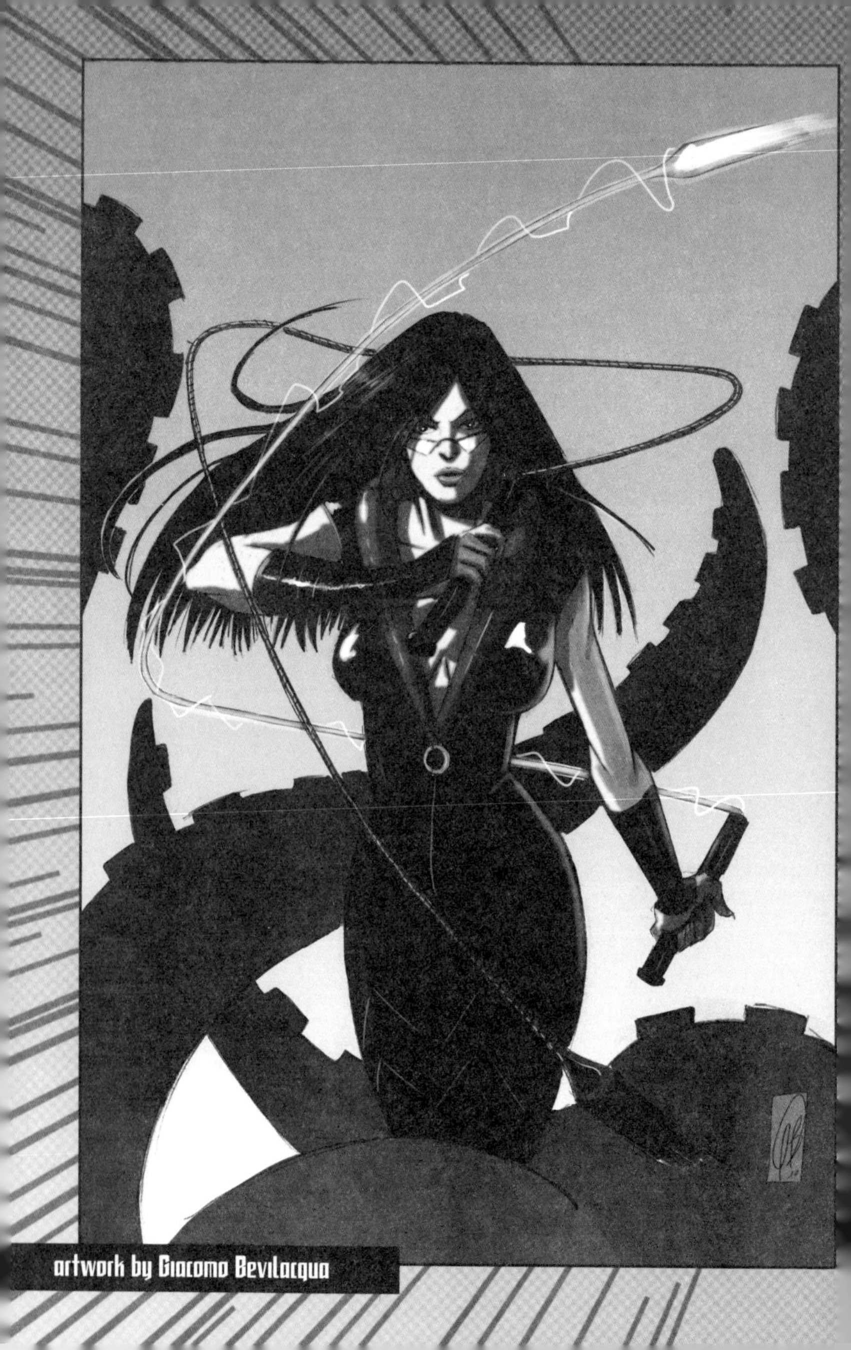

artwork by Giacomo Bevilacqua

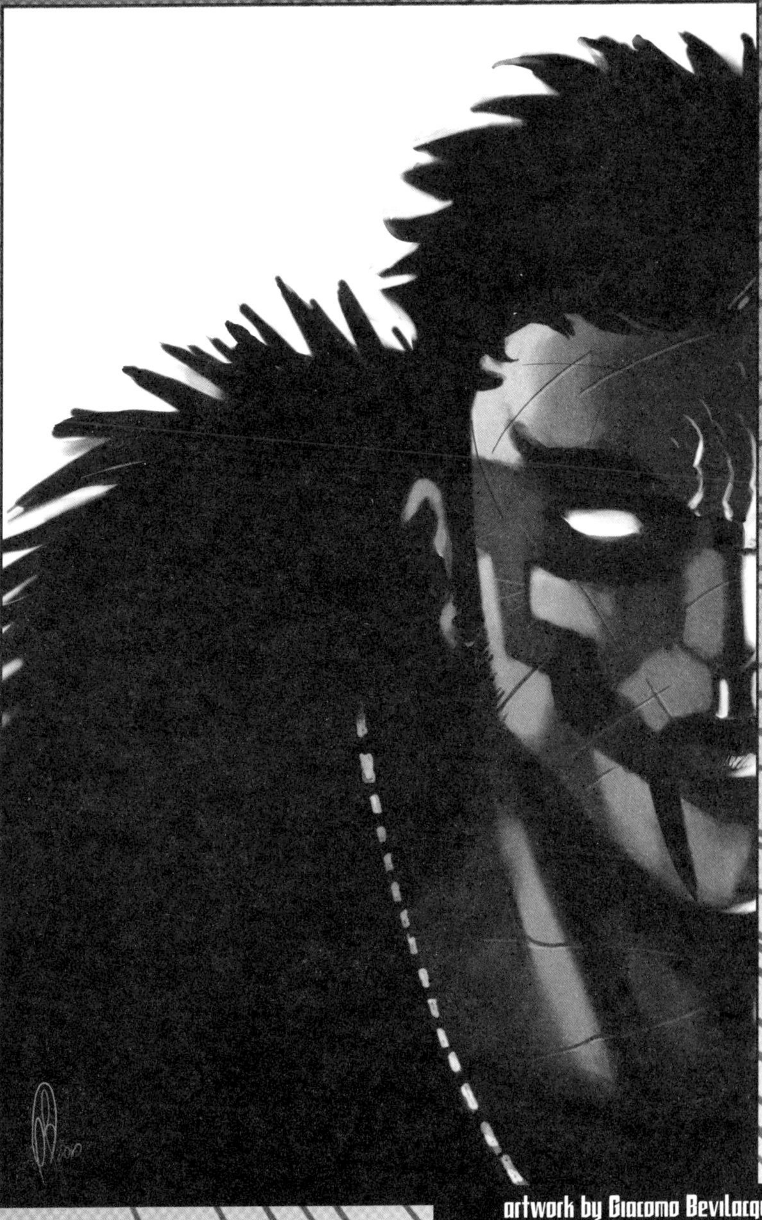

artwork by Giacomo Bevilacqua

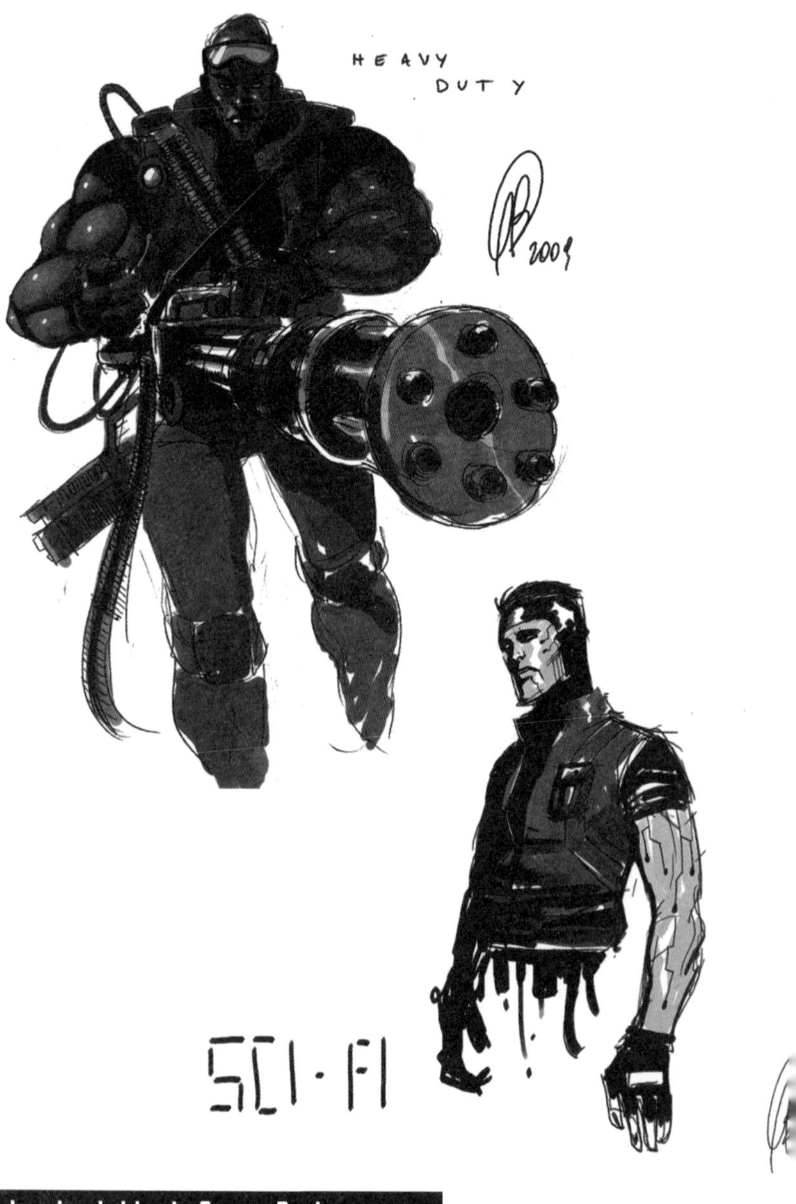
HEAVY DUTY
SCI-FI

character sketches by Giacomo Bevilacqua

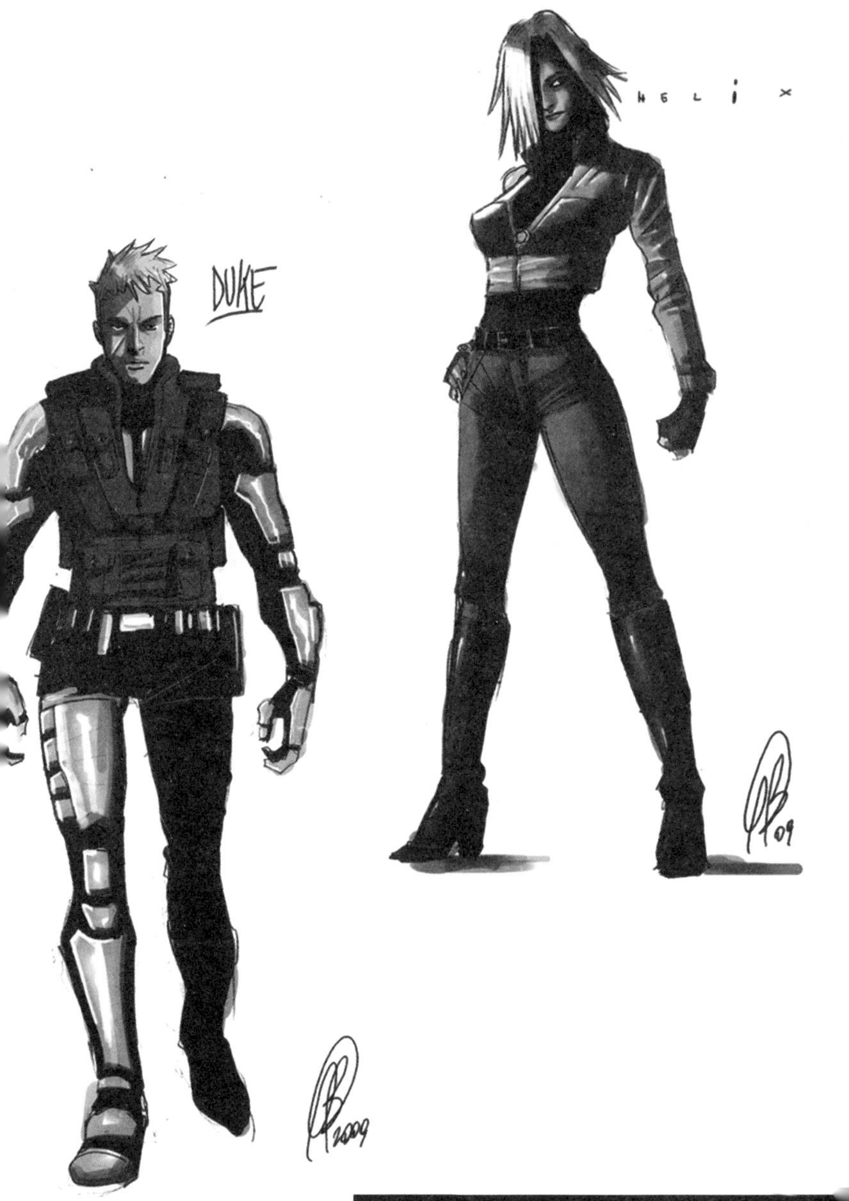
HELIX
DUKE

character sketches by Giacomo Bevilacqua

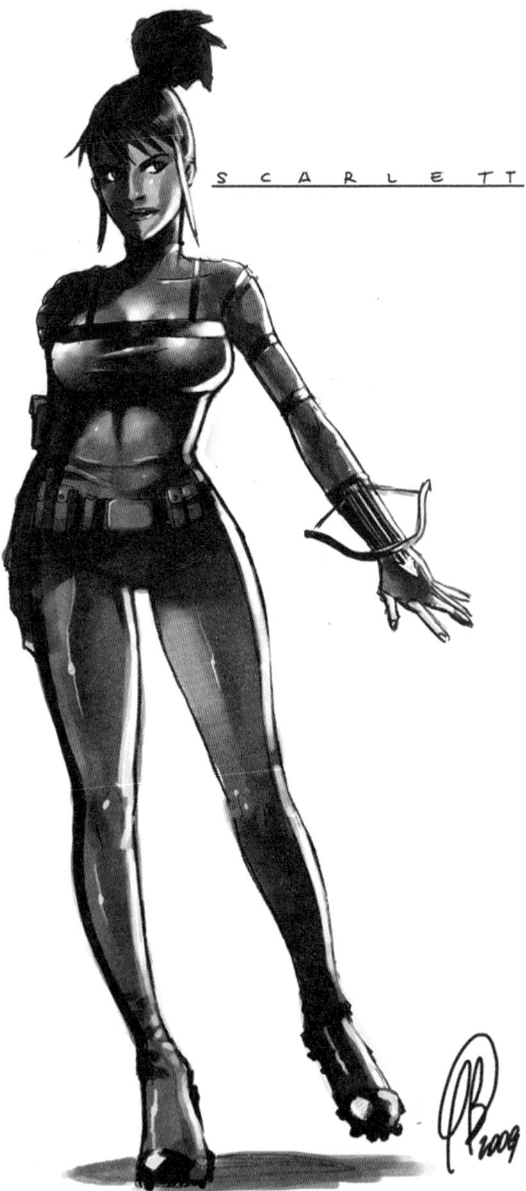
S C A R L E T T

character sketch by Giacomo Bevilacqua

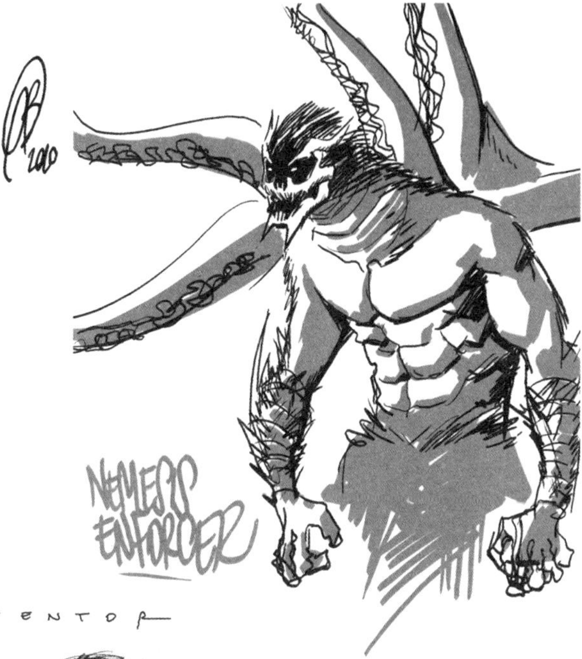
NEMESIS ENFORCER

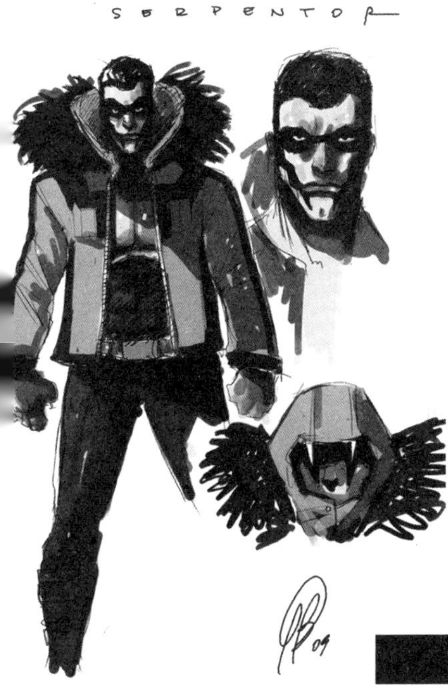
SERPENTOR

character sketches by Giacomo Bevilacqua

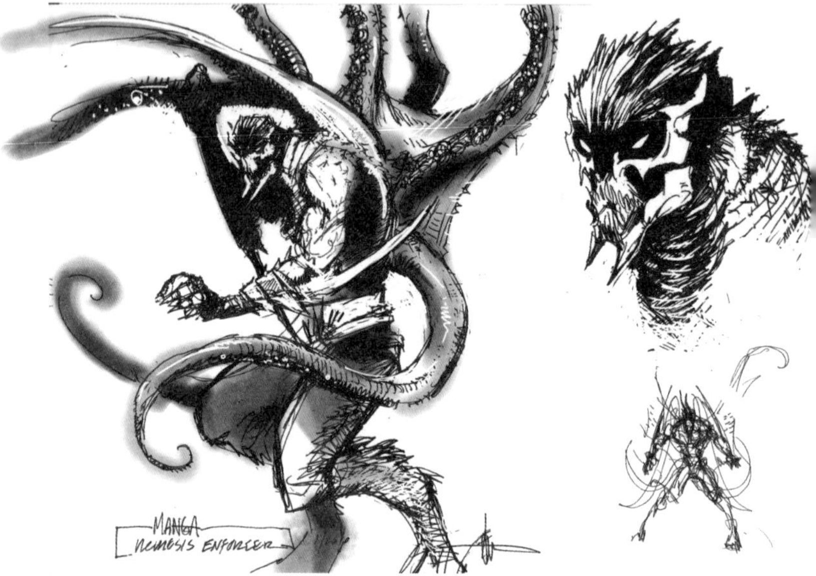
MANGA
NEMESIS ENFORCER

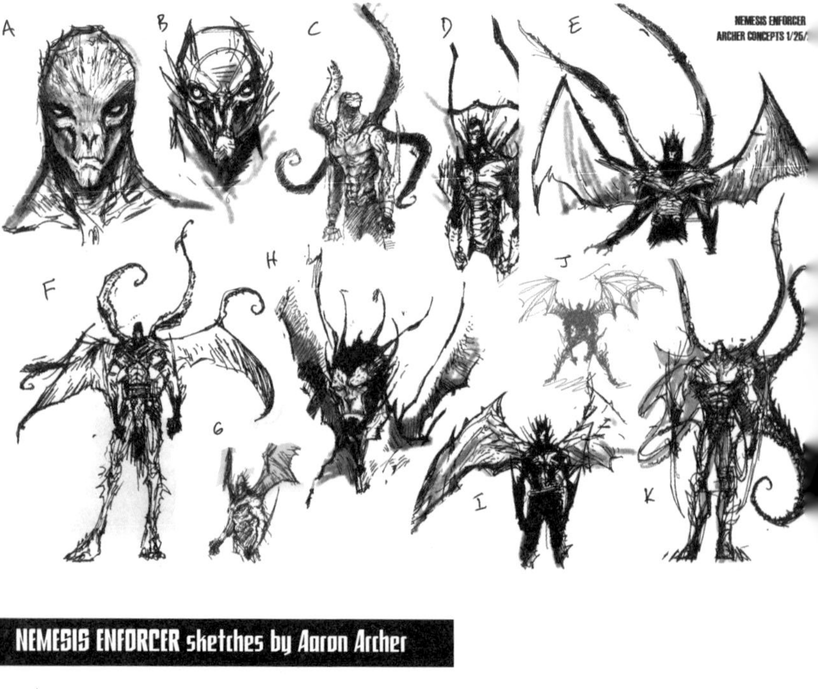
NEMESIS ENFORCER
ARCHER CONCEPTS 1/25/
A
B
C
D
E
F
G
H
I
J
K

NEMESIS ENFORCER sketches by Aaron Archer

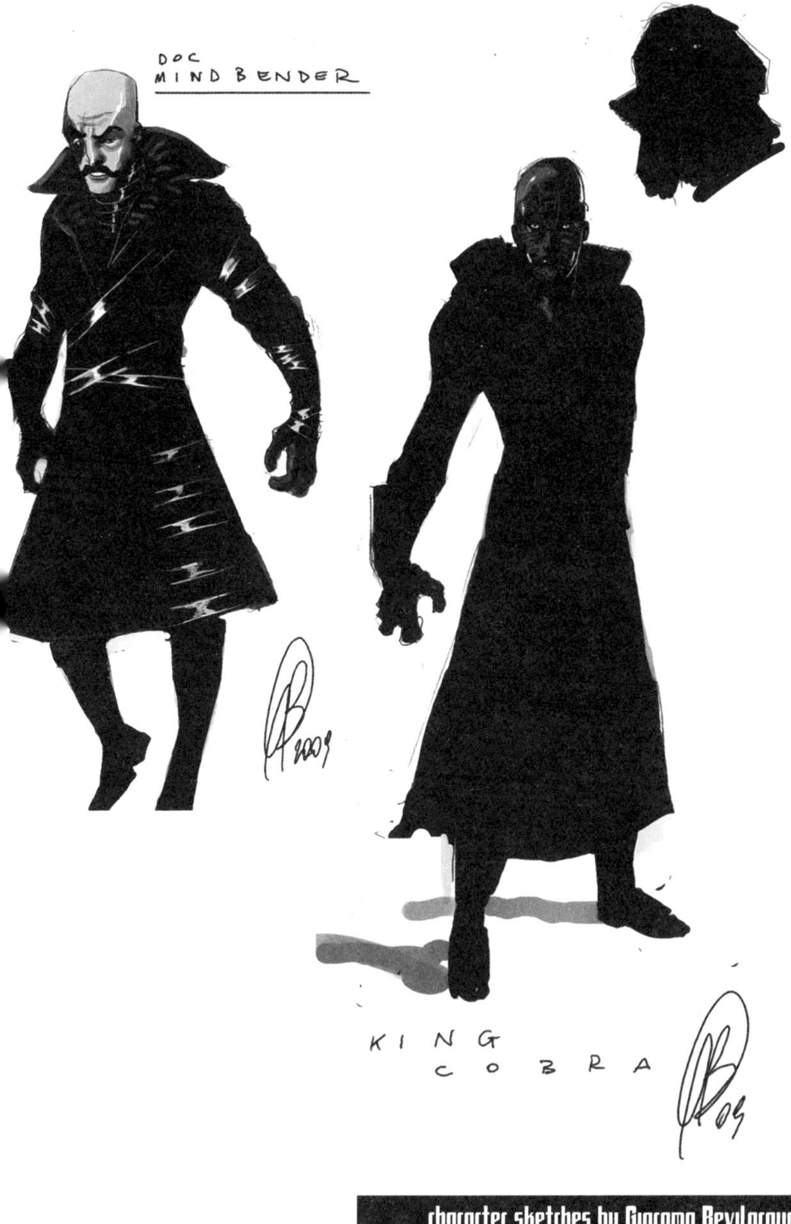
DOC
MINDBENDER
KING
COBRA

character sketches by Giacomo Bevilacqua

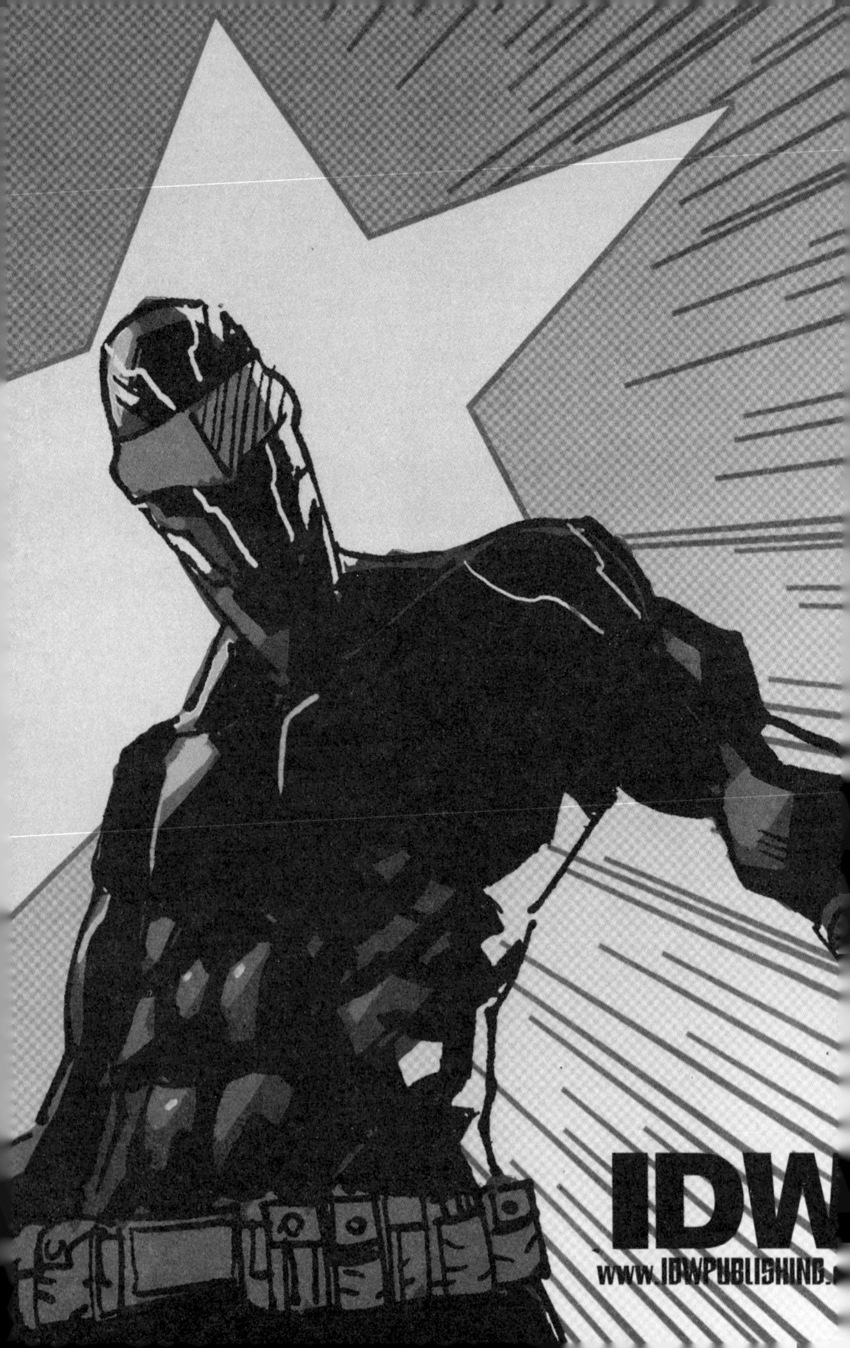
IDW
WWW.IDWPUBLISHING.